D0349131

READER'S DIGEST

all-season guide to gardening

late summer

READER'S DIGEST

all-season guide to gardening

late summer

PUBLISHED BY
THE READER'S DIGEST ASSOCIATION LIMITED
LONDON • NEW YORK • SYDNEY • MONTREAL

plant selector 76

a photographic guide to the best plants in late summer

garden projects 122

ideas and practical instructions on ways to improve your garden

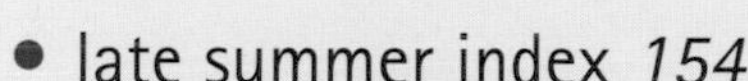

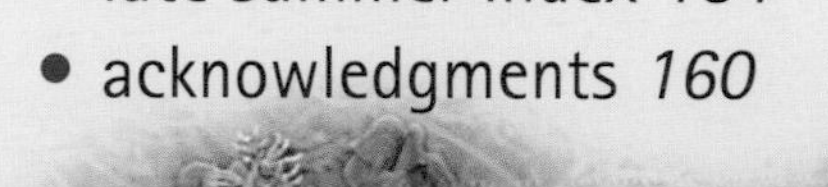

foreword

The *All-Season Guide to Gardening* provides a complete practical and inspirational guide to making the most of your garden season-by-season, with year-round detailed information to help you plan, plant and enjoy the garden of your dreams. Each of the volumes is presented in four key sections:

inspirations offers a source of design and planting ideas taken from contemporary and traditional gardens photographed during the season. The plants featured have been identified to enable you to re-create or adapt the ideas to your own garden scheme.

practical diary is a guide to the most important tasks to be done in the garden at this time of year. The information is divided into subject areas – such as Perennials, Climbers, or Patios & Containers – that reflect particular gardening interests. The headings appear in the same order in every volume in the series, so you can easily find the information you need. Under each heading is a list of the season's main tasks. The most important jobs are then explained in more detail, with step-by-step photographs and expert tips. The Healthy Garden, at the end of the section, is a full checklist of priority seasonal tasks for the whole garden. Since many jobs require follow-up attention in a later season, a 'Looking

useful terms

alpine Although this strictly refers to a mountain plant that grows naturally in free-draining soil at high altitude, the term is used by gardeners to mean any plant suitable for growing in a rock garden.

annual A plant that grows, flowers, sets seed and dies in one growing season.

anther The part of the flower that produces pollen.

aquatic plant In its widest sense, this can mean any water plant, but usually refers to plants such as water lilies that grow in deeper water, rooted in the bottom of the pond or in special baskets.

bareroot This refers to plants, usually trees and shrubs, that have been dug up and supplied to the customer without any soil on their roots. Roses are often supplied in this way.

bedding (plant) A plant used outdoors for temporary or seasonal display, often as part of a planned 'bedding scheme'.

biennial A plant that completes its life cycle in two growing seasons.

biological control The treatment or prevention of pests, diseases or weeds by natural, rather than chemical, methods, usually involving a naturally occurring parasite or predator.

cloche A glass or plastic cover used to shelter plants from cold or windy weather. Cloches are available as separate units or in tunnel form, often called 'continuous cloches'.

coldframe A low, unheated structure with a transparent top, in which plants can be grown in protected conditions.

cordon A plant restricted by pruning and training to a single, unbranching stem. Examples include apples, tomatoes and sweet peas grown on canes.

corm The swollen stem base of plants like crocuses and gladioli, where food is stored during winter. A new corm forms each year on top of the shrivelled remains of last year's.

cultivar A distinct, named plant variety that has originated in cultivation, rather than in the wild. Cultivars are often simply (but incorrectly) called 'varieties'.

deadhead To cut off the spent flowers.

die-back The result of attack by a fungal disease, which causes shoots or branches to die back from their tips.

direct sow To sow seeds in the ground where the plants are to grow, rather than starting them indoors or in a temporary seedbed for later transplanting.

drill A furrow or channel made in the soil at the correct depth for sowing seeds.

ericaceous Any plant belonging to the erica or heather family, for example pieris and rhododendrons. Also refers to the acid conditions these plants like and the special lime-free compost in which they are potted.

espalier A tree such as an apple or cotoneaster that is pruned and trained as a single upright trunk, with side branches extending horizontally to form symmetrical layers or 'tiers'.

foliar feed Liquid fertiliser sprayed or watered on the leaves of plants, usually applied for rapid results or when plants are not actively absorbing nutrients through their roots (after injury or in cold weather, for example).

glyphosate A chemical weedkiller that is absorbed through leaves and moves through the plant so that all parts, including roots, are killed (see systemic).

habitat The natural home of a plant growing in the wild. Not to be confused with habit, which is the typical form or shape of a plant.

harden off To gradually acclimatise a plant previously grown indoors to unprotected conditions outside in the garden.

hardwood cutting A piece of this year's shoot taken for propagation from a shrub, tree or climber during the autumn, when their stems are hard and ripe.

heel A small strip of bark torn from the main stem when a sideshoot is pulled off to make a (heel) cutting.

heel in To bury the roots of a plant in a temporary hole or trench when it is not to be planted immediately.

humus The dark, water-retentive component of soil that results from the decay of organic material.

in situ Literally, in position, or where plants are to grow permanently.

internodal cutting A cutting that is trimmed midway between two leaf-joints, rather than immediately below the leaves.

layering A method of propagation in which a shoot is rooted while still attached to the

ahead' feature indicates when you will find details of follow-up action in another volume.

plant selector is a directory of the plants which are at their best at this time of year, as selected by our gardening experts. Within each subject grouping the plants are arranged by colour, and within each colour sequence they are generally listed alphabetically by botanical name. Each plant is shown in a photograph, with information supplied including the plant's common name, size, site and soil preferences, best uses, general care and suggestions for good companions. Each plant is also given a 'hardiness' rating:

- 'Hardy' plants can be grown outdoors in all parts of the British Isles.
- Plants rated 'not fully hardy' can be grown outdoors in milder parts of the British Isles but elsewhere will need some protection in winter.
- 'Half-hardy' plants can withstand temperatures down to 0°C (32°F). They are often grown outdoors in summer displays, but propagated and kept under glass between autumn and late spring.
- 'Tender' plants require protection under glass for all or part of the year.

At the end of the section, there are lists of the plants best suited to different garden conditions and soil types.

garden projects offers ideas and instructions for garden improvements, ranging from building a patio, pergola or raised bed to designing and planting up a new border or pond. Major DIY projects are illustrated with step-by-step photographs and all the projects are within the capabilities of a fit, practical person. Although some projects are specific to a season, many of them can also be undertaken at other times of the year.

parent plant. Rooting a branch where it touches the ground is called simple layering, while serpentine layering involves rooting a long flexible stem in several places; long stems can be tip layered by burying their growing tips.

loam A type of soil that contains a balanced mixture of sand, clay and organic material.

marginal plant A waterside plant that is grown at the edge of the pond, either in shallow water or on the bank.

mulch Any material used to cover and protect the soil surface. Organic mulches include straw, manure and lawn mowings, while polythene sheet and stones are examples of inorganic mulches.

naturalise To deliberately plant, or allow plants to grow and spread, as in the wild.

node The place on a plant's stem where a leaf forms.

nursery bed A piece of ground specially reserved for raising young plants.

organic This literally refers to any material derived from decomposed animal or plant remains. It is also used to describe a gardening approach that uses little or no obviously chemical substances such as fertilisers and pesticides.

perlite A granular, absorbent soil or compost additive made from expanded volcanic rock.

perennial **(correctly herbaceous perennial)** A durable non-woody plant whose soft, leafy growth dies down in winter, but grows again the following year.

pinch out To remove a growing tip, using finger and thumb.

pot on To move a potted plant into a larger container.

pot (up) To transfer a plant from a seedtray or open ground into a pot.

prick out To transplant seedlings from where they have been sown to a container or piece of ground where they will have more space to grow.

rhizome An underground root (strictly, a stem) that behaves like a bulb by storing food from one season to the next. Also used to describe the buried creeping shoots by which some plants, especially grasses, spread underground.

rootballed This describes plants packaged for delivery by wrapping their mass of roots and soil or compost in a net bag.

rootstock (or stock) The rooted portion of a grafted tree. This usually influences the habit and ultimate size of the selected variety joined onto it (the scion).

seedbed A piece of ground for raising seeds, specially prepared by removing all weeds, stones and large lumps of soil.

semi-ripe cutting A section of this year's stem cut off for propagation, usually during summer while the tip is still soft but the base has become firm and woody.

softwood cutting A cutting prepared from a portion of a young new shoot that has not started to harden.

spit A measurement of depth equal to the length of a spade-blade (about 25cm/10in).

standard A trained form of woody plant with a single upright stem that is clear of all leaves and shoots. Full standard trees have trunks about 1.8m (6ft) high, half-standards 1.2m (4ft). Standard roses are about 1m (3ft) high, while half-standards have 75cm (2ft 6in) stems.

subsoil The lower layer of ground below the topsoil (see below). Often paler and relatively infertile, this is usually coarser in texture and hard to cultivate.

sucker A shoot growing from below ground and away from the main stem of a plant, sometimes from its rootstock.

systemic A type of pesticide, fungicide or weedkiller sprayed onto leaves and absorbed into all plant parts in its sap.

tender perennial A plant that can live for several years but cannot tolerate frost or very cold conditions.

thin out To reduce the number of plants, buds or fruit so that those remaining have enough room to develop fully.

tip cuttings Softwood cuttings (see above) formed from the outer ends of young shoots.

top-dressing An application of fertiliser, organic material or potting compost spread on the surface. Also refers to replacing the top layer of compost in a large container with a fresh supply.

topgrowth The upper, visible part of a plant above ground level.

topsoil The upper layer of soil, usually darker and more fertile than the layers below (see subsoil), and where plants develop most of their feeding roots.

tuber A fat, underground root (in dahlias, for example) or stem (begonias), constructed differently from a bulb or corm but used in the same way for storing food from one season to the next.

variety Botanically, a distinctly different variation of a plant that has developed in the wild, but commonly used to mean the same as cultivar (see left).

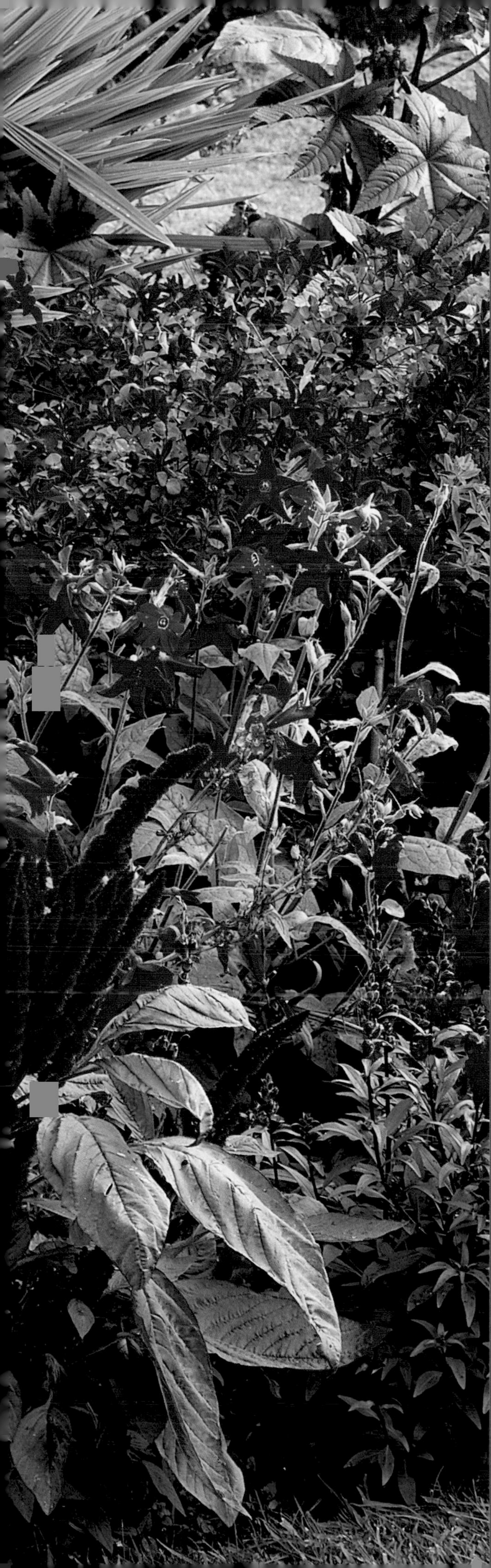

Late summer days may begin with early mists but often warm up to golden afternoons. Plants which have been biding their time come rushing into bloom, stimulated by the gradual change in day length. Colours tend to become stronger, with much red, rust and gold among late summer flowers, while foliage colour is toned down. As summer advances, the sense of urgency evaporates as the rate of growth slows. Tasks like weeding can be completed at a more sedate pace, giving you plenty of leisure time in which to enjoy the fruits of your earlier labours.

late summer glory

As summer progresses, the garden takes on richer, more mellow colours, and flowerbeds and borders become filled with clustered masses of warm-hued herbaceous perennials. The shortening of the days awakens some special late summer treasures and hardy cyclamen, colchicums and nerines all begin to appear.

Late flowering asters are joined by early autumn bulbs (left). Bright pink *Nerine bowdenii* clashes dramatically with pink *Aster novae-angliae* 'Alma Potschke' and purple-blue *A. amellus*.

Globe artichokes make superb decorative plants in a mixed border. They need rich soil, sun and plenty of space. The hybrid gladiolus makes a perfect companion.

Warm yellows, golds and oranges often predominate in late summer beds. In the foreground is *Ligularia clivorum* 'Desdemona'; on the right is rudbeckia, and behind are gaillardias and achilleas.

A single *Cordyline australis* makes a strong focal point in this informal border.

Heliopsis helianthoides 'Hohlspiegel'

Thoughtful planting and careful planning have produced a delightful flower garden (below left), with long-lived colour in a pink theme.

Hot-coloured cannas, *Fuchsia* 'Thalia' and red geraniums spill onto a patio (below). Standard mophead hollies add a formal touch to the lush perennials in the wide herbaceous border.

rich colour in flowerbeds & borders

Colour in the garden is never more glorious than in late summer. While random mixtures of colour work well in a cottage-style garden, careful blending of harmonious hues will have a more dramatic impact elsewhere.

Single colour borders can be effective but call for judicious planting. This superb all-red border uses a range of different flowers: penstemons, petunias, tobacco plants and dahlias provide the brightest reds, with dark-leaved *Amaranthus* to tone things down.

Dahlias are dependable perennials for late summer colour, but their flowers can be large and their hues strident, so careful siting is essential. Lift and divide dahlia tubers each autumn, and store.

Cannas are tropical plants (left), but grow so vigorously that they will develop and flower within a single summer, if planted out in May. They need moist, fertile soil and full sun. This is 'Rosemond Coles'.

An unusual mix of tropical and temperate-climate plants has been used here to develop a luxuriant display (left). The large banana leaves make a striking foil for *Lobelia* x *gerardii* and *Acanthus spinosus*.

Hot colours work well in full sunshine, and this double border at Great Dixter in Sussex is a shining example of bold planting (below). The large dahlia flowers harmonise with the soft, misty purple *Verbena bonariensis*, which seeds itself freely.

The bold curve enhances this mixed border and increases its length, providing more planting opportunities. The cool blue hydrangea at one end contrasts beautifully with the brilliant red and orange crocosmias at the other.

roses in bloom

Roses, the most romantic of all garden flowers, bring beauty and fragrance in summer. With care and the right selection, they will continue to bloom until the end of the growing season.

Bright, colourful floribunda roses line the path and provide a beautiful vista (right). With regular deadheading, they will flower more or less continuously from June to November, but may need to be treated against mildew and black spot.

Rosa Fellowship

Vigorous ramblers look their best when allowed to sprawl over a fence, like this 'Rambling Rector', or the top of a wall. Pruning involves removing any old or unproductive wood in winter and tying in long stems that might get in the way.

The exquisite blooms of the hybrid tea *Rosa* 'Lovely Lady' suit a formal garden.

Roses make good companion plants (far right). From midsummer, the cool spikes of delphiniums provide a contrast of colour and shape. For spring interest, underplant rose bushes with bulbs.

In a delightful combination, the rose 'Raubritter' trails its blooms through blue campanulas and parchment-coloured sisyrinchium (above).

The pink rambler rose 'Albertine' does not repeat, but has a long flowering spell. There is no need for deadheading, since whole stems that have finished flowering can be removed in the autumn. For a lovely display, plant with a rose of a different colour, such as the crimson gallica, 'Charles de Mills'.

aromatic herb beds

Herbs have a special beauty, whether they are growing wild on a Mediterranean hillside or planted in a formal herb garden. Bees find their blossoms irresistible and gardeners delight in their aromatic qualities.

Flowering chives, sage, golden marjoram and catmint provide colour in this herb garden (left). Pathways running through the herbs allow you to brush past their leaves and release their scent.

The domed shapes of the plants – santolinas, lavenders and convolvulus – are echoed in the rounded stones and paving. Trim herbs back in summer to promote fresh, healthy growth.

Basil can be a tricky herb to grow, especially in cold areas. It thrives best in a container, in full sun. Some varieties have coloured foliage, like this 'Purple Ruffles' form (right).

Sage is one of the most decorative of culinary herbs. The leaves are almost evergreen and the plants easy to keep compact. Here, four varieties nestle together (left), including two coloured leaf forms, which taste the same as the plain green sage.

If you do not have space for a herb garden, plant herbs in sunny borders. This border has a sage, *Salvia* 'Icterina', catmint and white rosebay willow herb (below).

The pleasure of a herb garden is enhanced by a chamomile path (above).

bringing interest to walls & fences

Walls and fences do far more than merely mark out a boundary. They can be important garden features, acting as a backdrop to plants or structures, or they can become attractive focal points in themselves.

The plain, stucco wall provides a neutral background for this formal planting of clipped photinias and white roses. An edging of annuals completes the picture.

The chromium-plated trellis shows how effective it can be to use new materials for a traditional structure. Man-made materials need siting with care but can be striking in a contemporary setting.

The strong colours and linear design of this extraordinary glass screen (above) make a sublime contrast with the natural growth of the climbing jasmine and hop.

Peepholes, gaps or gates tempt one to look through to see what lies beyond. This 'window', cut into the dividing wall covered by a climbing fig (*Ficus pumila*), frames a view through to a geometrically clipped photinia hedge.

Woven hurdles of willow (below) or hazel make beautiful informal screens that are easy to install – but will last for only about five years.

An espaliered apricot, in a Western American garden, makes a superbly decorative wall feature that is also highly productive. You could grow pears, apples, plums, figs or peaches in this way.

This freestanding blue-washed wall and large matching pot make an arresting focal point. When designing strong focal points, it is important to think big and to be very bold.

These withy panels, held in softwood frames, not only provide screening but filter the wind and afford shelter for developing plants.

decorative patios & terraces

The patio is at the very heart of a small garden, and the seats, tables and containers placed on it offer as much scope for interesting garden decor as they do for attractive planting.

This wholly original patio relies on a sunny climate. The simplicity of the floorboards and furniture, together with the restrained planting, brings the scene to life without distracting from the perfect setting (above).

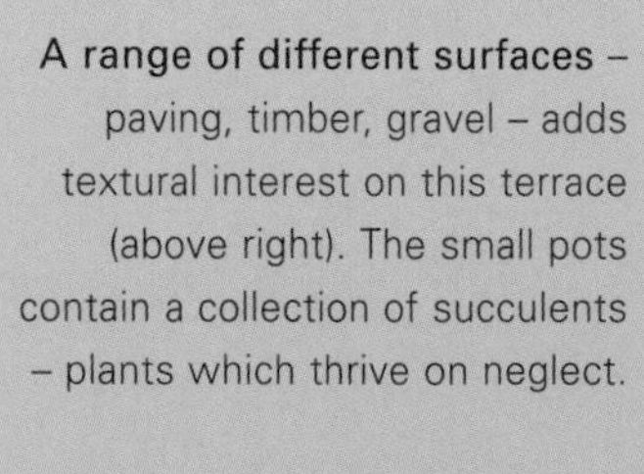

A range of different surfaces – paving, timber, gravel – adds textural interest on this terrace (above right). The small pots contain a collection of succulents – plants which thrive on neglect.

Shading is important both for people and some plants, making it possible to sit out at midday. Here, slatted bamboo on a metal frame blends well with the decking and assorted containers. In colder regions, an awning might be an alternative.

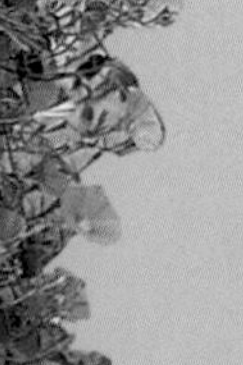

Convolvulus sabatius

In this rural garden, the unusual design of the cobbled floor and the bold blue of the table and chairs make for an individual terrace. The pot in the foreground holds a datura with trumpet-shaped flowers.

The choice of materials for garden flooring has never been more varied. In this narrow space, decking contrasts texturally with the path, which is surfaced with grey slate chips.

These oversized pots planted with clipped evergreens make a stylish permanent feature in the dining area of a small walled garden.

The dining area on this patio is covered with a pergola festooned throughout summer with *Solanum jasminoides* 'Album'. The surrounding containers are filled with soft-coloured argyranthemums and petunias.

late summer highlights

Eye-catching plants at this time of year include the tall spires of red hot pokers and the globe flowers of agapanthus, as well as the dreamiest of highlight flowers – the grasses.

Red hot pokers (*Kniphofia*) make a spectacular late summer highlight. Here, they are beautifully set off by the grass *Stipa tenuissima.*

Grass flowers are at their best with light shining through from behind them. *Pennisetum alopecuroides* (below) is one of many grasses to reach perfection in late summer. It is perennial but barely hardy, so will need protecting in winter with a thick, dry mulch.

Grasses for large borders include the vigorous *Miscanthus sinensis* and the lower-growing evergreen oat, *Helictotrichon sempervirens*. Both benefit from rich, well-drained soil that does not dry out too much in summer.

A South African native species, agapanthus is not fully hardy and in cool areas is best taken indoors in late autumn. Here, its blue flowers contrast with the vivid red of *Crocosmia* 'Lucifer'.

The stunning fan palm, *Trachycarpus fortunei*, is an architectural showpiece amid a collection of highlight plants (above). The vivid red garlands draping the evergreen shrubs are the annual climber *Tropaeolum speciosum*, a plant that flowers in the sun, but revels in cool shade for its roots.

The bold summer foliage of cannas (below) makes a strong highlight in its own right and a good foil for colourful dahlias. Dahlias need regular feeding and deadheading to prolong their flowering.

Large grasses, particularly such giants as *Cortaderia* (bottom) and *Spartina*, need plenty of space to allow for their arching growth without interfering with their neighbours.

the productive garden

A well-ordered kitchen garden is a joy to look at, as well as providing delicious food. Edible flowers such as violas or nasturtiums bring colour to border edges, and can be picked to decorate salads or confections.

Leafy vegetables such as chard (left), spinach or kale grow readily in containers. To harvest, cut the leaves as cleanly as possible near the base of the plants. Ensure a constant water supply, to prevent the plants from bolting.

In a display that is fruitful as well as decorative, trailing varieties of tomato happily share a hanging basket with trailing petunias. Varieties of tomato such as 'Tumbling Tom' and 'Tumbler' would be equally at home in pots and window boxes.

This productive corner, furnished with seats and filled with nasturtiums, bay, courgettes and a vine, is in fact part of a small roof garden.

Peach (*Prunus* 'Peregrine')

Groups of food crops in pots and containers on a patio, in a kitchen garden, or simply standing by the back door, will look charming and offer convenient pickings for the kitchen. This group (above) provides a selection of different chillies.

In this exuberant raised bed (left), courgettes, lettuce and spinach beet are ready for harvesting. Inverted terracotta pots, hung by string tied to the ends of canes, help to keep birds off the ripening produce.

Although marrows (above), melons and gourds are happy growing along the ground, they are easier to harvest, more attractive and more obviously impressive trained on a series of arches. Select long, trailing varieties rather than the bush kinds.

practical diary

A huge number of flowering plants are at their absolute best in late summer, providing a constant display of colour, but once flowering is over many will need to be cut back or lightly sheared. Roses benefit from deadheading now, if you want plenty of autumn blooms, and removing damaged stems will enhance the appearance of your borders. And there is much tidying to do around ponds and on the patio. But the most enjoyable work at this time of year is without doubt harvesting all the vegetables and fruit that you have been nurturing since the growing season began.

perennials

Give a little care to your flowering perennials and they will continue to perform well into autumn, although there is still time to fill gaps with new plants for late colour. With an eye to the future, take a few cuttings of tender perennials and prepare the ground for autumn planting.

now is the season to . . .

■ **deadhead border perennials regularly,** not only to improve their looks but also to encourage more flowers. Frequent deadheading of tender perennials is particularly worthwhile in order to prolong their display until the first frosts.

■ **stake late flowering tall perennials** such as cimicifugas, michaelmas daisies and phlox, before they start to topple. Surround clumps with a ring of short stakes and run garden string around the stakes. 'Grow-through' plant supports give the best results, but they need to be in place by early summer – something worth remembering for next year.

■ **cut back perennials that have finished flowering** and are flopping over, such as catmint (*Nepeta*), achilleas and hardy geraniums (see opposite).

Daisy-flowered *Echinacea purpurea* is one of the most colourful mainstays of the late summer border.

■ **water and feed** perennials in containers regularly.

■ **keep new plants moist** by watering thoroughly every couple of days if necessary. Established perennials that are not drought tolerant will benefit from a good soaking twice a week during prolonged periods of dry weather.

■ **hoe off weed seedlings** regularly when the weather is warm and dry. Every couple of weeks, look for larger weeds that may be growing unnoticed among mature perennials, and pull them up before they seed. Bindweed and ground elder are a real nuisance once established, so treat them with a weedkiller such as glyphosate. Take care to keep the chemical well away from other plants as it kills everything it touches. The alternative is to dig up every scrap of root.

■ **keep a look out** for pests and diseases.

■ **plant new perennials** for autumn flowers (see opposite).

■ **feed plants** that are coming up to flowering and tender perennials with a high-potash liquid fertiliser.

■ **pot up rooted cuttings** taken earlier and thin seedlings.

■ **propagate new perennials** by layering (see page 30) and taking cuttings (see page 31).

and if you have time . . .

■ **prepare the ground** for autumn planting.

■ **divide established clumps** of the very earliest spring-flowering perennials (see page 30).

■ **collect seed** for sowing or storing; pot up any self-sown seedlings you wish to keep.

pests and diseases

These can take hold very fast in warm weather, so inspect plants regularly and treat if necessary. While perennials are less susceptible than many other groups of plants, there are several problems that commonly occur at this time of year.

• **fungal diseases** include mildew (look out for this on michaelmas daisies) and rust, which can affect dianthus and campanulas. Limit the spread by removing affected foliage and spraying the plant with fungicide. Burn or bin the foliage, or the disease spores will overwinter and attack again next year.

• **vine weevil grubs** commonly feed on the roots of plants growing in containers. If your container plants show signs of ailing, remove them from the pot and look for the white comma-shaped grubs in the compost. Remove and destroy them and repot the plant in fresh potting compost.

Colourful perennials in the late summer border include red hot pokers (*Kniphofia*), seen here alongside the paler blooms of camassias.

Heliopsis

perennials for autumn colour

• heliopsis • kaffir lily (*Schizostylis coccinea*)
• lilyturf (*Liriope muscari*) • michaelmas daisies (*Aster*)
• rudbeckia

planting and transplanting

• **fill gaps in your border** with autumn-flowering perennials (see above right). They can make a handsome display this year provided you buy large plants in 15–20cm (6–8in) pots. Choose bushy, well-grown specimens with plenty of flower buds and avoid any that are tall, leggy or yellow leaved.

• **plant out young perennials** raised from seed or cuttings earlier in the year, so long as the roots are well developed in a minimum pot size of 8cm (3in). Alternatively, pot them on into 13cm (5in) pots and plant out next year.

• **transplant or pot up** young perennials that have self-seeded in the border or on gravel paths. It is worth looking out for such seedlings before hoeing or spraying with weedkiller. Either pot up plants into 8cm (3in) pots or grow them in a row in a nursery bed or a spare piece of ground and plant out next year.

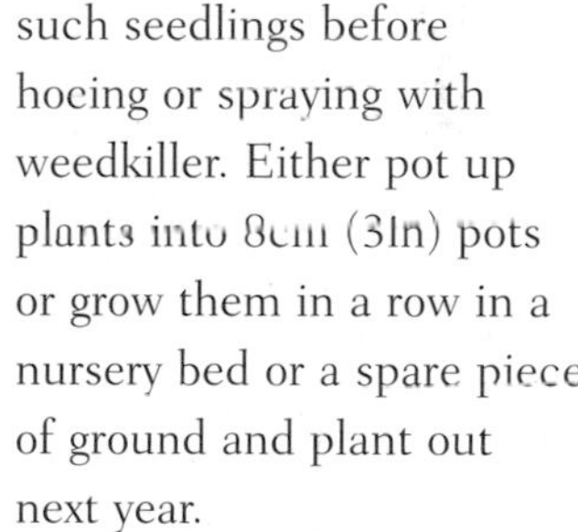

• **plan new borders** and prepare the ground for planting hardy herbaceous perennials. In early September the soil is warm and moist, which encourages plenty of root growth, while the shorter days and falling temperatures ensure the plants do not put their energies into making excess top growth.

cutting back untidy perennials

1 **Once early flowering** perennials like geraniums have finished blooming, they become straggly and untidy. To encourage new growth, cut them back to ground level using shears.

2 **Clear away the trimmings** – they can go on the compost heap – then cut off neatly any remaining straggly stems.

3 **Apply a sprinkling** of general fertiliser and water well. The plant will soon develop a tidy mound of fresh foliage and often more flowers.

perennials/2

propagation

Almost all herbaceous perennials are quick and easy to propagate by at least one method. Give priority to tender perennials, because taking cuttings now is insurance against the parent plant failing to survive the winter.

layering border carnations

Select non-flowering sideshoots for layering, then improve the soil around the plant by forking in some potting compost where the layer is to root.

- Use a knife to remove a small sliver, about 1cm (½in) long, from the underside of a sideshoot; the wound will stimulate root production. Peg the wounded area of the stem into the soil using a bent wire.
- Stake the end of the shoot to keep it upright. Lightly cover the wounded area with soil.
- Layers should be well rooted by autumn, when they can be detached, moved to a nursery bed then planted out next year.

raising from seed

You can raise many hardy perennials from seed, either those you have purchased or those you have collected yourself. Bear in mind when collecting seed that although the offspring of plant species come true, those of cultivated varieties are likely to be variable and often inferior to the parent plant.

Transfer collected seeds into used film canisters and store in the dark.

- Collect seed heads on a dry sunny day as soon as they have turned brown, which indicates the seeds are ripe. Either cover with a paper bag (see page 74) and shake, or cut off the heads and remove the seeds.
- Store seeds in paper bags, envelopes or used film canisters. Do not use polythene bags as the seeds could rot. Label each container with the plant name and the date.
- Sow seeds into pots or trays of moist compost and cover with a thin layer of perlite or horticultural vermiculite. Stand pots in a coldframe or a sheltered spot outside. Alternatively, sow seeds outside in rows in a well-cultivated nursery bed.

To divide pulmonaria, lift a clump and pull it apart into smaller pieces or individual plantlets. Discard the old central portion and replant the divisions. Water the plants well and keep them moist in dry weather.

helping seed germination

Most perennials are suitable for sowing immediately, but certain varieties need special treatment in order to germinate. The seeds of baptisia and lupin have a hard coating that needs to be chipped carefully with a sharp knife or rubbed with sandpaper to allow water to penetrate before germination can take place. Others, such as certain varieties of campanula and primula, require a cold period, known as stratification. To stratify seeds, mix them with damp potting compost in a plastic bag and keep in the fridge for several weeks. Then sow in autumn.

propagating by division

While most perennials are divided in autumn or spring, those that bloom early in spring, like bleeding heart (*Dicentra spectabilis*), leopard's bane (*Doronicum*) and pulmonaria do better if you divide them in late August or early September. Then they have time to establish before flowering next year. This easy method of propagation also rejuvenates old plants that have formed large congested clumps (see above).

taking cuttings of tender perennials

1 Select young healthy shoots, without flowers if possible. Remove the tip to make a cutting about 10cm (4in) long. Use a sharp knife to trim the base just below a leaf joint and remove the lower leaves. Dipping the base in hormone rooting powder improves the success rate but is not vital.

2 Fill a tray or 13cm (5in) pot with cuttings compost. Though not essential, it aids rooting if you mix compost with a third by volume of horticultural vermiculite or perlite. To reduce the risk of rot, space cuttings so that the leaves do not touch. Water with a fungicide and allow to drain, then cover with a lid or plastic bag.

Brightly coloured coleus come in many different leaf forms.

taking soft-tip cuttings

Take soft-tip cuttings to propagate woody-based tender perennials (see below) and varieties of herbaceous perennials that are difficult or impossible to raise from seed or division, such as penstemon and phygelius. Most tender perennials root easily from cuttings taken during summer (see above), though with non-woody herbaceous perennials it is important to select non-flowering shoots.

A high level of humidity is important for success, so either cover the pots with an inflated clear polythene bag secured with an elastic band or place them in a propagator out of the sun. The exception here is pelargoniums, which are prone to rotting and so best left uncovered.

After about eight weeks, carefully remove the pot to check whether the roots are well developed. If they are, pot up the cuttings individually into 8cm (3in) pots. Overwinter the young plants on a windowsill or in a greenhouse; the parent plant can be left to take its chances outside.

there is still time to . . .

- **divide bearded irises** after flowering (see Summer).
- **take cuttings of pinks** (*Dianthus*), known as 'pipings'.

perennials to raise from soft-tip cuttings

• achillea • anthemis • campanula • coleus • dianthus • diascia • erysimum • euphorbia • nepeta • parahebe • penstemon • phygelius • tanacetum • veronica

Anthemis tinctoria 'Sauce Hollandaise'

looking ahead . . .

☑ AUTUMN Pot up rooted cuttings individually.
☑ Pot up rooted layers of border carnations.
☑ Prick out seedling perennials in pots or thin those in a nursery bed.

annuals & biennials

Give your sweet peas more room to grow upwards and they will reward you with many more blooms, but only if you keep picking. Deadheading other annuals will keep them flowering until autumn approaches, but let some of them set seed for sowing next season.

now is the season to . . .

■ **water plants regularly** in dry weather, especially those growing in containers, and feed with a high-potash fertiliser, such as a tomato feed, every seven to fourteen days.

Cornflowers should be deadheaded as soon as their flowers start to fade, to extend the display.

■ **remove faded flowers** to prolong the display, unless you intend saving the seeds.

■ **control weeds** in beds and borders, if possible without treading on the soil between flowering plants.

■ **watch out for signs of seasonal problems** such as moulds, mildews and virus diseases, earwigs and red spider mites, and vine weevils in containers.

■ **cut and dry flowers,** such as 'everlastings', for long-lasting indoor displays (see Summer).

■ **fill gaps in your display** by planting late-sown annuals, and water them in with a diluted liquid feed.

■ **support tall flowers** such as sunflowers and hollyhocks, and continue tying in sweet peas and other annual climbers.

■ **lower cordon sweet peas** that have reached the tops of their canes (see opposite).

■ **select the best annuals** and allow them to set seed for gathering and drying for storage.

■ **sow some hardy annuals** in early September. These will overwinter and flower early next year (see opposite).

and if you have time . . .

■ **encourage bushy growth** by cutting back by half the long bare stems of sprawling annuals, such as petunias, and by pinching out the tips of long shoots of helichrysums and nasturtiums.

deadheading for long flowering

Some annuals will cease flowering once they have set their first seeds, and for this reason it is important to deadhead pansies, petunias and antirrhinums if you want them to continue into the autumn. Others, such as tagetes, begonias and impatiens, are either 'self-cleaning', dropping their faded flowers naturally, or are unaffected by seed development.

The glaucous seed heads of the annual poppy (*Papaver somniferum*) are eye-catching in the border and scatter seeds freely when ripe.

For these, deadheading is unnecessary, as it is for those special plants you have selected for saving seed.

Deadhead marigolds (*Calendula*) to stop them from seeding too prolifically.

collecting seeds

Many flowers start to set seeds from midsummer, and it is worth collecting the seeds of superior or unusual annuals for sowing next season – but not from F_1 hybrids, which rarely come true. Gather the seed heads before they are fully ripe and start shedding their seed.

annuals **to sow now**
- alyssum • bugloss (*Echium*) • calendula • candytuft • coreopsis • cornflowers • godetia (*Clarkia*) • larkspur • linaria • nigella • poppies (*Papaver*) • scabious • viscaria

Papaver nudicaule 'Summer Breeze'

Sweet peas, like these *Lathyrus* 'Violet Queen', can be encouraged to produce flowers for longer by lowering them.

- **as soon as the seed heads look dry** or start to change colour, cut them off carefully and invert them into paper bags.
- **tie the bags around the stems** and hang them upside down in a dry, airy place to finish ripening.
- **after a week or two,** shake out the dry seeds, gently blow away the chaff and store them in labelled envelopes in an airtight tin away from extreme cold and heat.

sowing annuals for early display

Although most hardy annuals are sown in spring, many produce larger, stronger plants if sown in late summer and early autumn, and will flower earlier next year, often bridging the gap between spring and summer bedding. Sow them outdoors *in situ* in mild areas, or in rows in a spare piece of ground where they can be covered with cloches or fleece in very cold weather, and thin the seedlings to 8–10cm (3–4in) apart when they are large enough to handle. Alternatively, start them under glass, prick out into trays or individual small pots, and keep these in a coldframe over winter.

lowering sweet peas

Sweet peas growing up individual vertical supports often have several more weeks flowering left after they reach the tops of their tall canes. The plants flower mostly at the top of their stems rather than along their length, so to prolong flowering, remove them from their canes and re-attach them to adjacent ones.

looking ahead . . .

☑ AUTUMN Continue collecting annual seeds.
☑ Thin late sowings of hardy annuals. Plant out biennials.
☑ EARLY SPRING Plant out remaining biennials.

- Carefully untie each stem and lay it neatly along the ground from its original cane to the next cane in the row. Re-attach the top 30–45cm (12–18in) of the stem to this new cane.
- Continue to do this with all the other sweet pea plants, moving them along the row to the next cane. The first cane will need to be moved to the end of the row.
- Continue watering and feeding regularly. Control slugs and cut flowers before they can set seed.

there is still time to . . .

- **transplant biennials** to spare ground (see Summer); even four to six weeks in a nursery bed will improve their quality.
- **use any spare bedding plants** and tender perennials to plant up containers for a late display.
- **pinch out the tips** of young wallflowers to make them bushy, if this was not done at transplanting time (see Summer).

Hollyhocks (*Alcea rosea*) are stately biennials, best suited to cottage-style gardens, but they have to be staked. Choose a rust-resistant variety.

bulbs & tubers

With summer bulbs in full bloom and autumn varieties safely tucked under ground, turn your attention to planting spring bulbs, both in the garden to flower naturally and in pots to force for winter enjoyment indoors.

One of the most colourful stars of the late summer border, *Crocosmia* 'Lucifer' blooms for weeks on end.

now is the season to . . .

- **finish lifting and drying tulips,** daffodils, hyacinths and other spring-flowering bulbs that are dying down in borders or were heeled in to spare ground by early August. Store them in a cool, dry place until planting time (see page 36).
- **lift and divide overcrowded clumps** of bulbs that failed to flower in spring. Discard them if they show signs of disease. You can also lift and divide three or four-year-old clumps of spring-flowering bulbs and reserve some of the largest for potting up to flower indoors.
- **water recently planted bulbs** in a dry season, especially those in containers or close to walls, and species such as galtonias that come from regions of high summer rainfall. A light mulch after watering helps to keep the ground moist.
- **feed summer flowering bulbs** in containers while they are in bloom and for three to four weeks afterwards.
- **cut gladioli spikes** low down the stem when the bottom flower is almost fully open and feed plants every seven to fourteen days with a high-potash fertiliser to encourage more blooms. The cut spikes will continue to bloom indoors.
- **deadhead and stake dahlias** and thin buds for larger flowers (see Summer). Continue feeding regularly, using only high-potash feeds from mid-August onwards.
- **plan spring bulb displays** and send off mail orders as soon as possible. From late August an increasingly diverse selection will be available in large garden centres (see page 36), but these will be more expensive.
- **begin planting spring bulbs** outdoors, starting in late August with daffodils, muscari and erythroniums, followed in September with most other kinds. Tulips are best left until November (see Autumn), as earlier planting only encourages diseases such as tulip fire.
- **consider naturalising** patches of spring bulbs in your lawn (see page 37).
- **begin potting up prepared bulbs** in early September to flower over Christmas and the New Year (see page 71).
- **pot up arum lilies** from early September for winter flowering under glass (see page 70).
- **collect lily bulbils** – dark, immature bulbs growing at the base of the leaves – and plant them 2–3cm (1in) apart in trays of compost in a coldframe or under glass.
- **check lilies for lily beetle,** signs of virus and other symptoms of pests and diseases.

Gladioli such as this *Gladiolus callianthus* benefit from a boost with a high-potash liquid fertiliser immediately after flowering.

and if you have time . . .

- **plant autumn flowering bulbs** like colchicums and autumn crocuses. Try to complete planting before the end of August.
- **feed autumn flowering bulbs** naturalised in grass with bone meal, applied once during August at 65g per m^2 (2oz per sq yd), or with a high-potash fertiliser at recommended rates.
- **collect seeds** of spring and summer bulbs and sow immediately in pots or trays, or outdoors in rows in a spare bed. Sow ripe lily seeds now, or keep them cold in the fridge and sow next spring.
- **foliar feed dahlias** using a general fertiliser, to boost late growth and flowering.

feeding summer bulbs in containers

Bulbs growing in containers that are repotted or top-dressed with fresh compost annually benefit from being given a single liquid feed with a high-potash fertiliser immediately after flowering, although this is not essential. However, bulbs left in the same compost for several years require regular feeding throughout their growing period if they are to flower well. This is particularly important for summer bulbs that share containers with bedding plants, as they are all competing for the same nutrients. Here, apply a high-potash liquid feed at recommended strength for alternate waterings, or at half strength every time you water the pot.

growing bulbs near trees and hedges

Although most bulbs prefer to grow in full sun, some kinds are unaffected by, and even appreciate, the shade cast by deciduous trees and hedges (see below). They have usually adapted to woodland conditions by producing flowers or foliage before the tree leaves open and cast shade, or by manufacturing food slowly and wilting if light and heat levels become too intense. Other bulbs grow happily anywhere, but their flowers often last longer out of bright sunshine.

- **before planting** enrich the top few centimetres of soil with moisture-retentive organic material such as garden compost or leaf-mould, and add more every autumn as a mulch.
- **relieve dense shade by thinning** branches unobtrusively to admit extra light and rainfall.
- **always check** the habits and preferences of a particular variety, as not all bulbs will perform well in shady or woodland conditions.

bulbs for beneath trees and hedges

• alliums, especially *Allium triquetrum* and *A. ursinum* • bluebell (*Hyacinthus non-scripta*) • chionodoxa • cuckoo pint (*Arum maculatum*) • cyclamen • dog's tooth violet (*Erythronium*) • Lent lily (*Narcissus pseudonarcissus*) • lilies, especially *L. auratum, L. henryi, L. martagon and L. pyrenaicum* • ornithogalum • snowdrop (*Galanthus*) • winter aconite (*Eranthis*) • wood anemone (*Anemone nemorosa*) • wood lily *(Trillium)*

Autumn-flowering cyclamen

bulbs & tubers/2

buying and planting bulbs

Whether you buy bulbs from a garden centre or by mail-order, plant them as soon as possible after delivery. Erythroniums, trilliums and other bulbs without a skin or 'tunic' should be kept in moist bark or compost.

The best flowers come from the biggest bulbs, so if your bulb catalogue offers a range of sizes, choose the largest you can afford. However, the lower grade or 'second-size' bulbs are more economical for naturalising in large quantities.

Distinguish between a mixture and a collection. A collection is a number of separate and labelled varieties (usually the supplier's choice) sold at a discount. Mixtures can be good value, but be prepared for an unpredictable range of colours. Inexpensive mixtures may comprise undersized bulbs or just a few common varieties.

If you prefer to buy loose and pre-packed bulbs in shops and garden centres, look for bulbs that are clean, firm and plump, with no obvious root or shoot growth. Avoid those that are dirty, soft, damaged, shrivelled, or showing signs of mould or pale, forced shoots and roots. Be wary of bulbs kept in warm conditions, as they are more likely to be soft and actively growing than those in a cool, dry atmosphere.

If you cannot plant your bulbs immediately, unpack them and spread them out in trays in a cool place.

bulbs to plant now

• alliums • early spring crocuses • erythroniums • grape hyacinths (*Muscari*) • dwarf bulbous irises (*Iris danfordiae, I. histrioides, I. reticulata*) • narcissus • ornithogalum

planting bulbs

Ideally, you should finish planting your daffodil bulbs by the end of August, as their roots start growing in late summer. However, there is usually no harm in waiting until September, the usual time for planting other spring-flowering bulbs (except for tulips). If you are planning a bedding display with wallflowers and other spring-flowering plants, you can even wait until early October in mild areas.

- **bulbs in borders** look more appealing flowering in informal groups rather than in symmetrical patterns. Before planting it is worth enriching a light soil with plenty of garden compost or well-rotted manure. Or, if your soil is heavy, dig in some coarse sand or grit to improve drainage.
- **many smaller bulbs,** such as fritillaries, snowdrops or crocuses, add charming informality to areas of a lawn or wild garden, especially under deciduous trees.
- **before planting in grass** first mow the area as short as possible. And remember that after flowering you must wait at least six weeks before mowing the grass, to allow the bulb foliage to die down naturally and ensure flowers in future years.

CYCLAMEN TIP You can plant dried tubers now, 15cm (6in) apart and 2–3cm (1in) deep, but the tubers take over a year to establish. A more reliable method is to buy 'green', or growing, plants in pots and plant them in well-drained soil in semi-shade.

spring bulbs for naturalising in lawns

• *Anemone blanda* • chionodoxa • crocus • dwarf narcissus • ornithogalum • puschkinia • *Scilla siberica* • snakeshead fritillary (*Fritillaria meleagris*) • snowdrop (*Galanthus nivalis*)

Fritillaria meleagris

planting bulbs in the border

1 **Dig out a large** planting hole. Check that it is wide enough for the bulbs to be at least their own width apart and deep enough so they are covered with soil to two or three times their height.

2 **Scatter a little bone meal** over the base of the hole and lightly fork in, then water gently before positioning the bulbs.

3 **Gently cover the bulbs** with soil, making sure you don't knock them over, then tamp the surface firm with the back of a rake and label the area.

rough guide to planting depth

Estimate the height of the bulb from tip to base, then cover it with two to three times that depth of soil, the deeper measurement on light soils.

Muscari botryoides 'Album'

naturalising bulbs in grass

1 **Cut the outline** of a large 'H' through the turf using a spade. This makes it easier to under-cut the turf from the middle and peel back two panels to expose a rectangle of soil. Loosen the soil underneath with a fork.

2 **Fork in bone meal** at a rate of 15g per m^2 (½ oz per sq yd). Then scatter the bulbs over the exposed soil and press each one in gently; they should be at least 2–3cm (1in) apart.

3 **Make sure the bulbs** are upright before carefully replacing the turf.

4 **Firm the turf gently** with your hand and, if necessary, fill the joints with fine soil.

roses

Gather roses for the house and deadhead them regularly to keep plants flowering for longer in the garden. Prune ramblers and remove suckers as soon as you see them then, as autumn looms, take some hardwood cuttings.

now is the season to . . .

■ **water recently planted roses** after 10–14 days without rain. Check those growing in containers daily in hot weather.

■ **stop feeding roses** at the beginning of August.

■ **continue to weed,** as weed seeds germinate quickly at this time. They are easily controlled by hoeing in dry weather.

■ **pull off suckers** as soon as you notice them (see right).

Cut roses for the house and at the same time deadhead any spent blooms.

■ **deadhead repeat-flowering roses** to encourage more blooms.

■ **gather blooms for vases** and combine this with light pruning, cutting the stems just above an outward-facing bud.

■ **prune ramblers and weeping standards** from late August onwards (see opposite).

■ **start taking hardwood cuttings** from early September.

■ **look out for signs of rust and red spider mite,** which are prevalent in late summer, as well as other seasonal pests and diseases (see page 75). Continue preventative spraying against black spot and mildew, if necessary, with a combined insecticide and fungicide every two weeks.

■ **disbud hybrid tea and floribunda roses** to encourage good-quality late blooms (see Summer).

■ **plan new plantings,** order roses and start getting beds ready for autumn planting (see opposite).

and if you have time . . .

■ **cut off developing seed heads,** unless the hips are decorative, especially if you are about to go away on holiday for any length of time.

■ **check supports and ties** are secure on standard, pillar and arch-trained roses, before early autumn winds start to blow.

■ **underplant roses** with untreated hyacinth bulbs, which make excellent edging or underplanting.

removing suckers

Suckers growing from the rootstocks of grafted roses are usually conspicuous at this time of year because of their paler colour and smaller, more numerous leaflets. If left uncontrolled they can come to dominate the plant, so remove each one promptly.

- **trace the sucker back** to where it joins the root and pull it off cleanly, wearing strong gardening gloves. Replace the soil and re-firm the rose in the ground (see Summer).
- **suckers on standard roses** sprout from the tall stem; remove any as soon as you spot them, using secateurs.

Rosa Lovely Lady

pruning a rambler on an arch

1 By the end of summer rambler roses have finished flowering and their growth will have become tangled. Untie all stems from their supports, and select about six of the strongest, new green stems growing from the ground to retain.

2 Prune out all the old, darker stems, cutting them close to ground level. If there is a shortage of new stems from ground level, cut back some of the older ones to a strong new shoot instead of cutting them right down.

3 Shorten all the fresh green sideshoots by at least two-thirds and ideally to leave only two to three buds, as shorter sideshoots will produce better regrowth next year. Tie in the retained shoots to their supports, spreading them out evenly.

taking hardwood cuttings

Most roses can be grown from hardwood cuttings. These root easily and the resulting plants grow on their own roots, so there will be no problem with suckers. Take the cuttings between late August and early October, selecting strong, well-ripened stems about the thickness of a pencil.

- Cut off and discard the slim, soft growth at the tip. Make the cutting about 30cm (12in) long and trim just below a leaf joint at the base. Remove all lower leaves, but not the buds.
- Prepare a narrow, V-shaped trench in the ground, about 23cm (9in) deep; half fill with sharp sand if the soil is heavy.
- Dip the base of the cuttings in hormone rooting powder. Plant upright, 15cm (6in) apart, buried to half their length.
- Replace the soil and tread it firm round the cuttings. Water them well and label clearly. Check whether they have rooted in April but, preferably, leave until next autumn.

late summer pruning

Prune rambler roses by the first half of September (see above). Weeping standards are also pruned now and in the same way, removing as much older growth as possible and leaving the best of this year's new growth as replacement.

preparing for new roses

Take the opportunity to visit rose gardens to see plants in bloom and read through some rose catalogues. Order plants in good time for autumn delivery. Before then you need to prepare the site thoroughly. Make a start in late summer by digging the soil, two spade blades (spits) deep. Remove weeds and root fragments and work in plenty of well-rotted manure or garden compost. Deep digging helps to improve drainage, but on very heavy ground it might be easier to create raised beds. Lightly fork in a top-dressing of rose fertiliser and leave the soil to settle for at least six weeks.

ROSE SICKNESS TIP Avoid planting new roses where roses grew before as they are unlikely to thrive. If you have nowhere else to plant, you must replace the soil. Dig a hole for each new plant, about 60cm (2ft) wide and 45cm (18in) deep. Remove the excavated soil to elsewhere in the garden and replace it with a mixture of fresh topsoil and garden compost or rotted manure.

there is still time to...

- **take bud cuttings** of most kinds of roses. Root them in a coldframe to make young plants next year (see Summer).
- **layer long flexible branches** of shrub and rambler roses to produce new plants for transplanting next spring.

looking ahead...

☑ EARLY SPRING Transplant rooted layers and pot up bud cuttings.

☑ SPRING OR AUTUMN Check hardwood cuttings.

climbers

Although the pace of growth has slowed, some regular attention in the form of watering, pruning and training continues to pay off. Take advantage of the maturing growth to make semi-ripe cuttings and prepare the ground now for planting new climbers in autumn.

now is the season to ...

- **prune wisteria** as soon as possible if not already done earlier in summer.
- **train in plant stems** regularly; use soft string where tying is necessary. As growth slows, attend to plants on a fortnightly, rather than a weekly, basis.
- **control self-clinging climbers,** which can damage woodwork and guttering.
- **in dry spells water** climbers in containers and any that are newly planted. Another priority group is established plants growing beside buildings where the soil is sheltered and gets little rain. Give them a soaking every couple of weeks; increase frequency in drought periods.
- **weed regularly** and watch out for bindweed in particular.
- **check leaf-bud cuttings of clematis** taken in late spring once new leaves begin to appear.
- **stay alert for signs of fungal diseases,** which are likely to be a problem if the weather has been extremely wet or dry. An application of fungicide usually limits further spread of the disease but does not cure affected foliage, which should be cut off and removed or destroyed.
- **watch out for pests.** Aphids often infest annual climbers, and nasturtiums are also susceptible to attack by the larvae of the cabbage white butterfly. Regular inspections and hand-squashing caterpillars can keep populations in check.
- **feed annual climbers** every seven to fourteen days with liquid fertiliser to keep them flowering. Do not feed permanent plants, though, as this encourages soft growth that could be damaged later by frost.
- **take semi-ripe cuttings** of many climbers (see opposite).

and if you have time . . .

- **prepare ground for autumn planting** of hardy climbers. Dig the soil to two spade blades deep and incorporate plenty of well-rotted organic matter.

controlling bindweed

Weeds often grow unnoticed through established climbers, and bindweed is a particular nuisance as it twines up their stems. Midsummer is a good time to apply the systemic weedkiller glyphosate to this and other tenacious perennial weeds, before they flower and set seed. Because the chemical kills any growth it touches, train the bindweed away from the host climber by sticking bamboo canes into the ground up which the weed can grow. Then slip the growth off the canes and apply the glyphosate within a polythene bag, to prevent it from coming in contact with other plants.

pruning guide

- **summer prune wisteria** if not already done (see Summer). Tie in new stems left unpruned and train them horizontally if possible, which will boost flowering by slowing the flow of sap along the branches.

The annual morning glory climber (*Ipomoea*) is intertwined with the growth of a grape vine (*Vitis vinifera* 'Olivette').

pruning and training climbers

1 Space out main stems evenly and at an angle from the vertical. Secure them to their support using soft twine tied in a figure of eight.

2 Trim back wayward stems to just above a leaf joint. You may need to do this regularly for vigorous climbers.

Cut back young stems of ivy that have insinuated their way between the wooden panels of sheds and fences. Unless they are cut back, they will eventually force the panels apart.

• **prune other climbers** if they are extending well beyond their allotted space, but remember that by pruning flowering climbers in late summer you are likely to be removing some of next year's blooms.

The climber *Parthenocissus henryana* clings by sucker pads.

• **cut back self-clinging climbers** like ivy, virginia creepers and *Parthenocissus henryana*. Keep these plants clear of window frames and other woodwork, as their clinging stem roots or sucker pads are likely to cause damage, particularly to paintwork. Trim back growth to at least 30cm (12in) from susceptible areas of the house. Train or prune the stems of all climbers to keep them clear of your roof edges, guttering and downpipes.

propagation

Many climbers can be raised now from semi-ripe cuttings. The chief exception is clematis, which are best propagated by internodal leaf-bud cuttings (see Late Spring). If you took any of these earlier in the year, check them once new leaves begin to appear by carefully taking off the pot. If roots are developing, pot up cuttings individually into 8cm (3in) pots.

semi-ripe cuttings

• Select healthy, non-flowering shoots when the stem is firm but not yet hard and woody. Sever them from the parent plant just above a leaf joint.

• Make the cuttings about 10–15cm (4–6in) long by trimming just below a leaf joint, using a sharp knife. Remove the leaves on the lower two-thirds of the shoot.

• Dip the base of each cutting in hormone rooting compound, then insert several cuttings around the edge of a 13cm (5in) pot filled with moist cuttings and seed compost. Rooting is improved if the compost is mixed with a third by volume of perlite or horticultural vermiculite.

• Stand the pot of cuttings in a propagator or coldframe shaded from the sun. Do not over-water, but do not let them dry out completely. Rooting usually takes between eight and twelve weeks.

looking ahead . . .

☑ AUTUMN Choose or order hardy climbers for autumn planting in prepared ground.

☑ Pot up rooted cuttings individually into 8cm (3in) pots.

☑ WINTER Winter-prune wisteria.

climbers **to raise from semi-ripe cuttings**

- honeysuckle (*Lonicera*)
- passion flower (*Passiflora*)
- solanum • summer jasmine (*Jasminum officinale*)
- trachelospermum

Jasminum officinale

shrubs & trees

Pruning shrubs and trimming hedges are the main activities this season. In addition, time spent weeding is never wasted and, if you want to make more of your plants, now is the perfect opportunity to propagate lots of different shrubs.

now is the season to . . .

- **trim hedges** to keep them neat (see page 44).
- **check variegated shrubs** and remove any all-green shoots.
- **prune shrubs** that flowered early in summer.
- **keep camellias moist** as they can suffer from bud drop and, consequently, loss of flowers in the coming spring, due to a shortage of water now. Take care not to let the plants dry out, and cover the soil with a 5cm (2in) layer of mulch to help maintain moisture in the soil.
- **water shrubs growing in containers** regularly to keep the compost moist at all times. In dry spells water any recently planted shrubs.
- **weed borders regularly** by hoeing or digging weeds up before they have a chance to establish. Look under spreading branches in case perennial weeds such as dock are growing and shedding seeds unnoticed; the old adage 'one year's seeding means seven years weeding' is a true one.
- **inspect plants for signs of pests or diseases.** These are more likely to be a problem if shrubs have been under stress due to drought or if the weather has been unduly wet. Established shrubs usually shrug off all but severe attacks, but it is worth checking young plants and those growing in containers, and controlling any attacks detected in the early stages.

and if you have time . . .

- **prepare ground** for autumn planting.

Buddleja davidii 'Black Knight' is a beautifully scented shrub. Propagate it now, from non-flowering shoots turning woody.

shrub pruning guide

- **prune early summer-flowering shrubs** such as deutzias, mock orange (*Philadelphus*) and weigelas as soon as possible. Cut back flowered shoots to strong, young lower growth and remove any dead, diseased or damaged stems.
- **trim lavender** and cotton lavender (*Santolina chamaecyparissus*) after their main flowering to keep them neat and bushy.
- **remove green-leaved, or reverted, shoots** that commonly occur on shrubs with coloured or variegated foliage. Prune these out as soon as possible, because they grow fast and, if left, will eventually dominate the coloured plant. Reversion is much less likely to occur on flowering shrubs, but tree mallow (*Lavatera*) may produce shoots with blooms of a different colour and you should prune these out if you wish to stop them dominating the plant.
- **thin out older plants** that are becoming overgrown. Remove a third of the thickest branches close to the ground.
- **assess plants for future pruning now,** while they are in full growth. This is the best time to decide on what action needs to be taken and make a diary note accordingly, rather than viewing leafless plants in winter when they look far less bulky.

shearing lavender

1 **Clip over lavender bushes** when they are coming towards the end of their flowering.

2 **Use shears to clip over** the whole plant, taking off the dead flowers complete with stems and the top few centimetres of long new shoots.

shrubs to propagate from semi-ripe cuttings

• aucuba • box • brachyglottis • buddleja • ceanothus • choisya • cistus • cotoneaster • deutzia • escallonia • euonymus • exochorda • hebe • helianthemum • hydrangea • hypericum • kerria • lavender • myrtle • philadelphus • potentilla • pyracantha • santolina • senecio • spiraea • tamarisk • teucrium • weigela

Santolina chamaecyparissus

Check at intervals to see whether cuttings have rooted by pulling one out at random and then replacing if necessary. These yew and box cuttings are now ready to be potted up.

semi-ripe cuttings

These cuttings are taken from this year's growth that is beginning to turn woody. They provide an excellent means of making more shrubs and ensuring the survival of those of borderline hardiness that could be killed in a severe winter. Choose healthy, non-flowering shoots that are starting to turn woody. Sever them from the parent plant by cutting just above a leaf joint to avoid leaving a stump of dead stem.

In some cases you can take cuttings with a 'heel', a strip of older wood at the base of the shoot (see right). These have an even better chance of success because the plant's growth hormones that stimulate rooting are concentrated in the heel.

After inserting the cuttings in a container filled with cuttings compost, water and cover the pot with an inflated clear polythene bag, or stand it in a propagator or coldframe, out of direct sun, and leave. Rooting usually takes from six to ten weeks, but longer in the case of evergreens.

leaf-bud cuttings

• Leaf-bud cuttings are an economical method of propagating evergreen shrubs where you want several cuttings from one shoot, or there is not enough suitable material on the parent plant (such as after a poor summer, producing little growth).

• Select semi-ripe shoots as described above, but cut each one into sections, 2–3cm (1in) below a leaf joint and immediately above the leaf.

• Wound the stem below the leaf joint to stimulate rooting by removing a sliver of bark.

• Insert the cuttings into a pot or tray filled with cuttings compost so that the top of the leaf joint is just visible above the surface of the compost. Then treat as described above.

taking heel cuttings

1 **Detach complete sideshoots** from a main stem by pulling gently. You want the shoot to come away complete with a heel where it joins the stem.

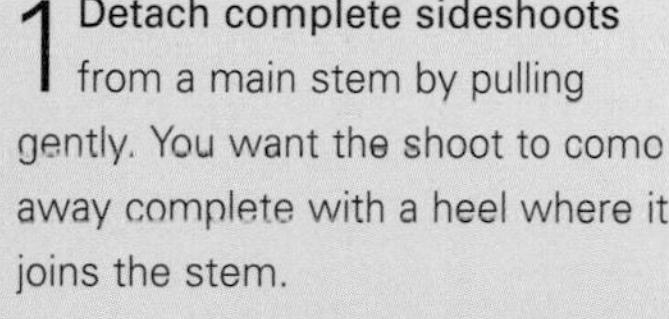

2 **Trim off** any bits of bark protruding from the heel.

3 **Dip the base** of each cutting in hormone rooting powder. Arrange in a tray or around the edge of a 13cm (5in) pot filled with seed and cuttings compost, either on its own, or mixed with a third by volume of horticultural vermiculite or perlite to aid rooting.

shrubs & trees/2

trimming hedges

Late summer is the time to give formal hedges their final trim for the year, as pruning in autumn encourages soft new growth that could be damaged by frost. Some informal hedges also benefit from attention now, notably those that have finished flowering.

Established formal hedges require regular trimming along the top and sides to maintain a neat shape, whereas informal hedges, mostly grown for their flowers or berries, should be left to grow more naturally. A neat formal hedge will need to be cut between one and three times during the growing season; the frequency depends on how quickly your chosen hedge plant grows.

Start trimming as soon as a recently planted hedge reaches the required height (except for conifers, see below). If allowed to get out of hand, the hedge may not regrow if pruned hard later on. By beginning regular trimming at an early stage, even leyland cypress (leylandii), that most rampant of hedge plants, can be kept compact. Shape the sides of the hedge so that the top is narrower than the bottom. This makes them less vulnerable to wind and snow.

If pernicious weeds such as bindweed have grown through the hedge, paint a systemic weedkiller onto their leaves. This will cause the plant to wither and die. Avoid getting any weedkiller on the hedge.

hedge-trimming tools

The choice of equipment depends on the size of hedge and the amount of energy you have. Garden shears for hand trimming come in lightweight and heavy-duty models. Choose light ones for a soft-stemmed hedge, but a heavier model for thicker growth. Shears with telescopic handles give extra long reach.

Hedge trimmers come in a range of sizes and are powered by petrol or electricity. For safety, use a circuit breaker, or residual current device (RCD) when operating an electric hedge trimmer from the mains. Wear protective clothing and do not work in wet conditions. Rechargeable battery-powered trimmers are safer.

trimming a formal conifer hedge

1 **Allow conifers to grow** about 60cm (2ft) above the desired height before cutting. Run a string between two canes at the cutting height, which will be around 15cm (6in) below the ultimate level. This will encourage new bushy growth at the top.

2 **Trim the sides,** starting at the bottom and working upwards, and making the hedge narrower at the top than it is at the base. Wear goggles and gloves when using a powered hedge trimmer and, if electric, always use a circuit breaker (RCD) for safety.

3 **Cut the top** of the hedge along your guideline, tapering the edges rather than leaving a flat, wide top. Do not overreach; if necessary, set up a ladder or trestles and make sure they stand on a firm, level base. Get a helper to steady the bottom of a ladder while you are working.

looking ahead . . .

☑ AUTUMN Pot up rooted cuttings to overwinter under cover.

☑ WINTER Renovate overgrown deciduous hedges.

☑ SPRING Renovate overgrown evergreen hedges.

Evergreen hedges and topiary, so characteristic of formal gardens, need regular clipping to maintain their sharp outline. They all need attention in late summer, when they have their final trim of the year.

hedge trimming times

FORMAL HEDGES	WHEN TO TRIM
BOX* (*Buxus sempervirens*)	once, late summer
HORNBEAM* (*Carpinus betulus*)	once, mid to late summer
LAWSON'S CYPRESS (*Chamaecyparis lawsoniana*)	twice, spring and autumn
HAWTHORN* (*Crataegus monogyna*)	twice, summer and winter
LEYLAND CYPRESS (x *Cupressocyparis leylandii*)	2–3 times in growing season
BEECH* (*Fagus sylvatica*)	once, late summer
HOLLY* (*Ilex aquifolium*)	once, late summer
PRIVET* (*Ligustrum ovalifolium*)	2–3 times in growing season
LAUREL* (*Prunus laurocerasus*)	once, spring
YEW* (*Taxus baccata*)	twice, summer and autumn
INFORMAL HEDGES	**WHEN TO TRIM**
BERBERIS*	immediately after flowering
ELAEAGNUS	remove straggly shoots only, in spring
ESCALLONIA*	late summer
*Griselinia littoralis**	remove straggly shoots in spring
LAVENDER (*Lavandula angustifolia*)	lightly in spring and again after flowering to remove dead flower stems and tips of new shoots
Pyracantha coccinea	summer
*Rosa rugosa**	remove thin shoots in spring
*Viburnum tinus**	thin out growth in spring

** plants that tolerate hard pruning and renovation*

PRUNING TIP Prune large-leaved hedges, such as laurel (*Prunus laurocerasus*), with secateurs to avoid shearing leaves in half and the unsightly browning remnants of severed leaf blades.

renovating overgrown hedges

Neglected and overgrown hedges can often be rejuvenated by hard pruning. However, there are some plants that do not regrow from old wood, notably the leyland and lawson's cypresses. Such plants are best cut down, dug up and replaced if they have become thin or bare at the base. The best time for hard pruning is mid-spring for evergreens and winter for deciduous plants.

alpine gardens

As the nights grow cooler and longer, many alpine plants come into flower, but their success depends on time spent weeding, checking invasive neighbours and watering alpine troughs. This is the best season to divide primulas and take cuttings of shrubby alpines.

now is the season to . . .

■ **keep a sharp eye open** for seedling weeds, which come thick and fast after rain, and remove them before they are big enough to cause trouble. Any overlooked weeds that have reached flowering stage must be removed before they have an opportunity to set seed.

■ **freshen up exhausted plants,** such as geraniums, thrift and alpine pinks that have finished flowering. Remove their stems, along with any unsightly dead or dying leaves and snip off any straggly parts. This not only tidies the plants, but also stimulates them into fresh growth.

Dianthus cuttings, as well as seedlings raised earlier in the year, can now be potted up singly in 8cm (3in) pots.

■ **propagate new alpines,** and plant up seedlings or cuttings that were sown or taken earlier in the year.

■ **restrain invasive plants** by taking action with any 'thugs'. Trim them hard back wherever they are threatening to engulf a neighbour and, in extreme cases, consider relocating the more sedate plants under threat – but defer the actual transplanting until autumn or spring.

■ **check creeping plants** that form wide mats, rooting as they go. Remove them from areas where they create a nuisance. Conversely, if you want to speed up their spread, tuck any loose stem ends into the ground and water thoroughly, to encourage extra rooting.

■ **if bare patches have developed** on spreading or ground-covering plants, cover them with a top-dressing of gritty leaf-mould or compost. This will stimulate new root growth, and should encourage the plant to regenerate.

■ **give attention to alpine sinks** and troughs, especially if the weather is hot and dry (see right).

■ **plant dwarf narcissus** at the end of August, when fresh bulbs arrive at garden centres. The tiny bulbs will dehydrate unless planted soon after purchase.

■ **guard against pests** such as vine weevil, particularly in containers. Slugs and snails can ruin delicate young plants, so surround the plants with slug-proof barriers, such as grit, and go out after dark with a torch and hand-pick any slugs and snails found feeding at night.

■ **gather seeds** from plants such as pinks, campanulas and geraniums, and be sure to label whatever you collect (see page 30).

and if you have time . . .

■ **consider building a raised bed** or new rock garden. Summer is a good time for construction and, if you complete the work within a few weeks, it will be ready for planting up in autumn.

Tidy alpine beds and borders by cutting the straggly stems off plants that have flowered. This will stimulate the plants into producing fresh growth.

looking after alpine containers

Although they require little maintenance at other times of the year, alpines in sinks or troughs can suffer in hot and dry summers if you fail to give them the care they need.

- **during the hottest part of the year** give containers an occasional thorough watering to guard plants against stress.
- **as the days shorten,** plants such as gentians and hardy cyclamen begin to grow again. Give your containers a penetrating soak after drought to stimulate this new growth and their flowering performance will be improved.
- **a single dilute liquid feed** will also help, particularly with gentians, but only if the soil has become impoverished. Do not overfeed, however. Late in the season, boost the organic level of the soil in permanent containers by working in a little leaf-mould or friable home-made garden compost.
- **watch out for vine weevil,** whose larvae may be active. The

symptoms are sudden wilting and death of formerly healthy-looking plants. If you search the soil and find the white, comma-shaped grubs among the roots, either re-pot the plant using new compost, or resort to using biological control such as watering with imidocloprid.

propagation

Cuttings of alpines taken in spring should be well rooted by now, and large and hardy enough to survive winter. Where several cuttings are in one pot, carefully turn them out, tease the young plants apart and replant each one in an 8cm (3in) pot filled with free-draining potting compost. Stand the pots in a coldframe or sheltered spot outside. Any plants that are large enough to handle, and have developed a good root system, can be planted directly into the rock garden.

taking semi-ripe cuttings

Woody plants such as dwarf willows, helianthemums, fuchsias and alpine penstemons are propagated in late summer from semi-ripe cuttings (see page 43 for details). Select stems that are just on the turn from soft to woody. Placed in a sheltered spot or a coldframe, the cuttings should develop roots over the coming autumn and winter.

Cut non-flowered helianthemum shoots that are just turning woody and remove the lower leaves. Place the cuttings round the edge of an 8cm (3in) container filled with cuttings compost and gently water them in.

dividing primulas

Most primulas divided now will have time to develop into healthy new plants before autumn advances.

- **primroses and their relatives** form clumps. Lift them, remove soil and dead foliage and gently pull apart the individual leaf 'rosettes'. Replant where you want them to grow.
- **auricula types** produce leaf rosettes at the ends of short, fleshy stems. Break off individual rosettes and use them as 'cuttings'. Insert up to five round the edge of a 8cm (3in) pot filled with gritty, free-draining compost.

A collection of succulents, including the almost black *Aeonium* 'Zwartkop', thrives in pots raised off the ground for free drainage. Again for drainage, the compost is mixed with grit, and more grit has been added as a mulch.

water gardens

Ponds and water features reach their peak of beauty this season, with water lilies in full bloom and marginal plants at their most luxuriant. The essential jobs are to remove dead and dying leaves and to top up water levels regularly.

now is the season to . . .

- **top up ponds and water features,** especially small ones, whenever levels drop. Where possible, do this with clean rainwater, collected in a water butt, rather than tap water. If tap water is used over prolonged periods, the level of dissolved mineral salts gradually increases, encouraging algae.
- **oxygenate your pond** in hot weather, especially if you have fish (see right).
- **keep pond water clear** and sweet by removing blanket weed.
- **remove dead or dying water lily leaves** and flowers; not only do they look unsightly but they can also foul the water. Take hold of each leaf in turn and pull away as much of its stem as you can.
- **tidy up marginal plants** by removing dead leaves and fading flowers. Use secateurs, or a pocket knife, to cut away dying leaves or stems from the base of the plants, but take great care not to puncture the pond liner.
- **thin out oxygenating plants** and surplus water lily leaves.
- **control weeds in your bog garden.** In lush, moist conditions, weeds can take hold quickly and with devastating results.
- **ensure that young frogs have an easy exit,** as tadpoles will be entering the last stage of their juvenile lives and, over a few days, will turn into tiny frogs. If your pond has no 'beach' area, rest a plank to bridge the gap from water to dry land to give them access.

Pontederia cordata

maintaining oxygen levels

As the water temperature rises the level of dissolved oxygen drops, which means that the ability of the water to sustain a rich variety of life forms also diminishes. There are several ways in which you can help to minimise the effects of reduced oxygen.

- **run fountains** and other moving water features at night, as well as during the day. As well as helping water to absorb oxygen, this will also bring down the temperature slightly.
- **oxygenate pond water** quickly in hot and sultry weather, especially if you see fish gasping for air at the surface, by playing a hose at least 60cm (2ft) above the water surface. This will carry oxygen down into the pond.
- **make sure oxygenating plants are healthy** and receive enough light to grow. They should be threatening to fill up the pond at this time of year, but if their growth is sparse, try some new species that may be better suited to your pond's conditions.
- **control water snails** if they are too plentiful. In moderate numbers, these are beneficial, helping to clean up algae, but in large numbers they will consume all green leaves under water, including those of oxygenating plants. Pick a few out of the pond every day.

NEW PONDS TIP Deep ponds, or those with relatively large volumes of water, warm up more slowly than do small ones, so if you are building a pond from scratch, or want to expand your existing pond, bear this in mind.

Keep a waterfall running as much as possible during spells of hot weather to lower the temperature and help to oxygenate the water.

controlling surplus growth

Plant growth reaches a climax in late summer, and in a small pond it may be necessary to thin the vegetation to avoid overcrowding. Water lilies can become so congested that the leaves lie on top of each other, or can rear up on their stems, hiding the flowers.

Fairy moss has been allowed to colonise the surface of this container pond. Though it looks pretty, it should be scooped out to control its spread.

- **skim off surplus floating plants,** not only from ponds and smaller water features, but also from water butts. Fairy moss and duckweed should not be permitted to cover every centimetre of the surface. Use a wire rake to pull weeds in one direction, but do this gently and carefully so that plants left behind are not messed up, then remove the weeds by hand to the compost heap. In small ponds a flour sieve does the job more effectively.
- **with water lilies** the aim is to cover no more than 70 per cent of the pond's surface. Remove any excess leaves, starting with older or damaged ones, by giving the stem below the water surface a brisk tug; take off as much of the stem as you can.
- **thin out submerged oxygenating plants** by simply hauling out handfuls at a time. Before taking them along to the compost heap, rescue any stranded fish and leave plants by the waterside for a few hours so that other pond life has a chance to crawl back in.
- **blanket weed,** the green filamentous algae with the texture and consistency of wet wool, can cause an unsightly problem in water features in late summer, especially during spells of hot weather. Remove it by winding up the long filaments round a rake or a strong stick, and take them away for composting.
- **green algae** that clouds the water may not look pretty, but is relatively harmless and a producer of oxygen in daylight. It is often a result of incorrect balance and, although there are chemical algae controls, it is better to allow your pond to develop a good balance naturally (see Late Spring).

Lush-growing marginal plants by a stream (above) include rodgersias, mimulus, primulas and daylilies. Thin out any that are spreading too far, to prevent overcrowding (left).

patios & containers

Now that the pace of work slows to a gentle crawl, take the opportunity to relax and enjoy your patio. Freshen up plants with regular watering and deadheading, and take some soft-tip cuttings of your favourite flowers for next year's tubs and window boxes.

now is the season to . . .

- **water each container** until you see the surplus running out through the drainage holes, as it is possible for large containers to dry out completely without you knowing.
- **feed flagging plants,** as the growth rate slows down in late summer. An extra boost of plant food should rejuvenate them and help them to flower on until the first frost.
- **deadhead all spent flowers,** and remove faded leaves and straggly stems.
- **trim overgrown topiary** (see right).
- **take soft-tip cuttings** of the tender plants you would like to keep and use again next year.
- **weed** the cracks between paving.

Hand-weed the cracks in between paving stones before plants set seed.

and if you have time . . .

- **plant up a container** or two in September for winter beauty (see Autumn).

survival guide for the holidays

This is the traditional season for getting away from the garden, but before you depart make provision for your patio plants so that they survive your absence.

- **arrange for a friend** or neighbour to come in and water your containers, or consider installing an automatic watering system (see Summer).
- **group containers together in one spot,** which is both out of the sun and sheltered from the wind. Not only does this make watering more convenient for your neighbour, it also means pots are less likely to dry out if left unattended for a day or two.
- **plunge small pots** into a bigger container filled with moist sand or potting compost.
- **incorporate water-retaining gel** into the compost of thirsty summer bedding when planting or repotting. The gel mops up excess moisture, preventing waterlogging, but roots are still able to extract the water when they need it.
- **cut off surplus growth,** as plants pruned quite hard will need watering less frequently than those with an excessive amount of leaves and stems. Feed and water plants thoroughly immediately after pruning, to initiate healthy re-growth.
- **pick off flowers and buds,** if these are likely to open while you are away. Removing young flower spikes from such plants as penstemons, phygelius, nemesias and diascias should stimulate a burst of fresh growth to greet your return.

trimming topiary

This is the best time for trimming topiary, as there is still enough growing season left for it to recover from being shorn, but not enough to grow untidy. In this way specimens will retain their neat shape until next summer. The number of trims per year depends on the plant (see Hedge Trimming Times chart on page 45).

keeping topiary in trim

1 **Use shears to trim** small-leaved topiary such as box. Trimming now will define the shape better and neaten the plant.

2 **Follow your eye** to maintain an established shape, like this bird.

tender **perennials suitable for soft-tip cuttings**

- coleus • fuchsia
- mexican salvia • mimulus
- nemesia • pelargonium
- verbena

Fuchsia 'Margaret'

POTTING UP TIP When potting up rooted cuttings, avoid using containers that are too large. The compost could become wet and stagnant, and the young roots rot off. It is better to pot them now into small containers and pot them on later, in February, when the days are lengthening and growth begins in earnest.

looking ahead . . .

☑ WINTER OR EARLY SPRING Pot up rooted cuttings taken in late summer.

Trimming by eye is usually sufficient for simple shapes, although you can use a wooden frame as a guide. More intricate designs are probably best trained on a wire-netting frame, which makes them easier to trim to shape. Shears or mechanical hedge clippers are suitable for topiary work, although shrubs with large evergreen leaves, like laurel, may look unsightly unless trimmed with secateurs. Shears cut across whole leaves, which stain and distort as they heal.

It is easier to trim topiary shrubs in containers than those in borders, which can grow very large. Keep the topiary form in harmony with the container's shape and in proportion to its size.

propagation

This is the season to take cuttings of tender perennials, which are so attractive just now, but so costly at garden centres. Taking soft-tip cuttings now will ensure that you have plentiful stocks of mature plants, ready to set out in beds and containers in late spring next year. Ideally, select non-flowering shoots. If this is not possible, remove the flowers before making and inserting the cuttings in a tray or round the edge of a container (see page 31).

If you plan to grow lots of cuttings, you will need a greenhouse or a well-lit conservatory. But even if you lack these facilities, and space is limited, it should still be possible to overwinter a few of your favourites for next year on a windowsill indoors.

Soft-tip cuttings of scented-leaved pelargoniums should root successfully within a few weeks.

Extend the flowering period of your patio plants by regular feeding, watering and deadheading. This will prolong the colourful display into autumn.

lawns

Regular cutting keeps your lawn looking smart, although if the summer is dry the growth may be very slow without generous watering. If you are planning a new lawn in autumn, prepare the ground well in advance to clear weeds and allow the soil to settle.

now is the season to . . .

- **mow regularly** to maintain a good quality lawn (see opposite).
- **trim edges** every three to four weeks, immediately after mowing. Cut as close to the lawn edge as possible and collect up the trimmings.
- **spike and scarify the grass** if it feels spongy to walk on, a sign that a layer of dead grass clippings, or thatch, has formed. Rake out the thatch with a fan-shaped wire rake, otherwise it can prevent water and fertiliser from reaching the soil around the roots.
- **water regularly** in dry periods, particularly if the lawn is in its first season.

Spiking the lawn with a special tool aerates it by removing small plugs of soil, and allows water and nutrients to reach the grass roots.

The grasses in new lawns will not have developed the large root systems found in established turf and this makes them more vulnerable to drought. The best times to water are in the cool early morning or late evening, so that as much water soaks in as possible rather than being lost through evaporation (see Summer).

- **at the end of summer, feed the lawn** with an autumn fertiliser containing phosphates and potash to help harden plant growth for autumn and winter. Apply two days after mowing, and be prepared to water the fertiliser in if it does not rain within two days.
- **start preparing the soil** for a new lawn.
- **examine your lawn** for signs of fungal disease, like red thread (see opposite).

FEEDING TIP Applying a soluble fertiliser through an 'in-hose' dilutor saves having to water the lawn after it has been fed by combining the two operations.

preparing for a new lawn

Whether you plan to sow seed or lay turf, you need to prepare the soil well in advance and clear the ground of weeds before laying a new lawn (see Late Spring).

Low box hedges frame this fresh green carpet of lawn. The smaller the garden, the more immaculate the lawn needs to look.

• Dig over the ground to at least the depth of a spade blade, and remove all traces of perennial weeds. Rake over the soil to break down lumps and level the surface.
• Allow weed seedlings to germinate and, when they have grown to about 8cm (3in) high, either hoe them off at soil level or kill them by spraying with a weedkiller.
• Repeat this process several times to kill off weed seeds that are close to the soil surface. When the time comes to sow, there will be fewer weeds germinating along with the grass seed, which will help the lawn to establish quickly.

A regular mowing regime is best, though the frequency will depend on weather conditions.

mowing frequency

How often you need to mow will vary according to the wetness or dryness of the season and the type of lawn you have. The points to remember, before following the guidelines given here, are never to reduce the height of the grass by more than a third at a single cut, and always to allow it to recover for a couple of days before cutting again.
• **fine ornamental lawns** need cutting as often as two or three times a week, to a height of about 6mm (¼in).
• **cut average-use lawns** once or twice a week to approximately 1cm (½in).
• **hardwearing lawns,** designed for play, need one cut a week to about 2cm (¾in).
• **for new lawns,** leave the grass slightly longer to reduce stress in dry weather. If you have a mower with a roller, alternate between mowing the grass and rolling it lightly. The rolling will bend over the grass shoots, encouraging them to form more leaves and shade for the roots.
• **avoid mowing too closely,** as this can reduce the vigour of the grass plants and make them more susceptible to attack from fungal diseases.
• **infrequent or erratic mowing** encourages moss and weeds to invade the lawn as it struggles to recover.

protecting lawn edges

By late summer, herbaceous plants will be flopping over the edges of borders unless you have put supports in place. This will cause the edges of the lawn to turn brown as well as making them difficult to mow. Insert either purpose-made support frames or twiggy 'pea sticks' (see Late Spring) to pull plants back, or use canes and string to keep leafy plants off the lawn. The alternative is to lay a hard 'mowing edge' between the edge of the lawn and any border (see page 150).

A home-made support using bamboo canes and hazel twigs stops tall perennials from falling onto the lawn.

red thread disease

This disease can appear as bleached patches of grass, with the leaves taking on a pinkish tinge as summer progresses. The incidence of red thread disease is more common on fine-leaved lawns and those that are underfed, and where soils are sandy as the fertilisers are easily washed through. If you start feeding the grass regularly (with a high-nitrogen fertiliser in spring and early summer and a high-phosphate plus potash feed in late summer and autumn), your lawn will gradually recover, but it can look unsightly for some time. You should also avoid cutting the grass too closely as this will lead to stress, which in turn makes the lawn more vulnerable to fungal diseases.

fruit

The fruit harvest is now in full swing, and in a good season there will be excess for you to store or preserve. In addition to enjoying your fruits, there is also pruning and training to be done, as well as planning new plantings.

now is the season to . . .

■ **continue watering** recently planted fruit in dry weather, especially those on light soils and those planted against walls. Mulch after watering to conserve soil moisture.

■ **keep on top of weeds** by hoeing or hand-weeding. Pay particular attention to young plants that are still establishing.

■ **stay vigilant** for late summer pests and diseases, and take appropriate measures immediately (see page 75).

■ **harvest fruit as it ripens.**

■ **plan new fruit plantings,** send off for nursery catalogues and explore locally available varieties. Pay particular attention to the soil, climate and pollination requirements (see right).

■ **start preparing** the site where new plants are to grow.

and if you have time . . .

■ **clear any fallen fruits,** as these invite pests and diseases.

■ **protect ripening fruit** from birds and wasps with fleece or fine-mesh netting. This is particularly important when signs of damage appear, as raiding will continue once started.

harvesting now

• early apples • blackberries
• blackcurrants • cherries
• red currants • white currants
• dessert gooseberries • grapes
• figs • loganberries and other hybrid berries • peaches
• early pears • plums
• raspberries • strawberries

Loganberries

ordering new fruit

It is wise to order new fruit plants early to allow yourself the widest possible choice. Popular varieties are usually available from many outlets throughout the planting season, but unusual, rare or old-fashioned varieties, as well as recent introductions, may sell out early or be available from a limited number of specialist nurseries. Send for catalogues now, and order before the end of September for satisfaction, but before you buy bear in mind the following points:

• **always buy from a reputable source** to avoid introducing diseases or poor quality plants. Where appropriate, choose certified plants: many fruits are inspected regularly to make sure they are healthy and true to type.

• **decide where you want to plant,** then match fruits to the aspect and exposure of your site, and the type of soil. There are some apple varieties, for example, that thrive best in areas of high rainfall; gooseberries enjoy cool districts; raspberries dislike chalky soils; and a single red currant variety can ripen early, mid-season or late according to how warm, sunny, cool or shady is the site.

• **check pollination requirements.** Fruits such as blackcurrants and acid cherries are self-pollinating and will crop well in isolation, whereas sweet cherries, apples, pears and most plums need at least one other compatible tree with which to exchange pollen at flowering time. If you have space for only one tree, make sure it is self-fertile.

Mesh netting will help to protect soft fruit, such as these ripe red currants, from attack by birds.

• **most fruit trees are grafted,** so when you buy avoid plants labelled simply 'bush' or 'standard'. The type of rootstock will decide your tree's vigour, ultimate size and start of cropping, and it is important to choose the appropriate type, identified by a name or number (see Autumn). A reputable garden centre or nursery will help you to make the right choice.

preparing for planting

As soon as you have ordered your new fruit, make a start on preparing the site so that the ground has time to settle before planting in autumn. Most kinds of fruit are long-lived and, like other trees and shrubs, grow best where the soil has been thoroughly cultivated.

Begin by clearing all the weeds, particularly perennial kinds. This may mean simply forking out a few weeds here and there, but where the ground is heavily infested, cut down the top growth by hand or with a rotary mower, then spray the entire area with a weedkiller such as glyphosate.

Once the site is cleared you can cultivate, but how you do this depends on your soil type and which fruits you intend to grow. The larger the plant, the deeper the soil needs to be; strawberries will grow in shallow ground 25–30cm (10–12in) deep, whereas tree fruits need 60–75cm (2ft–2ft 6in) of well-drained soil.

• **double dig sites** that are poorly drained or very weedy. This can be strenuous and the work is best tackled in stages.
• **single digging is sufficient** for bush and cane fruits on good soil or ground that has been cultivated previously.
• **fruit trees** need only individually prepared planting sites of about 1m (3ft) square.
• **all soils and sites** benefit from liberal additions of garden compost or rotted manure worked in well as you dig.
• **after cultivation** leave the ground to settle for at least six weeks and then, just before planting in the autumn, hoe or fork out any weeds that have emerged and rake in a dressing of fertiliser appropriate to the type of fruit (see Autumn).

there is still time to . . .

• **summer prune trained forms** of apples and pears (see Summer), especially in areas of high rainfall, but try to finish before the end of August.
• **prune plums and sweet cherries,** shortening new sideshoots by about a third. Tie in new extension shoots, unpruned.

Being trained against a warm wall helps peaches and other fruits to ripen, but they will also need frequent watering.

looking ahead . . .

☑ AUTUMN Finish preparing the ground and planting new fruits.
☑ Propagate cane fruits.

fruit/2

routine care

After your plants have fruited, keep on top of the pruning, training and tidying up; not only will your garden look neater but the plants will be more productive and easier to manage in future.

Remove suckers from the trunks of cherry and other fruit trees if they appear. Use secateurs and cut them cleanly against the trunk.

tree fruit

• **prune acid cherries.** 'Morello' and other culinary cherry varieties produce most of their fruit on shoots made the previous year, so pruning concentrates on encouraging a constant renewal of growth by cutting out old wood and replacing it with new. As soon as the crop is cleared, prune out the sideshoots that have borne cherries, cutting back to a young shoot left as a replacement during spring pruning. Restore weak-growing varieties that produce few new shoots, and neglected trees that only fruit on the outer fringe of the branches, by pruning out about a quarter of the old fruited wood, cutting where possible just above a young sideshoot.

• **prop up heavily laden branches.** Even when thinned to reduce a lavish crop of fruit, branches can be so heavily laden they may break unless supported. Prop them up with forked stakes, using pads of old blanket or sacking to protect the branch from injury, or support them with rope tied to a central stake. This is particularly important for plums, since damage can admit fungal diseases as well as spoiling the shape of the tree.

bush and cane fruits

• **prune blackcurrants** immediately after harvest. Cut out as many of the oldest branches as possible, removing about a third of all growth to make way for the new, more fruitful stems (see Summer).

BLACKCURRANT TIP If you notice blackcurrant stems wilting during August, prune them off halfway down. A dark hole down the centre is symptomatic of the clearwing moth, whose numbers are increasing. The grubs tunnel downwards, so cut back to clean sound wood, and burn the prunings.

• **prune summer raspberry canes** as soon as the remaining fruit has been harvested. Undo the ties attaching the exhausted canes to their training wires, and cut them off at ground level. Remove weak, spindly, damaged or overcrowded new canes (distinguished by their fresh green colour) to leave four to six of the strongest. Tie these to the wires with individual twists or a continuous string looped and knotted over the wires. Space canes evenly about 10cm (4in) apart. Pull up any suckers growing away from the row, and clear any weeds and plant debris.

After harvesting blackcurrants, cut out about a third of the oldest canes to leave room for the newer canes to develop and bear fruit.

• **finally tie in autumn-fruiting raspberry stems** once they reach the top wire. Water well in dry weather as plants come into flower, and mulch with grass cuttings. Birds are seldom attracted to late varieties, so netting is unnecessary.

• **loganberries and other hybrid berries** need to have their old fruited canes cut out; do this

Morello cherries fruit later than sweet cherries and are used for cooking. Pick them when, like these, they are fully coloured.

also for the earliest blackberries immediately after harvest. Trim them at ground level or just above a strong sideshoot if new growth is sparse. Tie the new green canes in place, evenly arranging them on the wires according to the training system used. If your garden is very cold, bundle the canes together for protection and tie them to the lowest wire.

strawberries

When all the fruits have been picked, remove any protective netting and shear off all the foliage and unwanted runners about 5–8cm (2–3in) above ground level; a rotary mower with the blade set high can be used for this on large beds. Remove, clean and store protective mats from around the plants, then rake off and burn the leaves, together with any straw used for mulching. Weed between the plants.

In the third year after planting, fruit quality and size decline, so plants are usually cleared after harvest, although some gardeners leave them for a further year to produce a large crop of small fruits for jam-making. Fork up the plants with all their roots, shake off the soil and burn them (composting can perpetuate diseases), together with all their foliage, unused runners and any straw. Then dig over the bed and manure it, ready for planting a late crop like spring greens.

Plant up new beds on a prepared site (see below) where strawberries have not grown before. The beds need to be dug over thoroughly with plenty of manure or compost worked in, as strawberries prefer organic manures to artificial fertilisers.

perpetual strawberries

These varieties will continue fruiting until the frosts. They benefit from regular watering in dry weather, together with a feed of general fertiliser in early August. As these are best grown for one or, at the most, two years, dig up the plants when cropping finishes, or pick off the oldest leaves and clear away loose debris to leave plants tidy for a second year.

planting a new strawberry bed

1 **Rake in a dressing** of general fertiliser just before planting, then mark out planting positions every 38–45cm (15–18in) in rows 75cm (2ft 6in) apart, using string and canes. Select plants that you have rooted from strong, healthy runners (see Summer) or have bought in as certified virus-free stock. Plant them carefully, at the same level as the compost in the pot.

2 **Firm the plants** in well and water regularly in dry weather during the first few weeks. Try to complete planting by mid-September.

fruit/3

harvesting and storing

With so many fruits ripening at this time of year, it is worth exploring the various methods of preserving and storing. If you harvest fruits gently and avoid bruising them, they will keep for longer.

apples and pears

- **the earliest apples** mature from late July and do not keep, so they should be eaten within a week or so of picking, before the flesh becomes soft and mealy. Some mid-season varieties, which mature in late August and the first half of September, are ripe enough to eat fresh, but others need storing first for a few weeks and will remain in good condition for another month or more.
- **the first pears** are ready to pick during August, but need a few weeks to finish ripening in store, as do all later varieties. Like apples, their harvesting time is indicated by a change of colour and readiness to part easily from the tree, rather than on their readiness for eating.
- **apples and pears ripen** over a long period, so test before you pick by lifting one or two fruits to see if they come away without twisting or tearing; windfalls lying on the ground can be a good indication of ripeness. You might have to spread the harvest over several days, because fruits in the sun or on the outside of the tree often ripen first.

Test apples for ripeness by lifting them gently, rather than by twisting.

- **store only sound fruits,** and reject any with holes, insect damage, torn stalks or bruises. Handle them carefully and spread them on slatted shelves, or in single layers in boxes, and make sure they do not touch each other. High-quality apples can be individually wrapped in newspaper. Or you can pack about 2kg (4–4½lb) in a clear polythene bag with the bottom corners cut off for ventilation.
- **store all fruit** in a cool but frost-free place with good air circulation. Check fruit every 10 days or so and remove any that are showing signs of rot.

cherries, peaches and plums

- **sweet cherries** are usually cleared in late July, but acid varieties do not ripen until August or early September. Pick when fully coloured; cut the stalks with scissors or secateurs. Bottle or freeze surplus fruits, with or without their stones.
- **plums, damsons and bullaces** continue to be available until late October. Pick them when soft and fully coloured for eating immediately and for freezing (halved and stoned). Or you can gather them slightly under-ripe for bottling and

Pick pears when they part easily from the tree and use only healthy, unblemished fruit for storing. This is 'Louise Bonn de Jersey'.

Tiny cracks in the well-coloured skin of figs indicate that they are ripe and ready to be picked.

jam-making, or for keeping in a cool place for two weeks and eating fresh.

- **late varieties of peaches and nectarines** continue ripening throughout August and into early September. Pick the fruits when they are fully coloured and soft around the stalk, and part easily when gently twisted. Handle them carefully as they bruise easily. They will keep for a few days in a cool place, and surplus fruits can be bottled or frozen.

cane fruits

- **late raspberry varieties** such as 'Leo' continue the summer season into August, often overlapping with the first autumn varieties. Check the ripening crops every two to three days and harvest all that are fully coloured and come away freely, without their stalks and plugs (autumn kinds are a little firmer and part from their plugs less readily). Bottle, freeze or preserve any surplus in syrup or alcohol.
- **hybrid berries** such as loganberries and tayberries ripen in mid to late summer, while the blackberry season extends from midsummer to the first frosts, according to variety. Pick them when fully coloured and soft, complete with their plugs. Check for ripeness every few days, especially in warm, sunny weather. Bottle, freeze or preserve in syrup.

bush fruits

- **black, red and white currants** ripen throughout late summer. Some varieties need harvesting immediately they are ripe, while others remain in good condition for weeks. Pick whole clusters when fully coloured and before they start to shrivel or fall. Cut the stalks with scissors if necessary to avoid damaging the fragile fruit, then use a table fork to strip individual currants from the stalks. Either use straight away, bottle or freeze.
- **any gooseberries** remaining in late summer will be larger, sweeter and of dessert quality, compared with the earlier varieties harvested in June and July. Their skins can be very fragile, so they need careful picking when fully ripe. Freeze or juice surplus fruits.

grapes and figs

- **indoor and outdoor grapes** mature throughout late summer depending on their variety and the amount of heat they receive. It is best to taste them to check for ripeness, as good colour is not a reliable indication and most varieties need several more weeks to develop their full sweetness. Handling grapes removes the bloom from their skins, so harvest by cutting through the stem a short distance away on both sides of the bunch. To store for a few weeks, cut a longer section of branch so that the lower end can be inserted in a jar or bottle of water, securely wedged on a shelf where the grapes can hang freely. Any surplus fruits can be dried or preserved in alcohol.
- **figs are ready to pick** in late summer when they are very soft and hang downwards, with fully coloured skin. Pick them carefully and eat them straight away or store them in a cool place for up to a week or so. You can bottle or freeze surplus fruits.

PRESERVING TIP Many of these fruits can also be preserved by candying or pickling, as well as by being processed into jams, jellies and purées.

vegetables

This is a time of plenty, with many crops approaching maturity. The real skill during late summer is to strike a balance between keeping plants growing rapidly, and encouraging them to crop. In addition, every time you water plants to keep them growing, a new crop of weeds emerges and has to be dealt with.

harvesting now

• aubergines • beetroot • broad beans • broccoli • carrots • chillies • courgettes • florence fennel • french and runner beans • globe artichokes • japanese onions • kohl rabi • lettuces and salad leaves • radish • shallots • spinach • spring onions • summer cabbages • summer cauliflowers • sweetcorn • sweet peppers • tomatoes • turnips

Purple-podded dwarf french beans

now is the season to . . .

■ **harvest crops** as they mature and water as necessary.

■ **hoe weekly** to kill weed seedlings as they emerge.

■ **apply a mulch** of well-rotted compost or other organic matter around the base of plants that occupy the ground for several months, to control weeds and to help keep the soil moist. Leave space to hoe through the centre of each row.

■ **control pests,** such as aphids and caterpillars, with sprays containing a non-persistent rapeseed oil at seven to ten day intervals, and cover plants with insect-proof mesh to deter root fly infestation.

■ **pick off any discoloured leaves** and other plant parts showing early signs of disease.

■ **cut down and burn** potato tops if the leaves show brown markings, the signs of blight.

■ **control caterpillars** by hand-picking or spraying affected crops with the biological agent *Bacillus thuringiensis*, which can prove effective without the risk of pesticide residues.

■ **sow a green manure** after crops have been cleared, to help improve soil texture and fertility (see opposite and page 73). Alternatively, sow a follow-on crop of quick-maturing peas or french beans, both of which add nitrogen to the soil as well as providing an edible crop.

there is still time to . . .

■ **plant winter brassicas:** cauliflower, cabbages and kale.

■ **make successional sowings** of lettuce, spinach, spring onions and salad radishes.

■ **sow carrots, fennel and turnips**.

watering

Use water efficiently, by applying generous amounts when the plants are going through critical stages of development.

• **water new plants,** both transplants and seedlings, in dry weather. Do this daily for the first four to five days until they have stopped wilting, a sign that new roots have formed and established.

• **leafy plants** and crops with soft, lush growth, such as celery, lettuce and spinach, as well as cabbages and cauliflowers, benefit from 4–5 litres per metre of row (1 gallon per yard) once a week to keep plants actively growing.

• **plants with edible fruits,** such as courgettes, tomatoes, peas and beans, should not go short of water at flowering time and when the fruits or pods are starting to swell.

• **potatoes** benefit from a heavy soaking just as the tubers begin to form, which for a number of cultivars coincides with the start of flowering. Watering at this stage increases the overall yield significantly.

• **water sweetcorn** when the silks (tassels) on the small cobs have just started to shrivel, and again about 10 days before the cobs are due to be picked.

BRUSSELS SPROUTS TIP The very firm planting of brussels sprouts, required to prevent them from falling over as they grow, means that they rarely need water unless the weather is extremely dry.

growing and harvesting

In late summer the work is divided between sowing and transplanting new or successional crops, and harvesting mature vegetables.

peas and beans

• **harvest peas** regularly while the pods are young, bright green and juicy. This encourages further yields and ensures tender peas of good quality. Peas will stop flowering if the pods are left on the plant.

• **harvest french beans** and runner beans every two to three days, and before the seeds start to swell prominently and the pods become stringy and tough.

green manures

Sow green manures on bare ground (see page 73) to improve the soil. They help to retain soil nutrients, the roots open up the soil, and the top growth, when dug in, adds organic matter. Members of the pea family, such as bitter lupins, fenugreek and winter tares, are particularly useful as a rich source of nitrogen.

cabbages, cauliflowers and broccoli

• **finish planting winter and spring cauliflowers** in July and space them 75cm (2ft 6in) apart in rows 75cm (2ft 6in) apart to give them plenty of growing room.

• **transplant winter cabbage** early in the season at a spacing of 50cm (20in) in rows 50cm (20in) apart. Choose the hardier 'January King' types for colder or more exposed areas.

• **transplant kale** into its cropping site in July, spacing plants 45cm (18in) apart in rows 60cm (2ft) apart. The purple forms tend to be less hardy than the green leaf forms.

• **earth up the soil** around the base of sprouting broccoli plants to a depth of about 15cm (6in). This helps to prevent them from falling over during winter if they become top-heavy.

• **sow spring cabbages** in seedbeds outdoors, with a second sowing 10 days later. Grow them as 'hearted' cabbages or cut as spring greens. Transplant spring cabbages sown in early summer, spacing plants 30cm (12in) apart in rows 30cm (12in) apart.

• **sow Chinese cabbage** in July or August. Transplant seedlings sown in modules at a spacing of 30cm (12in) in rows 45cm (18in) apart. Be prepared to protect them from frost in all but the mildest areas.

• **harvest summer cauliflowers,** cutting them with the outer leaves, which protect the curd.

• **continue cutting broccoli;** by now smaller sideshoots will be developing after the main shoots have been harvested.

Winter brassicas and trained runner beans make a colourful sight in the late summer garden.

vegetables/2

- **harvest summer cabbages** while their heads are still firm.
- **be vigilant for caterpillars** and mealy cabbage aphids, which can be a problem at this time, especially on broccoli. Hand-pick caterpillars or control both pests with spray containing a non-persistent rapeseed oil at seven to ten day intervals.

onions

- **lift onions** as soon as the tops have died down. Ease them out of the ground using a fork so as not to damage the roots, and leave them on the soil until the skins turn papery. If the weather is wet, remove them to the greenhouse staging or take indoors until the weather improves.
- **lift shallots** once the tops start turning yellow, if this has not yet been done (see Summer). Allow them to dry in the sun for four or five days, until the skins are papery. Then remove the tops and break the clumps apart.
- **continue to sow spring onions** at three-week intervals for successional crops.

Red-skinned onions (*Allium cepa* 'Noro')

- **sow next year's japanese onions** thinly in August or September about 1cm (½in) deep in rows 30cm (12in) apart. Sow them in the evening in a well-watered seedbed, as they germinate better in a cool soil.
- **lift japanese onions,** which have been growing through the winter. Allow the tops to die back, and leave the bulbs in the ground so that the skins ripen before they are dug up.

root crops

- **sow carrots** in July for a late crop of finger-sized roots.
- **sow turnips** in early August for winter use.
- **sow florence fennel** in July, 1cm (½in) deep, and thin seedlings in stages to 30cm (12in) apart in rows 40cm (16in) apart. You can also sow a little later, but these plants should be protected with cloches in September. Fennel sown at this time should produce good plants, but they rarely develop large bulbs as the days grow shorter.
- **water maincrop potatoes** thoroughly as the tubers are forming. The tubers of healthy plants can be left *in situ* and harvested in autumn or as they are required.
- **harvest immature turnips and carrots** as baby vegetables, as they are required. You can combine this with thinning if you leave thinning until later than normal, so the roots have had a chance to develop. The remaining plants will then have space to develop full-size roots for later harvesting.
- **sow hardy winter radishes** for harvesting over winter. Sow seeds thinly to give the seedlings plenty of room for the large roots to develop. Thin to a final spacing of 15–20cm (6–8in) in rows 25cm (10in) apart, depending on the variety and size of roots required.

tender crops

- **sow lettuce and salad radishes** at weekly intervals for successional crops. Sow radish seeds more thinly than usual. The lettuces will be ready to harvest in autumn.
- **harvest salad crops raised** from earlier sowings as they mature.
- **pick sweetcorn** when the tassels on the ends of the cobs have turned brown and the cobs are at an angle of 45 degrees to the plant's

For maximum sweetness, pick sweetcorn immediately before use, so that the sugar content has no time to convert into starch.

Chard can be grown in a variety of colours – red, yellow and pink – which makes it a decorative crop. Colour does not affect the flavour.

main stem. To be sure that sweetcorn is ready to harvest, press a thumbnail into a kernel – if the sap is creamy it is ready, if clear it is not.

• **pick tomatoes as they ripen.** If the weather is wet, pick the fruits just before they are ripe rather than leave them on the plant for too long, as they may split.

• **harvest peppers and chillies** when the fruits are swollen and the skin smooth. Cut them from the plant with a small stalk attached when green, or leave them until fully ripe and coloured.

• **harvest aubergines** when the fruits are swollen and the skin is clear and glossy, but before the flesh inside becomes soft.

• **gather courgettes** as soon as they reach the required size. If they are left too long the plants will stop producing flowers and cropping will be interrupted.

• **continue to train pumpkins and squashes** by nipping out any new sideshoots. Pinch out the tips of existing sideshoots once a fruit has started to develop.

spinach, celery and chicory

• **continue to sow spinach** at two-week intervals. Choose rough-seeded cultivars at this time of year as they are hardier than those with smooth seeds.

• **sow chicory in beds** for transplanting later. Choose the sugar-loaf types as they can tolerate light frost. They will crop through winter if you protect plants with cloches or a straw mulch in severe weather.

• **sow spinach beet** for early spring harvest. Make two or three sowings at three-week intervals. Sow seed 2cm (¾in) deep and thin plants to 15cm (6in) apart in rows 30cm (12in) apart. Be prepared to protect the plants in winter if the site is cold and exposed.

• **water celery** during dry periods, giving at least 1 litre (2 pints) per plant per week. Keep the plants growing rapidly and the sticks soft and succulent by applying a liquid feed of organic nitrogen every two weeks when you water.

looking ahead . . .

☑ AUTUMN Protect florence fennel from cold weather.

☑ WINTER Protect chicory and spinach beet if your garden is cold and exposed.

holiday care for vegetables

Before you go on holiday, water all plants thoroughly.

• **sink pipes or plant pots** close to the base of larger plants such as artichokes to make watering easier and get the moisture down to the plant roots.

• **lay a seep hose** along the rows or beds of vegetables and link it up to a timing device set to water plants automatically.

• **lay an organic mulch** around wide-spaced plants, such as cabbages, to retain moisture and suppress weeds.

• **remove flowers** from crops that may set seeds or develop fruits while you are absent. This is important if no one is harvesting your crops while you are away.

While you are away, arrange for a friend or neighbour to:

• **harvest vegetables** as they mature, particularly peas, beans, peppers and tomatoes.

• **water plants**, particularly root crops. Carrots often split when subjected to irregular watering, and potatoes will stop swelling if the soil becomes too dry.

perennial crops

• **cut the heads of globe artichokes** when they are plump and green, but before the scales start to open. Water the plants with a liquid feed after harvesting. This will stimulate the production of a second flush of smaller artichokes.

• **harvest late varieties of rhubarb** by cutting through the stalks at ground level.

Globe artichokes are handsome enough to combine with flowering plants and herbs in a border. Pick the heads for eating when plump.

vegetables/3

storing vegetables

One of the main problems at this time of year is what to do with surplus produce. All too often, the sign of a successful season for a particular crop is over-production. Rather than trying to eat your way through everything, consider which crops can be stored. Those harvested young and succulent are ideal for freezing, and gluts of almost any vegetable can be turned into delicious chutneys and pickles. Then you have the double satisfaction of enjoying produce out of season and knowing that you grew and preserved it yourself. After harvesting, inspect your produce and freeze or store only that which is in perfect condition.

If growing beans for drying, wait until the pods are mature and filled out before picking.

peas and beans

- **freeze french and runner beans** whole, after topping and tailing them, or sliced.
- **remove peas** and broad beans from their pods and freeze as soon as possible after picking.
- **for dried peas and beans,** lift whole plants laden with mature pods and hang them up to dry slowly in a cool, dry place, before removing the seeds from the pods. Store the dry seeds in sealed plastic containers or in coloured glass jars; keep them in a cool, dark room.

cabbage family

- **freeze broccoli** (calabrese) and sprouting broccoli as small florets or sideshoots.
- **slice or shred cabbage** and freeze; red cabbage also makes a tasty pickle.
- **winter cabbages** will keep well in the ground, or for two to three weeks after picking, suspended in a net in a cool, dry, dark place such as a shed.
- **although brussels sprouts and kale** can be frozen, there is little point as they are hardy plants and are better left in the ground for picking fresh, as required, from late summer through to winter.

onions

Bulb onions, shallots and garlic are grown with storage in mind. After lifting, leave the crop to dry so that the sun cures the skins. This will seal in the nutrients and improve the storage qualities.

- **once dry, store** the bulbs in a dry, dark, cool but frost-free place such as a shed or garage. Leave them loose in a box or rack, hang them in net bags, or tie them into strings, with the tops tied or plaited together with string.
- **small onions and shallots** can be pickled.

Lift onions and leave them on the soil to dry, a process which also improves their flavour.

root crops

Many roots are safe left in the ground during a mild winter, especially if the soil is light and free-draining. It is a good idea to cover them with straw or bracken against the occasional hard frost. On heavy soils, and for easy access if the ground is frozen, many roots can be dug up and stored in a cool, frost-free place in paper or hessian sacks or cardboard boxes lined with newspaper. Do not wash before storing.

- **maincrop carrots** can be stored in boxes of damp sand (see Autumn). Early carrots will keep in a plastic bag in the fridge for two to three weeks, after cutting their tops off.
- **parsnips taste best** after frost has enhanced their aromatic sweetness, so leave in the soil until needed. Mark the end of the rows with a cane as all top growth disappears from sight.
- **turnips and swedes** are best left in the ground until needed.
- **beetroot** may be left in the ground for use as required or dug up in autumn and stored in damp sand, like carrots. Alternatively, it can be pickled in vinegar.
- **kohl rabi** will keep in the fridge for two to three weeks.

potatoes

Maincrop potatoes keep quite well in the ground once they reach maturity. It is only as the weather gets colder and the soil becomes wetter that it is necessary to lift them. This may be well into autumn, unless the ground is required for other crops. But in a very wet September, or if blight has affected your potatoes, it is advisable to lift them early. After the skins have dried, store them in thick paper sacks to exclude light.

preserving vegetables

VEGETABLE	METHOD
ASPARAGUS	blanch and freeze spears
AUBERGINE	slice or dice, blanch and freeze
BEETROOT	store dry; freeze baby beets whole
BROAD BEANS	pod beans, blanch and freeze; dry
BROCCOLI	blanch and freeze florets
CABBAGE	slice or shred, blanch and freeze
CARROTS	slice or dice, blanch and freeze; freeze baby carrots whole; store in damp sand
CAULIFLOWER	blanch and freeze florets
CELERY	slice or dice, blanch and freeze
CHILLIES	hang up to dry, threaded together
COURGETTES	slice or dice, blanch and freeze
FRENCH BEANS	top and tail pods, blanch and freeze; dry
GARLIC	store dry
KOHL RABI	slice or dice, blanch and freeze
MARROWS	store dry
ONIONS	store dry
PARSNIPS	leave in ground; slice, blanch and freeze
PEAS	pod, blanch and freeze; dry
POTATOES	store dry in thick paper sacks
PUMPKIN	store dry
RUNNER BEANS	slice, blanch and freeze; dry
SPINACH	blanch and freeze whole leaves
SPROUTING BROCCOLI	blanch and freeze main shoots and sideshoots
SWEDE	leave in ground; store dry
SWEETCORN	strip off husks and silks; blanch and freeze whole cobs or kernels
SWEET PEPPERS	de-seed, slice or chop and freeze
TOMATOES	chop and freeze
TURNIPS	leave in ground; store dry

salad and fruiting crops

Many salad and fruiting crops can be frozen (see chart above), though some, like tomatoes and peppers, will only be suitable for cooking. Green tomatoes can be made into chutney.

- **store marrows and pumpkins** in a cool, dry, dark room once the skins have been allowed to 'ripen', or harden, in the sun.
- **lettuce and salad leaves** must be eaten fresh. Drench them in icy water and leave to drain, to preserve their freshness.

storing dry and freezing

The best store is a cellar, basement, unheated room or shed where it is cool, dry and inaccessible to mice. It needs to be dark, airy and, ideally, fitted with slatted shelves to keep the produce off the floor. You need wooden boxes or cardboard boxes lined with newspaper for storing root vegetables, net bags for onions, marrows and pumpkins, and hessian or paper sacks for potatoes; it is a good idea to keep the thick paper sacks in which potatoes are sold. Keep insulating materials such as straw, old blankets, rugs or newspapers handy in case temperatures fall. Check your stored produce every few weeks to see that there is no sign of decay.

Blanching involves immersing the prepared vegetables in boiling water for less than a minute, then plunging them into cold water and draining thoroughly. The best way to freeze is to spread the prepared vegetables in a single layer on a tray and open-freeze them, before putting them into plastic bags. In this way they freeze faster and do not stick together.

In a productive walled kitchen garden cabbages are grown in a block, making it easier to protect them from pigeons. Pick alternate plants while young, leaving others to heart up and grow on to maturity.

herbs

It is seed harvesting time in the herb garden, with seed heads ripening in readiness for you to collect for culinary use or for sowing. And it is time, too, to start tidying up and preparing plants for winter use.

now is the season to . . .

■ **continue harvesting** herbs while at their best. Pick small sprigs regularly for immediate use, larger quantities for preserving (see Summer).

■ **pot on rooted cuttings** taken earlier in summer.

■ **prick out seedlings** from sowings made the previous month, and pot up any needed for indoor use over winter.

■ **continue sowing parsley,** chervil and winter purslane for winter harvesting, indoors or in a coldframe.

■ **gather seed heads** as they near maturity and dry the seeds for storing or sowing (see right).

■ **clear leaves and old foliage** from around plants that are being left to self-sow, and lightly loosen the soil as a seedbed.

■ **begin tidying the herb garden** in September, deadheading or trimming tall plants and clearing exhausted annual herbs (see opposite).

■ **prepare the ground** for new herb beds and borders, early in September, ready for planting in early autumn (see page 132).

and if you have time . . .

■ **cut back tarragon** by half to stimulate young growth for late harvest or cuttings.

■ **select strong or bushy plants** of chives, parsley and marjoram to pot up later for winter use. Feed them now with a high-potash fertiliser and water in dry weather to maintain quality. You can also lift a few parsley and basil plants and replant in a coldframe or greenhouse border to re-establish before autumn.

A pot of lemon balm makes a centrepiece for a small geometric herb bed including silver thyme, purple sage, oregano and tarragon.

harvesting herb seeds

The seeds of many herbs are worth gathering for culinary use or for sowing later. Select from the largest, strongest plants if the seeds are for sowing; for culinary purposes you can gather seeds freely. Label varieties and keep them separate at all times.

- **harvest seeds** before they are fully ripe and shedding. As a guide, look for darkening stalks, seed heads turning yellow or brown, or a papery skin on the seed pods.
- **carefully cut the stems** and either dry the seed heads on trays lined with paper, or loosely bundle them inside paper bags and suspend them in a warm, airy place.
- **most seed heads** take two to three weeks to dry fully. Crush the pods or capsules, or shake out the dry seeds from their

Gather seed of biennial angelica now to sow in autumn. Winter temperatures encourage the seeds to germinate.

receptacles, and remove as much chaff and plant material as possible.

- **for kitchen use,** store the seeds in airtight tins or jars.

storing seeds to sow

Keep seeds for sowing in a cool, dry place, in small labelled envelopes or used film canisters (see page 30).

- **fresh seeds** usually germinate faster and more evenly than those kept for a year or more. Angelica seeds, for example, should be sown, either *in situ* or in small pots, within three months of gathering to avoid disturbing the taproots later. Alternatively, keep the seeds in a refrigerator through winter, and sow direct in early spring.
- **seeds of many umbellifers,** such as alexanders (*Smyrnium olusatrum*), angelica, aniseed, fennel, lovage and sweet cicely (*Myrrhis odorata*), need a period of cold before they will germinate, so are best sown in autumn or late winter to take advantage of frost and low temperatures.
- **leave one or two plants to self-sow** lavishly, such as angelica, parsley, borage or chervil. When the seedlings germinate, thin them or transplant elsewhere while small. However, results may be less predictable than saving and sowing seeds yourself.

tidying the herb garden

As you harvest seeds, leaves and flowers, start tidying plants and beds ready for autumn. Deadhead or cut back spent flower stems, remove dying leaves and broken stalks, and thoroughly weed around the herbs, especially if any are being left to self-sow. In early September, lightly clip over shrubby herbs such as lavender, hyssop and thyme. Give formal hedges their last light trim of the year.

Even the smallest herb bed is an ornamental as well as a functional asset in the garden. Start making plans for a new herb bed or border now (see page 132). Once you have decided on its site and layout, prepare the ground while the soil is still warm and there is time to control overlooked weed seeds and root fragments that may appear later.

there is still time to . . .

- **take semi-ripe cuttings** of non-flowering shoots of shrubby herbs such as cotton lavender, hyssop, lavender, rosemary, sage, thyme and winter savory (see page 43).

Take semi-ripe cuttings of shrubby herbs such as cotton lavender and thyme now to replenish your stocks for next year.

the greenhouse

Inside the greenhouse crops and flowers are at their peak, but in the midst of this bonanza plan ahead. Sow annuals, force bulbs and make time to give the greenhouse a thorough clean ready for the autumn intake of tender plants.

- **keep the greenhouse cool** by a combination of shading, ventilation and damping down.
- **water and feed plants regularly** and remove any dead leaves and flowers.
- **stay alert for diseases and pests;** red spider mite is most likely to appear during August and if it does, introduce biological control in the form of the *Photoseiulus* parasite (see page 75).
- **prepare for your holiday,** especially if you have to leave plants unattended (see opposite).
- **harvest crops** such as tomatoes, cucumbers, melons, peppers and early grapes, and continue training and supporting them as necessary.
- **prick out and pot on** flowering houseplants such as calceolarias and tender perennials as soon as they need more space. Feed them regularly, and stand in a cool, well-lit place.
- **pot up rooted cuttings** of houseplants and shrubs.
- **gradually cease watering amaryllis** (*Hippeastrum*) as their summer growth period ends, and allow the foliage to die down.
- **thoroughly clean and disinfect** inside the greenhouse in early September (see opposite).
- **bring indoors** all pot plants that have passed the summer outside, before the nights turn cold.
- **take semi-ripe cuttings** of your favourite shrubs, alpines and herbs (see pages 43 and 47).
- **propagate tender perennials** from soft-tip cuttings (see page 31).
- **sow annuals** for flowering under glass during winter and spring, and annual herbs for winter use.
- **plant bulbs in pots** for indoor display (see page 71).
- **pot up arum lilies** after their summer rest (see page 70).
- **collect lily bulbils** and plant in trays.
- **encourage poinsettias** and Christmas cacti to flower at Christmas (see page 71).

and if you have time . . .

- **select strong strawberry runners** and pot them up singly in 13–15cm (5–6in) pots. Stand them in a shaded place. In late November bring them into the greenhouse to force early fruits.
- **cut back violas** growing outdoors, and feed to stimulate plenty of young growth for autumn cuttings.

Anisodontea capensis

■ **plant** *Anemone coronaria* in early September for flowers from late winter on. Space tubers 10–15cm (4–6in) apart and 8cm (3in) deep in a coldframe or greenhouse border.

keeping the greenhouse cool

Temperatures under glass can soar alarmingly in late summer, and it is important to control this for healthy plant growth and to protect foliage from scorching

- **apply a further coat of shade paint** to the outside glass.
- **cover seedlings** with sheets of newspaper on bright days.
- **open all doors and ventilators** to prevent temperatures from rising much above 20°C (68°F); do this at night too in exceptional weather conditions.
- **damp down paths** and staging every day, especially if leaves look dull, a symptom of red spider mite infesting the underside of leaves (see page 75).
- **water once, preferably twice, daily,** and watch out for early signs of water stress such as flagging or lacklustre leaves and a dry, stale smell as you enter the greenhouse.

preparing for holidays

Before you go away take some of the following precautions.

- **fit automatic ventilators** to open at least one top and one side window above a pre-set temperature.
- **get up to date with your potting** and planting before you go.
- **harvest ripe or nearly ripe fruit;** cut off open flowers and any faded or discoloured leaves.
- **feed all plants** and spray them with a systemic insecticide or suspend sticky traps above their foliage.
- **install an automatic watering system,** using capillary matting or drip tubes, and fill all reservoirs (see Summer). Alternatively, take plants outdoors and group them together in a shady place where rain can reach them, and water them just before leaving.

cleaning inside the greenhouse

The most convenient time to clean out your greenhouse is on a mild day at the end of the season when most crops have finished and before you bring in tender plants for protection. Move any plants in pots outside before you start.

- **remove all used pots,** trays and labels. Clean and store them for later use. Clear out plant remains and brush down the inside structure and the staging to remove cobwebs, loose compost and other debris.
- **repair any broken glass** and make good structural defects.
- **wash inside the glass** using a cloth and warm water mixed with a little washing-up liquid and garden disinfectant; use a scrubbing brush or old toothbrush for the glazing bars. Clean dirt and algae from overlapping panes with a thin seed label. Rinse with a hosepipe or pressure sprayer and clean water.
- **brush down staging** and scrub it with warm water and garden disinfectant.
- **wash surface gravel** on the staging with a pressure sprayer. Sweep and scrub solid floors with water and garden disinfectant, and hose them clean.
- **wash or scrub** the outside of the pots in use before putting the plants back in the clean greenhouse. Shut ventilators in the evening and fumigate the greenhouse with a smoke cone.

cleaning inside the greenhouse

Wash the glass using a sponge and warm water mixed with washing-up liquid.

Brush down the staging with plenty of warm water and garden disinfectant.

Rinse clean using warm clear water and a cloth.

the greenhouse/2

crops and ornamental plants

Most crops under glass will be in full production now. Follow this quick reference guide to keep them in good shape and bearing healthy fruit.

- **peppers** Pick sweet peppers when they are green or have ripened to your preferred colour, and chillies when fully ripe. Water regularly, but decrease watering after the end of August. Maintain good air circulation to prevent grey moulds on leaves and stems.
- **cucumbers** Pick fruits as soon as they are large enough, to encourage further cropping. Continue watering regularly, and cover the surface roots with a top-dressing of fresh potting compost. Maintain high humidity by spraying and damping down regularly to control red spider mite.
- **tomatoes** Pick when fruits are fully coloured. Water regularly but, for maximum flavour, no more than necessary. Feed with a high-nitrogen fertiliser when four trusses have set, and pinch out growing tips after six trusses or, at the latest, by the end of August.
- **aubergines** Allow five or six fruits to set, then remove all others. Feed regularly with tomato fertiliser. Harvest fruits when fully coloured and glossy.

- **melons** Support ripening fruits with 'hammocks' or bags of soft plastic netting or muslin. Let four fruits mature on each plant; remove others and surplus growth. Pick when the stem cracks at the base of the fruit and sweet perfume fills the house.
- **grapes** Feed vines every 10–14 days while fruits are ripening, and ventilate the greenhouse freely to reduce risks of damp-induced fungal diseases. Cut whole bunches with a length of stem, and insert this in water if the fruit needs to be kept for several days (see page 59).

Grape 'Black Hamburg'

sowing for winter and spring

For pots of fragrant flowers in winter and spring, sow stocks (Brompton and Beauty of Nice), mignonette, schizanthus and cornflowers in a shaded coldframe. Prick them out separately into small pots, and pot on in early autumn into 13–15cm (5–6in) pots for flowering.

Sow basil, chervil and parsley in pinches in small pots and move unthinned clumps into 15cm (6in) pots for late autumn picking. Keep these herbs well ventilated at all times.

BULB TIPS

- To compose mixed arrangements in large bowls, start bulbs singly in 8cm (3in) pots, then choose those at the same stage of growth for planting together.
- Grow hyacinth bulbs and some narcissi, especially tazetta varieties, in jars of water or glass bowls filled with pebbles.

potting up arum lilies

The white arum, *Zantedeschia aethiopica*, will keep growing all year, but others, such as the brilliant yellow *Z. elliottiana*, require a dry summer rest. Repot them all in August, when you can also remove young offsets and pot them separately in rich soil-based compost such as John Innes No. 3.

- Use 15–23cm (6–9in) pots according to the size of rhizomes; position so the end buds are level with the surface.
- Stand pots outside until early October, keeping them moist.
- Then bring them indoors to a minimum temperature of 10°C (50°F). Higher temperatures will force earlier flowering.

A young cantaloupe melon ripening under glass.

forcing paper-white narcissi

1 **If the container** has drainage holes, fill it with ordinary moist potting compost; otherwise use prepared bulb fibre. Half fill the bowl with compost and arrange the bulbs in a single layer, close together. Cover with more compost and press it firmly around the bulbs so that their tips just show at the surface.

2 **Stand the container** in a dark shed or cupboard, no warmer than 4°C (40°F), or outdoors in a coldframe or shallow trench in the ground, the pot entirely covered with a 10cm (4in) layer of ash, leaves or sand. Check occasionally that the compost is still moist. When the shoots are about 5cm (2in) high, bring the container into a cool room or greenhouse at about 10°C (50°F). Once the flower buds begin to show colour, move the container to its flowering position.

3 **Twelve weeks after planting** the bulbs, these scented 'paper-white' narcissi are in full bloom and the flowering display should last for weeks.

forcing bulbs

You can force bulbs in pots and bowls to flower indoors in spring, or even earlier if you control temperatures carefully. For Christmas blooms, always choose prepared hyacinths, narcissi and tulips, and plant them by the third week in September. Choose a container at least 10cm (4in) deep. A 15cm (6in) wide bowl will hold three hyacinths, six narcissi or tulips, or 12 smaller bulbs like crocuses. All bulbs need a cold but frost-free period to initiate root growth: allow about 12 weeks for narcissi and hyacinths, 14–15 weeks for other bulbs.

preparing pot plants for Christmas

Poinsettias only start developing their colourful bracts once the flowers are initiated during a period of short days, which is why, left to their own devices, they flower in early spring. But you can trick them into flowering at Christmas by adjusting their growing conditions now.

- **In early September,** keep your poinsettia at 17°C (63°F) or more and expose it to light for a maximum of 10 hours each day, then cover it with a black plastic bag or move it into a dark cupboard for the remaining 14 hours. Do this for three weeks, then grow as normal in full light.
- **Christmas cactus** responds to similar treatment, but needs about 12 hours of darkness per day for six weeks. Keep plants cooler, between 10–15°C (50–60°F).

bulbs **suitable for forcing**

• crocuses • grape hyacinths • hyacinths • narcissi • reticulata irises • tulips

there is still time to . . .

- **propagate houseplants** from leaf or stem cuttings, including saintpaulias, streptocarpus, begonias (see Summer) and busy lizzies.
- **sow seeds of indoor cyclamen,** and restart old tubers.

the healthy garden

Although this is a time for lazing outdoors or taking a holiday break, the good gardener will still be monitoring plants for pests and diseases, coping with possible water shortages and planning ahead for autumn.

late summer checklist

Use this checklist to make sure you have not overlooked any important seasonal jobs.

- **continue watering** as often as necessary, focusing mainly on the most vulnerable plants and those in containers. In a dry summer, take steps to conserve water supplies (see opposite).
- **check the water quality** in ponds, especially where there are fish or vigorous floating plants and oxygenators. Keep levels of all water features topped up in hot weather.
- **harvest vegetables** while they are in peak condition, and sow or plant follow-on crops or green manures (see opposite).
- **pick fruit** as crops mature and protect ripening fruit from birds, squirrels and wasps.
- **finish summer-pruning** trained fruit trees and bushes.
- **prune rambler roses** after flowering (see page 39), together with other shrubs and climbers that have flowered.
- **trim hedges** regularly.
- **mow lawns** at the summer height setting as often as necessary for the kind of finish you prefer.
- **be extra vigilant** for pests and diseases, which often flourish in the late summer heat and humidity.
- **maintain** a congenial level of heat and humidity in the greenhouse, by means of ventilating and regular damping down.
- **keep on top of weeds,** especially tiny fast-growing annuals, which should be cleared before they have time to flower and shed their seeds all over the beds.
- **deadhead flowering plants regularly** to prolong their display.
- **support and feed** flowering plants if necessary.
- **thoroughly clean** the inside of the greenhouse before plants need rehousing in autumn (see page 69).
- **order spring-flowering bulbs,** prepare their sites and start planting. Pot up bulbs for forcing as soon as they become available (see page 71).
- **lift and divide** overcrowded perennials late in the season.
- **finish gathering herbs for preserving,** continue picking for immediate use and make the last sowings for continuity or winter use (see pages 66 and 70).
- **make plans for any new lawns** and beds for flowers, roses and fruit. Order the plants in good time, and start preparing the ground for autumn planting.
- **take soft-tip and semi-ripe cuttings** from all kinds of plants while there is enough warmth for them to root quickly (see pages 31 and 41).
- **collect seeds** from selected plants, dry them thoroughly and store in a safe place (page 74).

Take cuttings from healthy sage bushes for new young plants next year.

Use a string line to help you achieve a precise outline when clipping formal hedges, such as these box hedges.

making the most of the weather

Late summer is a time of transition, with long days and often hot, dry weather at the start, changing by the end of the season to more unpredictable conditions of shorter days, cooler nights and the first hints of autumn. Resourceful gardeners plan for all eventualities, conserving water supplies and soil moisture levels during drought, while organising cloches, fleece and space indoors by early September in case the summer ends early. This is particularly important in cooler districts and exposed gardens, where conditions can change surprisingly quickly. As the season progresses, make the most of good weather.

- **prepare the ground** for new plantings while there is no pressure to make haste and, if you need to dig, do so after late summer rain when the soil will be easier to work.
- **check that plant supports** and ties are secure before the strong autumn winds arrive.
- **take cuttings** and make late sowings while the air and soil are still warm, but be prepared to water the ground first in dry weather and continue watering regularly afterwards.

conserving water

You can reduce the impact of prolonged drought in late summer by following these simple steps, especially if you are asked to economise on water use.

- **top up mulches** applied earlier in the year, but keep enough organic material for mulching new plants and sowings.
- **continue controlling weeds,** which compete with other plants for soil moisture.
- **make sure the greenhouse** is fully shaded in hot weather and, on windy days, ventilate freely on the leeward side to reduce water loss.
- **install water butts** or use other containers, such as dustbins, to collect rainwater from downpipes.
- **save 'grey' water** (bath and washing-up water) for use around flowering and ornamental plants.
- **direct water to plant roots** rather than irrigating large areas. You can limit the spread of water by sinking a flowerpot or length of waste pipe near the stem, or making a saucer-shaped depression in the soil around a plant.
- **water in dull or cool weather,** and fit a timer to automatic irrigation systems to regulate the amount delivered.

sowing green manures

Try not to leave kitchen garden soil vacant during the growing season because, apart from wasting space, it is a prime seedbed for weeds and rain will wash away nutrients. If you do not intend to sow more vegetables, you can improve the soil and add nutrients by sowing a green manure while the ground is still warm.

- **to protect soil over winter** sow alfalfa, field beans, clover, tares or grazing rye. In early spring dig in the plants two or three weeks before the ground is needed.
- **short-term green manures** include buckwheat, fenugreek, mustard and phacelia. Grow these for one to three months on soil prepared for autumn planting.

Regular watering will ensure that your container plants bloom through into autumn. These pelargoniums and marguerite daisies brighten the late summer patio.

the healthy garden/2

storing your produce

Suitable varieties of fruit and maincrop vegetables can be stored from late summer onwards for use during the coming months (see pages 58–9 and 64–5), but they will need the right surroundings to stay in good condition. Produce can be readily damaged by frost, for example, while too much warmth tends to encourage diseases.

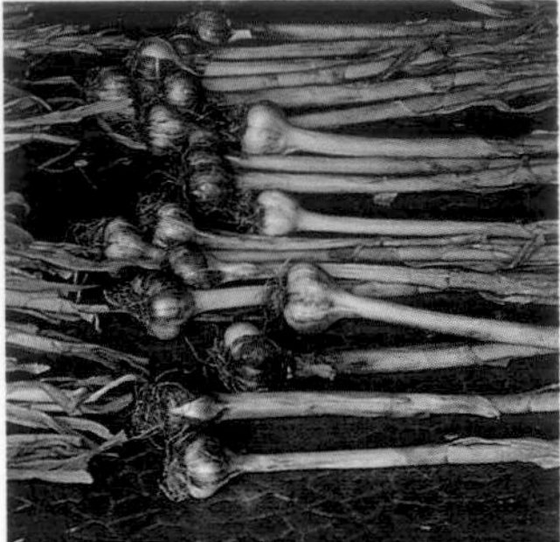

Garlic 'Ail Violet' set out to dry after harvesting. When fully dry, it can be strung up for storing in a cool place.

STORING TIP Starting with healthy produce is the best insurance against rotting and other problems. Harvest fruit and vegetables as soon as they are ripe, handle them with care and store only those that are unblemished.

Tie a paper bag over ripe seed heads to catch the seed as soon as it is released. Cut the seed head off with the bag in place.

storing seeds

Even when fully dried, seeds remain living organisms with a limited life span, so store them carefully to keep them in peak condition.

- Separate dry seeds from their casings and other seed-head fragments by hand picking, sieving or blowing away debris.
- Seal the seeds in paper envelopes labelled with the name, date and origin, and pack them in an airtight container. Alternatively, use old lidded film canisters.
- Prevent dampness, the greatest enemy of stored seeds, by including sachets of silica gel in the container. Silica gel absorbs moisture and turns pink in its presence. (You can dry the sachets gently in a very low oven until the silica gel is blue again, then re-use them.)
- Keep the seeds in a cool place where they are not exposed to fluctuating temperatures. Any surplus bought seeds remaining in opened packets can be stored in exactly the same way.

dealing with pests and diseases

It is tempting to relax your vigilance, especially once the main fruit and vegetable harvest begins and the end of the flowering season approaches. But late summer pests and disease may lie dormant until next year if left untreated.

- **dry conditions** in August favour red spider mites, under glass and outdoors. Once established, they can be hard to eradicate.
- **warm humid days** encourage the spread of fungal and bacterial diseases, such as mildew on gooseberries, plums, peas and chrysanthemums; rust on roses; and fireblight on cotoneasters and apples.
- **continue with preventative measures** taken earlier in the season, and maintain precautionary insecticide/fungicide spray routines if you have adopted these for roses and fruit.
- **develop the habit** of lifting the leaves as you work among plants, checking the undersides for insect pests and spores or other signs of fungal infections.

Gather sunflower seeds once the large flowerheads turn brown and dry.

- **late in the season** it is often more effective to cut off and burn leaves, shoots or flowerheads affected by disease or aphids, rather than attempt treatment with slow-acting systemic sprays.
- **as temperatures drop** under glass so too does the efficacy of biological controls, most of which require consistent warmth for the predator or parasite to feed and multiply rapidly.

seasonal threats

- **brown rot** Soft brown patches develop on fruits such as apples, plums and pears. Prune off affected shoots, pick up and destroy windfalls, and do not store infected fruit. Remove any shrivelled fruits from the tree in winter.
- **fireblight** A bacterial disease causing shoots and leaves to wither and turn brown, as if scorched. Cotoneasters, apples, pears and *Sorbus* and their relatives are vulnerable. Cut out affected shoots about 60cm (2ft) below the wound to clean the wood. Dip tools in garden disinfectant during and after use. Badly affected plants are better dug up and destroyed.
- **greymould (botrytis)** The fluffy, off-white mould develops in damp conditions on the stems, flowers and leaves of most plants. Clear up all loose dead material from around plants. Pull up dying plants or cut off affected portions and destroy. Improve ventilation under glass.
- **downy mildew** In damp, humid conditions yellowish patches develop on upper leaf surfaces with mealy white outgrowths on the undersides. Remove affected leaves, improve air circulation in the greenhouse by better spacing and ventilation, and grow resistant varieties.
- **powdery mildew** In dry conditions foliage and stems develop a greyish white, powdery coating that later turns brown. Pick off affected leaves, water and mulch in dry weather, and avoid using high-nitrogen fertilisers after the longest day. Some fruit varieties can be sprayed with sulphur.
- **cabbage whitefly** Tiny delta-shaped flies are easily disturbed from cabbage and other brassica crops. Remove lower or outer leaves, spray in the early morning with insecticidal soap, and burn or compost plants immediately after cropping.
- **caterpillars** These may still be a problem late in the season. Examine plants, especially the undersides of the leaves, when the adult moths and butterflies are seen on the wing. Crush the egg clusters and pick off the grubs by hand.
- **earwigs** A useful insect that feeds on aphids, but also damages flowers such as dahlias and chrysanthemums. Clear loose plant debris from around plants. Trap the earwigs in upturned pots stuffed with straw, and empty them well away from the affected plants.
- **red spider mites** The minute mites suck sap from the leaves, which turn pale and mottled. Fine webs may be visible on badly affected plants. These pests are encouraged by dry conditions under glass and also occur outdoors in dry summers, especially on fruit trees. Introduce the predatory *Phytoseiulus* mite under glass up to the end of August, and raise humidity levels by damping down. Outdoors, spray plants with insecticidal soap.

A tiny hoverfly rests on the petals of a plumbago flower. Hoverfly larvae are useful predators of aphids.

plant selector

Perennials come into their own in late summer, with a host of American prairie species such as solidago, asters and eupatoriums. Purple coneflowers bloom ahead of their yellow, tan and orange cousins, the rudbeckias, but there are also huge sunflowers, heleniums that look like flights of bumble bees and gaillardias which just won't stop blooming. It is a quieter time for shrubs, apart from roses and the buddleias, on whose blossoms hundreds of butterflies will be feasting. The rose season reaches its peak a little after the longest day, but most varieties will produce second and third flushes, and some will go on flowering into winter.

Aster x *frikartii* 'Mönch'

perennials

Durable perennials are the mainstay of attractive summer borders. A few of these non-woody plants are evergreen, but most are herbaceous, that is they die down in winter. Plant when dormant, in autumn or early spring.

3

purple, blue and violet

1

4

1 Acanthus mollis Latifolius Group
Bear's breeches

The mound of glossy lobed leaves, each as much as 1m (3ft) long, makes this an impressive foliage plant. It is stately in flower, too, with erect stems stacked with white flowers sheltering under purple bracts from early summer onwards. Hardy.

Height: 1.2m (4ft) **Spread:** 1m (3ft)
Site: Sun, partial shade. Well-drained soil
Use: Sunny or lightly shaded border
Good companions: *Fritillaria imperialis, Helleborus argutifolius, Viburnum opulus* 'Compactum'

2 Aconitum 'Bressingham Spire'
Aconite, Monkshood

Above a base of deeply cut, dark green leaves, sturdy stems carry spires of violet-blue hooded flowers. 'Spark's Variety' has branched stems and is taller and wider. Staking is not normally necessary. Highly poisonous if ingested. Hardy.

Height: 1.5m (5ft) **Spread:** 45cm (18in)
Site: Partial shade, full sun. Moist but well-drained soil
Use: Shady or sunny border, woodland garden
Good companions: *Erythronium dens-canis, Hydrangea* 'Preziosa', *Kirengeshoma palmata*

2

3 Agapanthus 'Blue Giant'
African blue lily

The somewhat stiff, strap-shaped leaves of this deciduous fleshy-rooted perennial form a rich green, leafy clump. Tough stems carry rounded heads of bell-shaped blue flowers from mid to late summer. Not fully hardy.

Height: 1.2m (4ft) **Spread:** 60cm (2ft)
Site: Sun. Fertile and moist but well-drained soil
Compost: Soil-based (John Innes No. 3)
Use: Container, sunny border
Good companions: *Dierama pulcherrimum, Galtonia candicans, Salvia uliginosa*

4 Agapanthus 'Lilliput'
African blue lily

Fleshy-rooted plant with narrow leaves and heads of trumpet-shaped flowers that are rich blue and darkly veined. Not fully hardy.

Height and spread: 40cm (16in)
Site: Sun. Fertile and moist but well-drained soil
Compost: Soil-based (John Innes No. 3)
Use: Container, sunny border
Good companions: *Agapanthus* 'Blue Giant', *Kniphofia* 'Royal Standard', *Kniphofia triangularis*

5 Aster x frikartii 'Mönch'

The flowering season of this hybrid aster extends into autumn with long-lasting, violet-mauve flowerheads. Disease resistant. Hardy.

Height: 75cm (2ft 6in) **Spread:** 40cm (16in)
Site: Sun. Fertile and well-drained soil
Use: Sunny border
Good companions: *Centaurea hypoleuca* 'John Coutts', *Delphinium* Belladonna Group 'Atlantis'

6 Clematis x durandii

This non-clinging herbaceous clematis has flexible stems. The single saucer-shaped flowers are 10cm (4in) across and indigo blue with a near-white eye. Good for cutting. Not fully hardy.

General care: Subject to mildew if trained against a wall, so tie up to a support in the open garden or drape over a shrub.
Height: 1.5m (5ft) **Spread:** 1m (3ft)
Site: Sun. Fertile, humus-rich and well-drained soil
Use: Sunny border
Good companions: *Delphinium* Belladonna Group 'Cliveden Beauty', *Rosa* 'Céleste', *Weigela* 'Victoria'

7 Delphinium Belladonna Group 'Cliveden Beauty'

This forms a base of deeply cut leaves over which branching wiry stems carry loose spikes of sky blue, spurred flowers from midsummer to autumn. Hardy.

Height: 1m (3ft) **Spread:** 45cm (18in)
Site: Sun. Well-drained soil
Use: Sunny border
Good companions: *Centaurea hypoleuca*

'John Coutts', *Paeonia lactiflora* 'Festiva Maxima', *Phlox paniculata* 'Fujiyama'

8 Echinops ritro 'Veitch's Blue'
Globe thistle

Jagged grey-green leaves, which are white and downy on the underside, are the base for erect stems that carry spherical flowerheads. These are metallic blue in bud and a softer blue when the tiny florets open. Good for cutting. Hardy.
Height: 1m (3ft) **Spread:** 45cm (18in)
Site: Sun. Well-drained, even poor soil
Use: Gravel garden, sunny border, wild garden
Good companions: *Artemisia* 'Powis Castle', *Gladiolus communis* subsp. *byzantinus*, *Helleborus argutifolius*

9 Eryngium alpinum
Eryngo, Sea holly

From basal heart-shaped leaves rise stiff branching stems that carry deeply cut leaves and numerous cone-shaped flowerheads, which are surrounded by ruff-like, exquisitely cut bracts. These look spiny but are soft to the touch. The flowerheads, bracts and the upper parts of stems are metallic blue. Suitable for drying. Hardy.
Height: 75cm (2ft 6in) **Spread:** 45cm (18in)
Site: Sun. Fertile and well-drained soil
Use: Sunny border
Good companions: *Artemisia ludoviciana* 'Valerie Finnis', *Geranium sanguineum*, *Sedum* 'Vera Jameson'

10 Eryngium x tripartitum
Eryngo, Sea holly

Wiry stems branch widely above a basal rosette of coarsely toothed leaves and carry many small cones of violet-blue flowers. Each of these sits on a sparse ruff of grey-blue spines and the broad effect is of hazy metallic blue. Suitable for drying. Hardy.
Height: 75cm (2ft 6in) **Spread:** 50cm (20in)
Site: Sun. Well-drained soil
Use: Gravel garden, sunny border, wild garden
Good companions: *Allium cristophii*, *Festuca glauca* 'Elijah Blue', *Ruta graveolens* 'Jackman's Blue'

11 Gentiana asclepiadea
Willow gentian

A woodland gentian with arching stems, narrow pointed leaves arranged in pairs and rich blue trumpet-shaped flowers that grow from the junction of leaves and stems. Hardy.
Height: 75cm (2ft 6in)
Spread: 45cm (18in)
Site: Partial shade, shade. Fertile, humus-rich and moist but well-drained soil
Use: Shaded border, woodland garden
Good companions: *Dryopteris wallichiana*, *Geranium sylvaticum* 'Mayflower', *Smilacina racemosa*

12 Geranium wallichianum 'Buxton's Variety'
Cranesbill

The trailing stems of this geranium work their way out from the central cluster of marbled leaves and insert the white-centred blue flowers among other plants. Flowers from midsummer to mid-autumn. Hardy.
Height: 30cm (12in) **Spread:** 1.2m (4ft)
Site: Sun, partial shade. Well-drained soil
Use: Sunny or partly shaded border
Good companions: *Diascia rigescens*, *Penstemon* 'Evelyn', *Spiraea japonica* 'Anthony Waterer'

purple, blue and violet
(continued)

1 Platycodon grandiflorus
Balloon flower

Fleshy-rooted perennial that comes into leaf in late spring. Above the blue-green foliage ballooning buds open to blue or violet bell-shaped flowers. Veining intensifies their colour and adds a shadow to white-flowered cultivars. Hardy.

General care: Mark the plant's position so that it is not damaged by digging in spring.

Height: 50cm (20in) **Spread:** 30cm (12in)

Site: Sun. Fertile, reliably moist but well-drained soil

Use: Front of sunny border, raised bed, rock garden

Good companions: *Geranium cinerium* subsp. *subcaulescens*, *Tulipa clusiana*, *Veronica peduncularis* 'Georgia Blue'

2 Salvia uliginosa
Bog sage

This airy and graceful perennial flowers from the end of summer until mid-autumn. The branching, leafy stems wave loose spires of sky-blue flowers above the heads of most border plants. Not fully hardy.

Height: 2m (6ft) **Spread:** 1m (3ft)

Site: Sun. Reliably moist soil

Use: Sunny border

Good companions: *Anchusa azurea* 'Loddon Royalist', *Miscanthus sinensis* 'Variegatus', *Thalictrum aquilegiifolium* 'Thundercloud'

3 Scabiosa caucasica 'Clive Grieves'
Pincushion flower, Scabious

Almost leafless stems rise from a basal clump of long grey-green leaves carrying flowerheads composed of a pale dome of tiny fertile flowers edged with frilly, lavender-blue, petal-like ray-florets. In 'Moerheim Blue' the ray-florets are dark blue. There are also white varieties. All are attractive to bees and butterflies and excellent for cutting. Hardy.

Height: 75cm (2ft 6in) **Spread:** 50cm (20in)

Site: Sun. Well-drained soil. Good on lime

Use: Sunny border, wild garden

Good companions: *Achillea* 'Taygetea', *Artemisia stelleriana* 'Boughton Silver', *Lavandula angustifolia* 'Nana Alba'

4 Thalictrum delavayi 'Hewitt's Double'
Meadow rue

A woodland plant of airy refinement with prettily divided grey-green leaves. Purple-tinted stems carry large open heads composed of tiny 'pompom' flowers, which create a haze of mauve-blue. Hardy.

General care: Avoid staking but position plants so that they are supported by neighbouring perennials or shrubs.

Height: 1.2m (4ft)

Spread: 60cm (2ft)

Site: Partial shade. Humus-rich and moist but well-drained soil

Use: Shaded border, woodland garden

Good companions: *Cornus alba* 'Elegantissima', *Gentiana asclepiadea*, *Viburnum carlesii* 'Aurora'

5 Verbena bonariensis
Stiff branching stems carry clusters of small, scented purple-pink flowers during late summer and autumn. This perennial is often short-lived, but reaches flowering maturity in its first year and self-seeds freely. Not fully hardy.

Height: 2m (6ft) **Spread:** 45cm (18in)

Site: Sun. Well-drained soil

Use: Gravel garden, sunny border

Good companions: *Lavandula* x *intermedia* Dutch Group, *Papaver orientale* 'Black and White', *Stipa gigantea*

pink and mauve

6 Anemone hupehensis 'Hadspen Abundance'
Windflower

This woody-based perennial flowers freely into autumn on erect dark stems rising above the divided leaves. The stems branch to carry more than a dozen single flowers, with light and dark pink around a boss of yellow stamens. Hardy.

Height: 75cm (2ft 6in) **Spread:** 40cm (16in)

Site: Sun, partial shade. Humus-rich and moist but well-drained soil

Use: Sunny or lightly shaded border

Good companions: *Anemone* x *hybrida* 'Whirlwind', *Thalictrum aquilegiifolium* 'Thundercloud', *Tiarella cordifolia*

7 Argyranthemum 'Vancouver'

Woody-based plant with soft stems and deeply cut grey-green leaves. The double flowerheads consist of a bright pink disc of crowded short florets surrounded by well-spaced petal-like ray-florets that fade to pale pink. Half hardy.
General care: In frost-prone areas treat as an annual, or grow in a container and overwinter under glass.
Height: 1m (3ft) **Spread:** 75cm (2ft 6in)
Site: Sun. Well-drained soil
Compost: Soil-based (John Innes No. 2)
Use: Container, sunny border, patio
Good companions: *Convolvulus sabatius, Diascia rigescens, Helichrysum petiolare*

8 Aster novi-belgii 'Heinz Richard'

Michaelmas daisy, New York aster

There are numerous cultivars of michaelmas daisy, a fibrous-rooted perennial that flowers from late summer to mid-autumn. The low leafy clump of 'Heinz Richard' is almost hidden by a mass of bright pink, yellow-eyed semi-double flowers, up to 8cm (3in) across. Hardy.
Height: 30cm (12in) **Spread:** 45cm (18in)
Site: Sun, partial shade. Fertile and moist but well-drained soil
Use: Front of sunny or lightly shaded border
Good companions: *Anemone hupehensis* 'Hadspen Abundance', *Anemone* x *hybrida* 'Honorine Jobert', *Aster divaricatus*

9 Astilbe 'Bronce Elegans'

Compact hybrid with finely divided, bronze-tinted leaves. Arching red-green stems carry sprays of tiny salmon-pink-flushed cream flowers. Hardy.
Height: 30cm (12in) **Spread:** 25cm (10in)
Site: Partial shade, sun. Fertile and humus-rich, reliably moist soil
Use: Bog garden, moist border, waterside, woodland garden
Good companions: *Alchemilla conjuncta, Asplenium scolopendrium, Hosta* 'Royal Standard'

10 Astilbe chinensis var. taquetii 'Superba'

Tall erect stems carry fluffy spires of reddish pink flowers over the clump of ferny leaves. Blooms when most astilbes have finished. Hardy.
Height: 1.2m (4ft) **Spread:** 75cm (2ft 6in)
Site: Sun, partial shade. Humus-rich and moist but well-drained soil
Use: Moist border, waterside, woodland garden
Good companions: *Asplenium scolopendrium, Astilbe* x *arendsii* 'Irrlicht', *Astrantia major* subsp. *involucrata* 'Shaggy'

11 Centaurea hypoleuca 'John Coutts'

Knapweed

Clump-forming perennial valued for its long flowering season in summer and autumn. Stiff stems carry deep pink flowerheads, paler at the centre, above light green lobed leaves. Hardy.
Height: 60cm (2ft) **Spread:** 45cm (18in)
Site: Sun. Well-drained soil
Use: Sunny border
Good companions: *Echinacea purpurea* 'Magnus', *Eryngium* x *tripartitum, Geranium* x *riversleaianum* 'Russell Prichard'

12 Chrysanthemum 'Clara Curtis'

Rubellum Group chrysanthemum

The Rubellum Group chrysanthemums are bushy, clump-forming woody-based plants. They flower generously into early autumn. 'Clara Curtis' has pink flowerheads with a central disc that changes from green to yellow. Excellent for cutting. Hardy.
Height: 75cm (2ft 6in) **Spread:** 60cm (2ft)
Site: Sun. Well-drained soil
Use: Sunny border
Good companions: *Anemone* x *hybrida* 'September Charm', *Aster ericoides* 'Pink Cloud', *Penstemon* 'Stapleford Gem'

pink and mauve (continued)

1 Diascia rigescens

Semi-evergreen trailing perennial that sends up stiff erect stems, which are clothed with small heart-shaped leaves and terminate in dense spikes of short-spurred pink flowers. In flower from early summer to mid-autumn. Not fully hardy.

General care: Overwinter cuttings as a precaution against loss.
Height: 30cm (12in) **Spread:** 60cm (2ft)
Site: Sun. Moist but well drained soil
Use: Base of warm wall, front of sunny border, raised bed, rock garden
Good companions: *Geranium* 'Johnson's Blue', *Rosa* Mary Rose, *Spiraea japonica* 'Anthony Waterer'

2 Echinacea purpurea 'Magnus'
Coneflower

Stiff-stemmed plant with rough dark leaves topped by flowerheads that consist of a ring of pink-purple, petal-like ray-florets surrounding a dark orange cone-shaped disc. Hardy.

Height: 1m (3ft) **Spread:** 45cm (18in)
Site: Sun. Humus-rich and well-drained soil
Use: Sunny border
Good companions: *Campanula lactiflora*, *Salvia* x *sylvestris* 'Mainacht', *Sedum* 'Herbstfreude'

3 Geranium 'Ann Folkard'
Cranesbill

From a central clump lax stems make long trails of lobed and toothed leaves. These are an acid yellow-green when young and become greener as they age. From midsummer to mid-autumn the stems also carry numerous dark-eyed magenta flowers. Hardy.

Height: 60cm (2ft) **Spread:** 1m (3ft)
Site: Sun, partial shade. Moist but well-drained soil
Use: Sunny or lightly shaded border
Good companions: *Epimedium* x *versicolor* 'Sulphureum', *Hosta* 'Gold Standard', *Milium effusum* 'Aureum'

4 Geranium x riversleaianum 'Russell Prichard'
Cranesbill

This vigorous perennial sends out trailing stems from a central clump of grey-green lobed leaves. The stems carry light magenta, funnel-shaped flowers throughout summer and into autumn. Hardy.

Height: 30cm (12in) **Spread:** 1m (3ft)
Site: Sun, partial shade. Well-drained soil
Use: Ground cover, sunny or light shaded border
Good companions: *Artemisia ludoviciana* 'Valerie Finnis', *Digitalis purpurea*, *Sedum spectabile* 'Brilliant'

5 Gypsophila 'Rosenschleier'

From mid to late summer the mound of narrow blue-green leaves is enveloped by a cloud of very small double flowers that open white but turn pale pink as they age. Hardy.

5

6

1

3
4

7

2

8

9

10

12

11

Height: 40cm (16in) **Spread:** 75cm (2ft 6in)
Site: Sun. Well-drained, preferably limy soil
Use: Sunny border
Good companions: *Allium cristophii*, *Lavandula angustifolia* 'Hidcote', *Lychnis coronaria*

6 Hosta 'Honeybells'
Plaintain lily

Good foliage plant with a clump of fresh green, lustrous leaves. These are nearly heart shaped with slightly wavy margins and are deeply veined. Stems of fragrant white to mauve bells appear in late summer. Hardy.

Height: 75cm (2ft 6in) **Spread:** 1m (3ft)
Site: Partial shade, sun. Fertile and moist but well-drained soil
Use: Ground cover, sunny or shady border, waterside, woodland garden
Good companions: *Astilbe* 'Fanal', *Dicentra spectabilis*, *Tiarella wherryi*

7 Liatris spicata
Gayfeather

From a base of linear leaves rise sturdy upright stems ringed at intervals with short narrow leaves and packed buds in the top two-thirds. In late summer and early autumn these open from the top down to make mauve-pink plumes. Hardy.

Height: 1.2m (4ft) **Spread:** 45cm (18in)
Site: Sun. Moist but well-drained soil
Use: Sunny border
Good companions: *Astilbe* 'Professor van der Wielen', *Geranium* x *riversleaianum* 'Russell Prichard', *Macleaya cordata* 'Flamingo'

8 Monarda 'Prärienacht'
Bergamot

The bergamot hybrids are aromatic perennials that flower over a long period in late summer and early autumn. The flowering stems of 'Prärienacht' end in heads of purple-mauve flowers arranged in rings. The leaves are prominently veined. Hardy.

Height: 1m (3ft) **Spread:** 45cm (18in)
Site: Sun, partial shade. Humus-rich and moist but well-drained soil
Use: Sunny or lightly shaded border
Good companions: *Anemone* x *hybrida* 'Whirlwind', *Aster* x *frikartii* 'Mönch', *Phlox paniculata* 'Eventide'

9 Origanum laevigatum 'Herrenhausen'
Marjoram, Oregano

Woody-based plant with purplish young leaves that turn dark green with age and are retained in winter. The foliage is not aromatic. Throughout summer and into autumn wiry stems carry dense clusters of small pink flowers, which are surrounded by red-purple bracts. Hardy.

Height: 45cm (18in) **Spread:** 40cm (16in)
Site: Sun. Well-drained soil. Good on lime
Use: Gravel garden, sunny border
Good companions: *Artemisia* 'Powis Castle', *Perovskia* 'Blue Spire', *Verbena bonariensis*

10 Osteospermum 'Jucundum'

Sprawling, woody-based evergreen plant with greyish, aromatic lance-shaped leaves and mauve-pink to magenta daisy-like flowerheads, each on a single stem. The purplish central discs turn gold with age. Blooms throughout summer and into autumn, but buds remain closed in dull weather. Not fully hardy.

General care: In cold areas treat as an annual, or overwinter container-grown plants under glass.
Height: 20cm (8in) **Spread:** 60cm (2ft)
Site: Sun. Well-drained soil
Compost: Soil-based (John Innes No. 2)
Use: Container, front of sunny border
Good companions: *Argyranthemum* 'Vancouver', *Diascia barberae* 'Ruby Field', *Petunia* Surfinia Purple

11 Pelargonium 'Apple Blossom Rosebud'
Rosebud zonal pelargonium

This bushy evergreen perennial has aromatic, green, rounded leaves and produces rounded heads of double flowers with central petals that remain unopened. The outer petals are pink, the central ones white. Plants flower freely in summer and autumn if deadheaded regularly. Tender.

General care: Overwinter in frost-free conditions.
Height: 35cm (14in) **Spread:** 25cm (10in)
Site: Sun. Well-drained soil
Compost: Soil-based (John Innes No. 2) or soil-less with added grit
Use: Conservatory or greenhouse minimum 2°C (36°F), container, formal bedding, sunny patio
Good companions: *Helichrysum petiolare*, *Pelargonium* 'L'Elégante', *Scaevola aemula* 'Blue Fan'

12 Penstemon 'Evelyn'

From a neat bush of narrow leaves rise spires of deep pink, slender tubular flowers that are paler in the throat. Flowering starts before midsummer and continues into autumn. Hardy.

Height: 50cm (20in) **Spread:** 30cm (12in)
Site: Sun, partial shade. Fertile and well-drained soil
Use: Sunny or lightly shaded border
Good companions: *Aquilegia* 'Hensol Harebell', *Paeonia lactiflora* 'Bowl of Beauty', *Penstemon* 'Stapleford Gem'

pink and mauve (continued)

1 Phlox paniculata 'Eventide'

Perennial phlox

The perennial phloxes are erect plants with linear leaves, often somewhat bare at the base, and rounded heads of scented flowers in a wide range of colours that are good for cutting. The flowers of 'Eventide' are a startling pink. Hardy.

Height: 1m (3ft) **Spread:** 60cm (2ft)

Site: Sun, partial shade. Fertile and moist but well-drained soil

Use: Sunny or lightly shaded border

Good companions: *Geranium psilostemon*, *Phlox paniculata* 'Fujiyama', *Tradescantia* Andersoniana Group 'Osprey'

2 Sedum spectabile 'Brilliant'

Ice plant

Succulent perennial with fleshy grey-green leaves arranged in rings on erect stems. Flat terminal heads are packed with starry mauve-pink flowers. Attractive to bees. Hardy.

Height and spread: 45cm (18in)

Site: Sun. Well-drained soil

Use: Sunny border

Good companions: *Agapanthus* 'Lilliput', *Caryopteris* x *clandonensis* 'Heavenly Blue', *Perovskia* 'Blue Spire'

bronze and maroon

3 Deschampsia cespitosa 'Goldschleier'

Tufted hair grass, Tussock grass

From a dense evergreen tussock of narrow arching leaves emerge tall stems carrying plumes of silver-purple flowers. In late summer these bleach to straw yellow. Suitable for drying. Hardy.

Height and spread: 1.2m (4ft)

Site: Sun, partial shade. Moist but well-drained soil

Use: Sunny or lightly shaded border

Good companions: *Miscanthus sinensis* 'Variegatus', *Monarda* 'Prärienacht', *Salvia uliginosa*

4 Heuchera micrantha var. diversifolia 'Palace Purple'

Coral flower

This richly textured, evergreen foliage plant is at its best in summer. The jagged, deeply veined leaves have a sheeny bronze-red surface and magenta-pink underside. Showers of tiny white flowers, carried on wiry stems in early summer, are followed by bronze-pink seed pods. Hardy.

Height: 45cm (18in) **Spread:** 60cm (2ft)

Site: Sun, partial shade. Fertile and moist but well-drained soil

Use: Ground cover, sunny or lightly shaded border, woodland garden

Good companions: *Asplenium scolopendrium*, *Hosta* 'Honeybells', *Tiarella cordifolia*

5 Macleaya cordata 'Flamingo'

Plume poppy

Tall and sometimes invasive perennial but handsome at the back of a border. The large deeply lobed leaves are grey-green, pale grey on the underside. Strong stems carry airy plumes of tiny cream and soft apricot flowers.

Height: 2.5m (8ft) **Spread:** 1m (3ft)

8

9

10

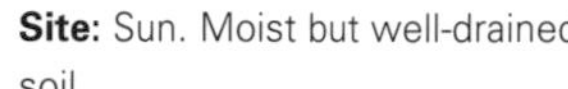

Site: Sun. Moist but well-drained soil
Use: Sunny border
Good companions: *Anemone* x *hybrida* 'September Charm', *Campanula lactiflora, Monarda* 'Prärienacht'

6 Phormium 'Sundowner'
New Zealand flax

Large evergreen foliage plant that forms a jagged clump of erect or slightly arching, leathery, broad strap-shaped leaves. These are bronze-green with cream and pink lengthwise stripes. In summer yellow-green tubular flowers are arranged in a zigzag along tall woody stems. Not fully hardy.
General care: In cold areas apply a dry winter mulch around the base.
Height and spread: 2m (6ft)
Site: Sun. Moist but well-drained soil
Use: Specimen clump, sunny border
Good companions: *Choisya ternata, Cotoneaster conspicuus* 'Decorus', *Hebe* 'Autumn Glory'

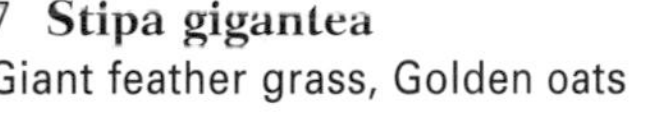

7 Stipa gigantea
Giant feather grass, Golden oats

This evergreen or semi-evergreen grass has a mid-green base of arching linear leaves. Tall stems, which stand erect above the clump, carry silver-purple plumes that ripen to spangled gold and remain a feature for many weeks. Plumes can be dried. Hardy.
General care: Cut out dead growths in early spring.
Height: 2m (6ft) **Spread:** 1.2m (4ft)
Site: Sun. Well-drained soil
Use: Gravel garden, sunny border
Good companions: *Anthemis tinctoria* 'E.C. Buxton', *Eryngium alpinum, Verbena bonariensis*

11

12

red and russet

8 Helenium 'Moerheim Beauty'
Helen's flower, Sneezeweed

The hybrid heleniums are late-flowering upright perennials with narrow leaves and daisy-like flowerheads of petal-like ray-florets around a central disc. They are long-lasting and good for cutting. 'Moerheim Beauty' has a dark brown disc surrounded by copper-red ray-florets. Hardy.
Height: 1m (3ft) **Spread:** 60cm (2ft)
Site: Sun. Fertile and moist but well-drained soil
Use: Sunny border
Good companions: *Helenium* 'Wyndley', *Helianthus* 'Loddon Gold', *Miscanthus sinensis* 'Zebrinus'

9 Hemerocallis 'Pardon Me'
Daylily

In midsummer leafless stems rise from a clump of strap-like leaves carrying red trumpet-shaped flowers that are green-throated with darker veining. Individual flowers are short-lived, but the season lasts for weeks. Hardy.
Height and spread: 60cm (2ft)
Site: Sun. Fertile and moist but well-drained soil
Use: Sunny border
Good companions: *Deschampsia cespitosa* 'Goldschleier', *Helenium* 'Moerheim Beauty', *Thalictrum flavum* subsp. *glaucum*

10 Knautia macedonica
In late summer and early autumn branching stems carry crimson 'pincushion' flowerheads above lobed leaves. Attractive to bees. Hardy.
Height: 75cm (2ft 6in) **Spread:** 45cm (18in)
Site: Sun. Well-drained soil. Good on lime
Use: Sunny border, wild garden
Good companions: *Echinops ritro* 'Veitch's Blue', *Lavandula* x *intermedia* Dutch Group, *Scabiosa caucasica* 'Moerheim Blue'

11 Pelargonium 'Rouletta'
Ivy-leaved pelargonium

This trailing evergreen perennial belongs to a group of hybrid pelargoniums with fleshy ivy-shaped leaves. Throughout summer and autumn it bears rounded clusters of semi-double flowers that are vivid crimson streaked white. Tender.
General care: Overwinter in frost-free conditions.
Height: 20cm (8in) **Spread:** 45cm (18in)
Site: Sun. Well-drained soil
Compost: Soil-based (John Innes No. 2) or soil-less with added grit
Use: Conservatory or greenhouse minimum 2°C (36°F), container, raised bed, sunny patio
Good companions: *Argyranthemum* 'Vancouver', *Convolvulus sabatius, Verbena* 'Silver Anne'

12 Penstemon 'Andenken an Friedrich Hahn'
Spires of small, garnet-red bell-shaped flowers rise from this bushy narrow-leaved plant from midsummer until late autumn. Not fully hardy.
General care: In cold areas protect over winter with a dry mulch.
Height: 30cm (12in) **Spread:** 60cm (2ft)
Site: Sun, partial shade. Fertile, well-drained soil
Use: Sunny or lightly shaded border
Good companions: *Anaphalis triplinervis* 'Sommerschnee', *Paeonia lactiflora* 'Karl Rosenfield', *Thalictrum aquilegiifolium* 'Thundercloud'

red and russet (continued)

1 Sedum 'Ruby Glow'
Stonecrop

Succulent perennial with red stems carrying fleshy, purplish green leaves. In late summer and early autumn plants are topped by packed heads of wine-red starry flowers. Hardy.

Height: 25cm (10in) **Spread:** 45cm (18in)
Site: Sun. Well-drained soil
Use: Front of sunny border, raised bed, rock garden
Good companions: *Gypsophila* 'Rosenschleier', *Lavandula angustifolia* 'Hidcote', *Scabiosa graminifolia*

yellow and orange

2 Achillea 'Coronation Gold'
Yarrow

Evergreen perennial with feathery grey-green leaves and flat heads of densely packed, tiny yellow flowers. Flowerheads can be dried for winter decoration. Hardy.

Height: 1m (3ft) **Spread:** 60cm (2ft)
Site: Sun. Well-drained soil
Use: Sunny border
Good companions: *Erysimum* 'Bowles' Mauve', *Potentilla fruticosa* 'Tangerine', x *Solidaster luteus* 'Lemore'

3 Coreopsis verticillata 'Grandiflora'
Tickseed

The finely cut mid-green leaves of this bushy perennial are covered by a profusion of rich yellow daisy-like flowerheads over many weeks. 'Moonbeam' has creamy yellow flowers, which team with a wider range of colours. Hardy.

Height: 60cm (2ft) **Spread:** 40cm (16in)
Site: Sun. Well-drained soil
Use: Sunny border
Good companions: *Aster* x *frikartii* 'Mönch', *Eryngium alpinum*, *Origanum laevigatum* 'Herrenhausen'

4 Hemerocallis 'Stella de Oro'
Daylily

This low-growing evergreen daylily flowers over many weeks in mid to late summer. The yellow trumpets are a little over 5cm (2in) across and the mouth is almost circular in outline.

Height: 30cm (12in) **Spread:** 45cm (18in)
Site: Sun, partial shade. Fertile and moist but well-drained soil
Compost: Soil-based (John Innes No. 2)
Use: Container, sunny or lightly shaded border
Good companions: *Astilbe* 'Professor van der Wielen', *Carex oshimensis* 'Evergold', *Iris sibirica 'Ego'*

5 Hosta fortunei var. aureomarginata
Plantain lily

The yellow variegation of many hostas fades as summer advances, but in this case the creamy edge of the deeply veined leaves remains distinct until autumn. Mauve flowers in summer. Hardy.

Height and spread: 75cm (2ft 6in)
Site: Sun, partial shade. Fertile and humus-rich but well-drained soil
Use: Ground cover, sunny or partially shaded border, woodland
Good companions: *Milium effusum* 'Aureum', *Tiarella wherryi*, *Viola riviniana* Purpurea Group

6 Kirengeshoma palmata

This elegant woodland perennial forms a clump of attractively lobed, pale green leaves. In late summer and early autumn black stems carry widely spaced tubular flowers that are composed of fleshy, pale yellow petals. Hardy.

Height: 1.2m (4ft) **Spread:** 75cm (2ft 6in)
Site: Partial shade. Humus-rich and moist soil that is well-drained and lime-free
Use: Peat bed, shady border, woodland garden
Good companions: *Hosta* 'Gold Standard', *Rhododendron luteum*, *Uvularia grandiflora*

7 Kniphofia 'Royal Standard'
Red hot poker, Torch lily

From a clump of arching narrow leaves rise stiff stems brandishing torches of tubular flowers. These are orange in bud but open yellow from the bottom up. Hardy.

Height: 1m (3ft)
Spread: 60cm (2ft)
Site: Sun, partial shade. Humus-rich and moist but well-drained soil
Use: Sunny or lightly shaded border
Good companions: *Agapanthus* 'Lilliput', *Coreopsis verticillata* 'Grandiflora', *Helenium* 'Wyndley'

8 Rudbeckia fulgida var. sullivantii 'Goldsturm'
Black-eyed susan

This bushy perennial has pointed leaves and slightly hairy branched stems that carry numerous

daisy-like flowerheads up to 8cm (3in) across. The orange-yellow, petal-like ray-florets radiate around an eye-catching, dark brown disc and last well into autumn. Hardy.
Height: 60cm (2ft) **Spread:** 45cm (18in)
Site: Sun, partial shade. Moist but well-drained soil
Use: Sunny or lightly shaded border, wild garden
Good companions: *Deschampsia cespitosa* 'Goldschleier', *Helenium* 'Moerheim Beauty', *Helenium* 'Sonnenwunder'

9 x Solidaster luteus 'Lemore'

These clump-forming perennials are a cross between a golden rod (*Solidago*) and an aster. In late summer and early autumn 'Lemore' bears dense sprays of small daisy-like flowerheads composed of pale yellow ray-florets around a darker central disc. Excellent for cutting. Hardy.
Height and spread: 75cm (2ft 6in)
Site: Sun. Well-drained soil
Use: Sunny border
Good companions: *Achillea* 'Coronation Gold', *Anthemis tinctoria* 'E.C. Buxton', *Helianthus* 'Lemon Queen'

cream and white

10 Anaphalis triplinervis 'Sommerschnee'

Pearl everlasting, Summer snow

Spreading clumps of grey-green spoon-shaped leaves are topped by white, papery everlasting flowerheads. Suitable for drying. Hardy.
Height: 40cm (16in) **Spread:** 50cm (20in)
Site: Sun, partial shade. Moist but well-drained soil
Use: Sunny or lightly shaded border.
Good companions: *Anemone hupehensis* 'Hadspen Abundance', *Aster divaricatus*, *Heuchera* 'Plum Pudding'

11 Anemone x hybrida 'Whirlwind'

Japanese anemone

This woody-based perennial forms an attractive mound of lobed leaves from which rise erect stems carrying white semi-double flowers with yellow centres in late summer and early autumn. Hardy.
Height: 1.2m (4ft) **Spread:** Indefinite
Site: Sun, partial shade. Humus-rich and moist but well drained soil
Use: Sunny or lightly shaded border, woodland garden
Good companions: *Anaphalis triplinervis* 'Sommerschnee', *Anemone* x *hybrida* 'September Charm', *Aster novi-belgii* 'Heinz Richard'

12 Argyranthemum 'Snow Storm'

Compact woody-based plant with soft stems and deeply cut grey-green leaves. Through summer and into autumn it bears white daisy-like flowerheads with yellow central discs. Tender.
General care: In frost-prone areas treat as an annual, or grow in containers and overwinter under glass.
Height and spread: 30cm (12in)
Site: Sun. Well-drained soil
Compost: Soil-based (John Innes No. 2)
Use: Container, sunny border, patio
Good companions: *Argyranthemum* 'Vancouver', *Scaevola aemula* 'Blue Wonder', *Verbena* 'Silver Anne'

cream and white (continued)

1 Astilbe 'Professor van der Wielen'

This large, graceful astilbe hybrid makes mounds of mid-green divided leaves. In midsummer tall stems bear long-lasting arching plumes of tiny creamy flowers. Attractive seed heads in autumn and winter. Hardy.

Height: 1.2m (4ft) **Spread:** 1m (3ft)
Site: Sun, partial shade. Humus-rich and reliably moist soil
Use: Bog garden, moist border, waterside, woodland garden
Good companions: *Miscanthus sinensis* 'Variegatus', *Rheum palmatum* 'Atrosanguineum', *Rodgersia pinnata* 'Superba'

2 Gaura lindheimeri

White flowers hover around the clump of erect or gently arching, slender stems set with narrow leaves. The buds are tinted pink and the flowers age to pale pink. Flowers into autumn. Hardy.

Height: 1.2m (4ft) **Spread:** 1m (3ft)

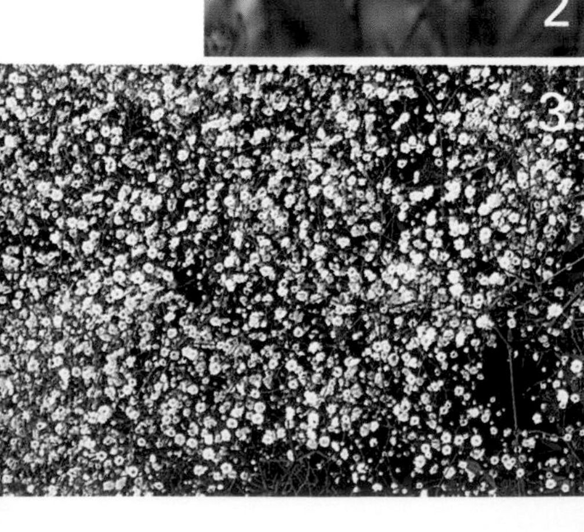

Site: Sun. Well-drained soil
Use: Gravel garden, sunny border
Good companions: *Artemisia* 'Powis Castle', *Ruta graveolens* 'Jackman's Blue', *Stipa gigantea*

3 Gypsophila paniculata 'Bristol Fairy'
Baby's breath
The base of grey-green grass-like leaves is topped by a tangle of slender branching stems. From mid to late summer these support an airy cloud of small, white double flowers. Good for hiding plants past their best and for cutting. 'Flamingo' has pale pink double flowers. Hardy.
Height and spread: 1m (3ft)
Site: Sun. Well-drained soil. Good on lime
Use: Sunny border
Good companions: *Acanthus spinosus*, *Papaver orientale* 'Black and White', *Verbascum* Cotswold Group 'Gainsborough'

4 Hosta 'Snowden'
Plantain lily
An impressive clump of foliage with elegant white flowers in mid to late summer. The long pointed leaves are grey-green and deeply veined. Hardy.
Height and spread: 1m (3ft)
Site: Sun, partial shade. Fertile and humus-rich but well-drained soil
Use: Ground cover, sunny or partially shaded border, woodland
Good companions: *Astilbe chinensis* var. *taquetii* 'Superba', *Hosta* 'Ginko Craig', *Pulmonaria* 'Mawson's Blue'

5 Phlox paniculata 'Fujiyama'
Perennial phlox
This erect plant has linear leaves and rounded heads of scented ivory-white flowers. Good in the border and for cutting. Hardy.
Height: 75cm (2ft 6in) **Spread:** 50cm (20in)
Site: Sun, partial shade. Fertile and moist but well-drained soil
Use: Sunny or lightly shaded border
Good companions: *Aster novi-belgii* 'Heinz Richard', *Geranium* 'Johnson's Blue', *Phlox paniculata* 'Eventide'

6 Romneya coulteri
Matilija poppy, Tree poppy
The deeply lobed, grey-green leaves of this deciduous woody-based plant have a blue-grey bloom. Tall stems carry white flowers, which have a boss of yellow stamens and are often more than 10cm (4in) across. Slow to get established, but later may spread vigorously. Not fully hardy.
General care: Grow in a warm, sheltered position and apply a dry mulch in winter. Cut down all of the surviving growth to the ground in late winter.
Height: 2m (6ft) **Spread:** Indefinite
Site: Sun. Humus-rich but well-drained soil
Use: Base of sunny wall, sunny border
Good companions: *Buddleja crispa*, *Clematis* 'Huldine', *Solanum laxum* 'Album'

7 Tradescantia Andersoniana Group 'Osprey'
Spiderwort, Trinity flower
The tradescantia hybrids grown in borders are leafy plants with pointed strap-shaped leaves that arch away from erect stems. Small sprays of three-petalled flowers emerge at the junction of leaf and stem. 'Osprey' has white flowers with a haze of blue filaments at the centre. Hardy.
Height and spread: 60cm (2ft)
Site: Sun, partial shade. Moist, well-drained soil
Use: Sunny or lightly shaded border
Good companions: *Aconitum* 'Spark's Variety', *Anemone* x *hybrida* 'Honorine Jobert', *Fuchsia magellanica* 'Versicolor'

silver and grey

8 Cortaderia selloana 'Sunningdale Silver'
Pampas grass
Evergreen grass suitable for a large garden. It forms a substantial mound of narrow arching leaves from which emerge erect stems carrying feathery heads of silky, creamy white flowers. These stand up well to weather and can be used fresh or dried in flower arrangements. Hardy.
General care: Cut down all the old stems in late winter.
Height: 3m (10ft) **Spread:** 2.5m (8ft)
Site: Sun. Well-drained soil
Use: Specimen clump, sunny border
Good companions: *Ceanothus thyrsiflorus* var. *repens*, *Cortaderia selloana* 'Aureolineata', *Stipa gigantea*

9 Cynara cardunculus
Cardoon
Magnificent foliage plant with large, jagged, grey-green leaves, sometimes grown as a vegetable for the edible leaf-stalks and midribs, which are eaten blanched. In summer and early autumn the violet-purple thistle-like flowerheads are impressive. They are also suitable for dried flower arrangements. Hardy.
Height: 2m (6ft) **Spread:** 1.2m (4ft)
Site: Sun. Fertile and well-drained soil
Use: Sunny border
Good companions: *Artemisia* 'Powis Castle', *Erysimum* 'Bowles' Mauve', *Sedum* 'Herbstfreude'

green

10 Carex comans 'Frosted Curls'
Sedge
This evergreen grass-like sedge makes a dense tuft of arching, pale silvery green, thread-like leaves. There are inconspicuous green cylindrical flower spikes in summer. Not fully hardy.
Height: 60cm (2ft) **Spread:** 45cm (18in)
Site: Sun, partial shade. Moist but well-drained soil
Use: Sunny or lightly shaded border
Good companions: *Miscanthus sinensis* 'Silberfeder', *Molinia caerulea* subsp. *arundinacea* 'Windspiel', *Panicum virgatum* 'Rubrum'

11 Hosta lancifolia
Plantain lily
Grown mainly as a foliage plant, this hosta makes dense dark green clumps of narrow pointed leaves. In late summer numerous stems carry purple, slender funnel-shaped flowers. Hardy.
Height: 45cm (18in) **Spread:** 75cm (2ft 6in)
Site: Shade, partial shade. Humus-rich and moist but well-drained soil
Use: Ground cover, shady border, woodland garden
Good companions: *Dryopteris wallichiana*, *Viola riviniana* Purpurea Group, *Waldsteinia ternata*

12 Kniphofia 'Percy's Pride'
Red hot poker, Torch lily
From arching leaves that are markedly keeled along the midrib rise upright stems carrying spikes of narrow tubular flowers, which hang down in dense ranks. When open the flowers are pale cream, but there is a strong green tint in the unopened buds. Hardy.
Height: 1.2m (4ft) **Spread:** 60cm (2ft)
Site: Sun, partial shade. Humus-rich and moist but well-drained soil
Use: Sunny or lightly shaded border
Good companions: *Helenium* 'Moerheim Beauty', *Hemerocallis* 'Stella de Oro', *Rudbeckia fulgida* var. *sullivantii* 'Goldsturm'

annuals & biennials

Annuals and biennials often give good value over many weeks. In late summer in particular they brighten beds and containers over a long period if regularly deadheaded.

purple, blue and violet

1 Brachyscome iberidifolia Splendour Series
Swan river daisy

Free-flowering dwarf annual with finely divided leaves and small yellow-centred daisy-like flowers in purple, blue, mauve, pink or white. Half hardy.
General care: Sow seed under glass at 18°C (64°F) in mid-spring. Plant out when there is no longer a risk of frost.
Height and spread: 30cm (12in)
Site: Sun. Well-drained soil
Compost: Soil-based (John Innes No. 2) or soil-less
Use: Container, formal bedding, front of sunny border
Good companions: *Callistephus chinensis* Princess Series, *Lavatera trimestris* 'Mont Blanc', *Nigella damascena* 'Miss Jekyll'

2 Lathyrus odoratus 'Noel Sutton'
Sweet pea

Sweet peas are annual tendril climbers. Modern cultivars have large scented, ruffled pea flowers, which in 'Noel Sutton' are mauve-blue. Hardy.
General care: Sow seed under glass in autumn or early spring and plant out in spring. Or sow *in situ* in mid-spring. Deadhead regularly.
Height: 2m (6ft) **Spread:** 60cm (2ft)
Site: Sun. Humus-rich, fertile and well-drained soil
Use: Screen, tripod climber
Good companions: *Cleome hassleriana* 'Rose Queen', *Lavatera trimestris* 'Mont Blanc', *Penstemon* 'Evelyn'

3 Lobelia erinus 'Crystal Palace'

A bushy narrow-leaved cultivar of a popular bedding and container perennial normally grown as an annual. Covered with dark blue flowers throughout summer and into autumn. Half hardy.
General care: Sow seed under glass at 16–18°C (61–64°F) in late winter. Plant out when there is no longer a risk of frost.
Height and spread: 15cm (6in)
Site: Sun or partial shade. Moist, well-drained soil
Compost: Soil-based (John Innes No. 2) or soil-less
Use: Container, front of sunny or lightly shaded border, formal bedding
Good companions: *Cosmos bipinnatus* Sensation Series, *Impatiens walleriana* Tempo Series, *Nicotiana* Domino Series

4 Salvia viridis 'Oxford Blue'
Annual clary

Erect hairy annual with insignificant flowers, but darkly veined, violet-blue leaf-like bracts. Good for cutting. Hardy.
General care: Sow seed *in situ* in early autumn or mid to late spring. Plant out when there is no longer a risk of frost.
Height: 30cm (12in) **Spread:** 25cm (10in)
Site: Sun. Well-drained soil
Use: Formal bedding, herb garden, sunny border
Good companions: *Allium cristophii*, *Gladiolus* 'Charm', *Verbena bonariensis*

5 Scaevola aemula 'Blue Wonder'
Fairy fan-flower

Shrubby evergreen perennial commonly grown as an annual for containers. The stiff trailing stems carry a profusion of violet-blue fan-shaped flowers from late spring until the first frosts. Tender.
General care: Sow seed at 19–24°C (66–75°F) in spring. Plant out when there is no risk of frost.
Height: 50cm (20in) **Spread:** 75cm (2ft 6in)
Site: Sun. Humus-rich, moist but well-drained soil
Compost: Soil-based (John Innes No. 2) or soil-less
Use: Conservatory or greenhouse minimum 5°C (41°F), container
Good companions: *Anagallis monellii*, *Verbena* 'Peaches and Cream', *Viola* Crystal Bowl Series

6 Viola x wittrockiana Crystal Bowl Series
Pansy

Pansy cultivars are short-lived evergreen perennials grown as annuals or biennials. Their flat flowers are often strongly marked, but some cultivars have single colours. Those of Crystal Bowl are purple, deep blue, rose or white. Hardy.
General care: Sow seed in a coldframe in late winter. Plant out in late spring. To prolong flowering, deadhead regularly.
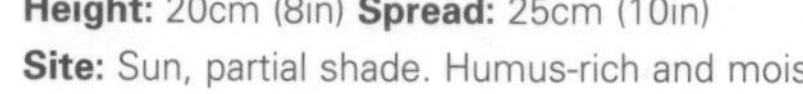
Height: 20cm (8in) **Spread:** 25cm (10in)
Site: Sun, partial shade. Humus-rich and moist but well-drained soil
Compost: Soil-based (John Innes No. 2) or soil-less
Use: Container, formal bedding, front of border
Good companions: *Lobelia erinus* 'Cobalt Blue', *Nemesia* Carnival Series, *Nicotiana* Domino Series

pink and mauve

7 Cleome hassleriana 'Rose Queen'
Spider flower, Spider plant

Erect annual with a base of 'fingered' leaves topped by rounded heads of fragrant, strong pink spidery flowers. Other colours available. Tender.
General care: Sow seed under glass at 18°C (64°F) from late winter to early spring. Plant out when there is no longer a risk of frost.
Height: 1.2m (4ft) **Spread:** 45cm (18in)
Site: Sun. Free-draining soil
Compost: Soil-based (John Innes No. 2)
Use: Container, sunny border, formal bedding
Good companions: *Antirrhinum* Sonnet Series, *Artemisia* 'Powis Castle', *Verbena bonariensis*

3

4

1

2

5

6

7

8

8 Cosmos bipinnatus Sensation Series

Erect annual with feathery foliage and tall wiry stems supporting large cupped flowerheads that are white or pink and yellow centred. Half hardy.
General care: Sow seed under glass in mid-spring and plant out when there is no longer a risk of frost, or sow *in situ* in late spring.
Height: 1m (3ft) **Spread:** 40cm (16in)
Site: Sun. Moist but well-drained soil
Use: Sunny border, formal bedding
Good companions: *Brachyscome iberidifolia* Splendour Series, *Delphinium* 'Faust', *Lathyrus odoratus* 'Noel Sutton'

9 Dianthus chinensis Baby Doll Series

Chinese pink, Indian pink

Short-lived perennial or biennial grown as an annual. Branching stems carry purplish red to pink and white flowers, usually patterned. Hardy.
General care: Sow seed *in situ* in mid-spring.
Height and spread: 15cm (6in)
Site: Sun. Well-drained soil. Good on lime
Compost: Soil-based (John Innes No. 2)
Use: Container, formal bedding, front of border
Good companions: *Antirrhinum* Sonnet Series, *Convolvulus cneorum*, *Matthiola incana* Ten Week Series

10 Impatiens walleriana Tempo Series

Busy lizzie

The busy lizzies are brittle-stemmed perennials widely grown as annuals. They offer a vast range of intense single colours and mixtures and are free flowering in shade. Tempo Series includes pink, orange, mauve and bicolours. Tender.
General care: Sow seed under glass at 16–18°C (61–64°F) from late winter to early spring. Plant out when there is no longer a risk of frost.
Height: 25cm (10in) **Spread:** 45cm (18in)
Site: Partial shade. Humus-rich and moist but well-drained soil
Compost: Soil-based (John Innes No. 2) or soil-less
Use: Conservatory or greenhouse minimum 10°C (50°F), container, formal bedding
Good companions: *Lobelia erinus* 'Cobalt Blue', *Nicotiana* Domino Series, *Viola* x *wittrockiana* Crystal Bowl Series

9 10

11 Petunia Surfinia Series

Grandiflora petunia

The Surfinia petunias are perennial hybrids grown as annuals, but available only as young plants raised from cuttings. They are vigorous, branch freely and produce numerous trumpet-shaped flowers on trailing stems throughout summer and early autumn. The colour range includes various shades of pink, red, blue, purple and white. Half hardy.
General care: Plant out when there is no longer a risk of frost.
Height: 35cm (14in) **Spread:** 1m (3ft)
Site: Sun. Well-drained soil
Compost: Soil-based (John Innes No. 1) or soil-less
Use: Container or formal bedding
Good companions: *Helichrysum petiolare*, *Isotoma axillaris*, *Verbena* 'Silver Anne'

11

12

12 Verbena 'Silver Anne'

In summer and autumn this stiff-stemmed sprawling plant bears heads of sweetly scented flowers that open bright pink and fade to silvery white. Perennial, but plants raised from cuttings are widely grown as annuals. Not fully hardy.
General care: To propagate take cuttings in late summer, overwinter under glass and plant out in late spring.
Height: 30cm (12in) **Spread:** 60cm (2ft)
Site: Sun. Moist but well-drained soil
Compost: Soil-based (John Innes No. 2) with added sharp sand
Use: Container, formal bedding
Good companions: *Diascia rigescens*, *Helichrysum petiolare*, *Scaevola aemula* 'Blue Wonder'

red and russet

1 Amaranthus caudatus
Love-lies-bleeding, Tassel flower

Bushy annual with large, heavily veined light green leaves. In summer and early autumn tassels of tiny red-purple flowers hang from erect stems. Suitable for cutting and drying. Half hardy.
General care: Sow seed under glass at 20°C (68°F) in mid-spring. Plant out when there is no longer a risk of frost.
Height: 1.2m (4ft) **Spread:** 75cm (2ft 6in)
Site: Sun. Humus-rich, moist but well-drained soil
Compost: Soil-based (John Innes No. 2)
Use: Conservatory or greenhouse minimum 7°C (45°F), formal bedding, sunny border
Good companions: *Cosmos bipinnatus* Sensation Series, *Dahlia* 'Porcelain', *Lathyrus odoratus* 'Noel Sutton'

yellow and orange

2 Calendula officinalis 'Fiesta Gitana'
English marigold, Marigold, Pot marigold

Easy, fast-growing compact annual that bears daisy-like flowers, usually double, above spoon-shaped leaves. Colours are soft yellows and oranges, with some bicolours. Self-seeds. Hardy.
General care: Sow seed *in situ* in early to mid-autumn or in early spring.
Height and spread: 30cm (12in)
Site: Sun. Well-drained, even poor soil
Compost: Soil-based (John Innes No. 2)
Use: Container, front of sunny bed or border
Good companions: *Nigella damascena* 'Miss Jekyll', *Salvia farinacea* 'Victoria', *Salvia viridis* 'Oxford Blue'

3 Nemesia Carnival Series

The cultivars and hybrids of *N. strumosa* are low-growing annuals that produce two-lipped flowers in summer, often with contrasting colours. Carnival Series includes purple-veined orange, yellow, white, pink or red blooms. Half hardy.
General care: Sow seed under glass at 15°C (59°F) in early spring and plant out when there is no longer a risk of frost.
Height: 20cm (8in) **Spread** 15cm (6in)
Site: Sun. Moist but well-drained soil
Compost: Soil-based (John Innes No. 2) or soil-less
Use: Container, edging, front of sunny border, formal bedding
Good companions: *Lobelia erinus* 'Crystal Palace', *Nicotiana* 'Lime Green', *Verbena* 'Peaches and Cream'

4 Tagetes tenuifolia Favourite Series
French marigold

The French marigolds are long-flowering hybrids with divided leaves and upstanding single or double flowerheads in colour mixtures that include yellow, orange and red-brown. Plants in this selection are relatively tall. Half hardy.
General care: Sow seed under glass at 18°C (64°F) in early to mid-spring. Plant out when there is no longer a risk of frost.
Height: 35cm (14in) **Spread:** 30cm (12in)
Site: Sun. Well-drained soil
Compost: Soil-based (John Innes No. 2) or soil-less
Use: Container, formal bedding, front of border
Good companions: *Bidens ferulifolia* 'Golden Goddess', *Felicia amelloides* 'Santa Anita', *Tagetes tenuifolia* 'Lemon Gem'

5 Tagetes tenuifolia 'Lemon Gem'
Signet marigold

The Signet marigolds are low bushy annuals with slender divided leaves. Over a long season they bear sprays of small single flowers in yellow and orange. 'Lemon Gem' is the coolest. Half hardy.
General care: Sow seed under glass at 18°C (64°F) in early to mid-spring. Plant out when there is no longer a risk of frost.
Height: 25cm (10in) **Spread:** 35cm (14in)
Site: Sun. Well-drained soil
Compost: Soil-based (John Innes No. 2) or soil-less
Use: Container, formal bedding, front of border
Good companions: *Bracteantha bracteata* Monstrosum Series, *Convolvulus sabatius*, *Nemesia* Carnival Series

6 Tropaeolum Alaska Series
Nasturtium

Compact variegated version of what is often a vigorous scrambling annual. The scented spurred flowers, in shades of yellow, orange and crimson, stand above wavy-edged leaves that are speckled or blotched with creamy white. Flowers throughout summer and into autumn. Half hardy.
General care: Sow seed under glass at 13°C (55°F) in early spring and plant out in late spring, or sow *in situ* in mid to late spring.
Height: 30cm (12in) **Spread:** 45cm (18in)
Site: Sun, partial shade. Well-drained soil
Compost: Soil-based (John Innes No. 2)
Use: Container, formal bedding, front of border
Good companions: *Bidens ferulifolia* 'Golden Goddess', *Calendula officinalis* 'Fiesta Gitana', *Tagetes tenuifolia* 'Lemon Gem'

1

2

3

4

5

6

7 Verbena 'Peaches and Cream'

Hybrid verbenas raised annually from seed include upright and sprawling plants that produce crowded heads of small flowers throughout summer. 'Peaches and Cream' is a rather stiff sprawling plant with relatively large flowers that combine cream, yellow, orange and salmon-pink. Half hardy.

General care: Sow seed under glass at minimum 18°C (64°F) in late winter or early spring and plant out in early summer.
Height: 45cm (18in) **Spread:** 50cm (20in)
Site: Sun. Moist but well-drained soil
Compost: Soil-based (John Innes No. 2) or soil-less
Use: Container, sunny bed
Good companions: *Brachyscome iberidifolia* 'Purple Splendour', *Helychrysum petiolare, Heuchera micrantha* var. *diversifolia* 'Palace Purple'

cream and white

8 Lavatera trimestris 'Mont Blanc'
Mallow

Erect bushy annual with hairy lobed leaves and white funnel-shaped flowers from midsummer to early autumn. Hardy.

General care: Sow seed *in situ* in early autumn or mid-spring.
Height: 50cm (20in) **Spread:** 35cm (14in)
Site: Sun. Well-drained soil
Use: Formal bedding, sunny bed or border
Good companions: *Echinops ritro* 'Veitch's Blue, *Eryngium* x *tripartitum, Perovskia* 'Blue Spire'

9 Nicotiana Domino Series
Tobacco plant

Upright annual with sticky leaves and stems. Throughout summer and into autumn it bears upward-facing tubular flowers in white, lime-green, pink or purple. Half hardy.

General care: Sow seed under glass at 18°C (64°F) in late winter or early spring. Plant out when there is no longer a risk of frost.
Height: 40cm (16in) **Spread:** 20cm (8in)
Site: Sun or partial shade. Moist but well-drained soil
Compost: Soil-based (John Innes No. 2) or soil-less
Use: Container, sunny or lightly shaded border
Good companions: *Alcea rosea* 'Nigra', *Amaranthus caudatus, Clarkia amoena* 'Satin'

10 Sutera cordata
Bacopa

Trailing perennial grown as an annual and sold as plants, mainly for edging containers. It has small leaves, and throughout summer and into autumn bears numerous tiny white flowers. Tender.

General care: Pinch back stems to encourage branching.
Height: 8cm (3in) **Spread:** 30cm (12in)
Site: Sun, partial shade. Moist but well-drained soil
Compost: Soil-based (John Innes No. 2) or soil-less
Use: Container, sunny or lightly shaded bed
Good companions: *Fuchsia* 'Red Spider', *Petunia* Surfinia Series, *Verbena* 'Silver Anne'

green

11 Molucella laevis
Bells of Ireland, Shell flower

The erect stems of this annual rise above scalloped leaves and are set with numerous shell-like green bracts, each harbouring a small white fragrant flower. Good for cutting and can be dried for winter decoration. Half hardy.

General care: Sow seed under glass in early spring and plant out in late spring, or sow *in situ* in mid-spring.
Height: 60cm (2ft) **Spread:** 20cm (8in)
Site: Sun. Moist but well-drained soil
Use: Sunny border, cutting garden
Good companions: *Alcea rosea* 'Nigra', *Amaranthus caudatus, Tropaeolum majus* 'Empress of India'

12 Zinnia 'Envy'

The annual zinnias usually have double daisy-like flowers that are valuable at the end of summer. Often sold as mixed colours in various heights. 'Envy' is an unusual lime green and readily available as a separate colour. Tender.

General care: Sow seed under glass at 13–18°C (55–64°F) in early spring and plant out when there is no longer a risk of frost, or sow *in situ* in late spring.
Height: 75cm (2ft 6in) **Spread:** 25cm (10in)
Site: Sun. Humus-rich and well-drained soil
Compost: Soil-based (John Innes No. 2) or soil-less
Use: Container, formal bedding, sunny border
Good companions: *Calendula officinalis* 'Fiesta Gitana', *Tagetes* 'French Favourites', *Tagetes tenuifolia* 'Lemon Gem'

bulbs

Perennials with underground food-storage organs – true bulbs, corms, tubers or rhizomes – are a varied group. Many flower in spring, but some of the most distinguished, including lilies, are summer flowering.

pink and mauve

1 Alstroemeria ligtu hybrids
Peruvian lily

These fleshy tubers form extensive colonies. Erect stems carry the narrow leaves and showy flowers, which are pink, purple, red, white or yellow with dark markings. Not fully hardy.
General care: Plant in late summer or early autumn with the top of the tuber about 20cm (8in) deep.
Height: 50cm (20in) **Spread:** 75cm (2ft 6in)
Site: Sun, partial shade. Fertile, moist but well-drained soil
Use: Sunny or lightly shaded border
Good companions: *Alchemilla mollis, Convallaria majalis, Macleaya cordata* 'Flamingo'

2 Cyclamen purpurascens
Sowbread

This tuberous evergreen or deciduous species has lightly silvered leaves and sweetly scented flowers in pink, carmine or white. Hardy.
General care: Plant in autumn with the top of the tuber about 5cm (2in) deep.
Height and spread: 10cm (4in)
Site: Partial shade. Humus-rich, moist but well-drained soil, preferably containing lime
Use: Shady border, woodland garden
Good companions: *Anemone blanda, Helleborus orientalis, Muscari armeniacum*

3 Dahlia 'Kiwi Gloria'
Cactus-flowered dahlia

Tuberous dahlia with small, pink-tinted double flowerheads. The petal-like ray-florets are rolled or 'quilled' for half their length. Half hardy.
General care: Plant in mid to late spring with the top of the tuber 10–15cm (4–6in) deep. Lift tubers in autumn and store in frost-free conditions.
Height: 1.2m (4ft) **Spread:** 60cm (2ft)
Site: Sun. Fertile, humus-rich, well-drained soil
Use: Formal bedding, sunny bed or border
Good companions: *Dahlia* 'Peach Cupid', *Dahlia* 'Porcelain', *Penstemon* 'Stapleford Gem'

bronze and maroon

4 Cosmos atrosanguineus
Chocolate cosmos, Chocolate plant

Tuberous perennial with chocolate-scented divided leaves and in late summer and autumn red-brown cupped flowers. Not fully hardy.
General care: Plant in mid to late spring with the top of the tuber about 10cm (4in) deep. Lift in autumn and store in a frost-free place. In a mild climate leave in ground over winter.
Height: 75 cm (2ft 6in) **Spread:** 45cm (18in)
Site: Sun. Moist but well-drained soil
Use: Sunny border
Good companions: *Echinacea purpurea* 'White Lustre', *Pennisetum alopecuroides* 'Hameln', *Sanguisorba obtusa*

red and russet

5 Begonia 'Memory Scarlet'
Tuberous begonia

Upright tuberous hybrid begonia, suitable for outdoor containers or formal bedding in summer. Branching stems carry white-edged, red double flowers over a long season. Tender.
General care: Start tubers into growth under glass and plant outdoors in early summer. Lift in autumn and store in frost-free conditions.
Height: 75cm (2ft 6in) **Spread:** 45cm (18in)
Site: Partial shade. Humus-rich, well-drained neutral to acid soil
Compost: Soil-based (John Innes No. 2) or soil-less
Use: Conservatory or greenhouse minimum 10°C (50°F), container, formal bedding
Good companions: *Fuchsia* 'Red Spider', *Petunia* Surfinia Series, *Verbena* 'Silver Anne'

6 Crocosmia 'Lucifer'
Montbretia

The sword-like leaves of this vigorous crocosmia develop from a corm. In mid to late summer arching stems bear sprays of upward-facing, vivid orange-red flowers. Not fully hardy.
General care: Plant in spring. Divide congested clumps in spring or autumn. Dry mulch over winter.
Height: 1.2m (4ft) **Spread:** 10cm (4in)
Site: Sun, partial shade. Moist but well-drained soil
Use: Sunny or lightly shaded border
Good companions: *Agapanthus* 'Blue Giant', *Cynara cardunculus, Kniphofia* 'Royal Standard'

7 Dahlia 'Moor Place'
Pompom dahlia

Tuberous hybrid dahlia with small, deep

1

2

3

4

burgundy round flowerheads packed with incurved petal-like florets. They are produced from midsummer until the first frosts occur. Half hardy.
General care: Plant in mid to late spring with the top of the tuber 10–15cm (4–6in) deep. Put in supporting stakes before plants make growth. Lift in autumn and store in frost-free conditions.
Height: 1m (3ft) **Spread:** 60cm (2ft)
Site: Sun. Fertile, humus-rich and well-drained soil
Use: Formal bedding, sunny bed or border
Good companions: *Dahlia* 'Kiwi Gloria', *Dahlia* 'Porcelain', *Penstemon* 'Raven'

yellow and orange

8 Begonia 'Orange Cascade'
Tuberous begonia

Trailing tuberous begonia with double orange flowers, 8cm (3in) across, over a long season. Suitable for growing under glass or for tall pots and hanging baskets outdoors in summer. Tender.
General care: Start tubers into growth under glass and plant outdoors in early summer. Lift in autumn and store in frost-free conditions.
Height and spread: 60cm (2ft)
Site: Partial shade
Compost: Soil-based (John Innes No. 2) or soil-less
Use: Conservatory or greenhouse at minimum 10°C (50°F), container
Good companions: *Bidens ferulifolia* 'Golden Goddess', *Helichrysum petiolare, Tropaeolum majus* 'Empress of India'

9 Crocosmia x crocosmiiflora 'Emily McKenzie'
Montbretia

Small corms produce the sword-like leaves. The sprays of star-shaped orange flowers, splashed mahogany in the throat, appear from late summer and into autumn. Not fully hardy.
General care: Plant in spring. Divide congested clumps in spring or autumn. Dry mulch over winter.
Height: 60cm (2ft) **Spread:** 10cm (4in)
Site: Sun, partial shade. Moist, well-drained soil
Use: Sunny or lightly shaded border
Good companions: *Agapanthus* 'Lilliput', *Deschampsia cespitosa* 'Goldschleier', *Hemerocallis* 'Stella de Oro'

10 Gladiolus 'Green Woodpecker'
Medium-flowered grandiflorus gladiolus

A fan of sword-like leaves grows from a flattened corm. In summer it produces green-yellow, ruffled trumpet-shaped flowers with a deep red mark in the throat. One stiff stem carries up to 25 buds arranged in a closely packed zigzag. The bottom bud opens first and produces the largest flower, about 10cm (4in) across. Ten flowers may be open at a time. Excellent as a cut flower. Half hardy.
General care: Plant in spring with the top of the corm about 15cm (6in) deep. Lift in autumn and store in frost-free conditions.
Height: 1.5m (5ft) **Spread:** 15cm (6in)
Site: Sun. Fertile well-drained soil
Use: Cutting garden, sunny bed or border
Good companions: *Euphorbia marginata, Tropaeolum* 'Alaska', *Zinnia* 'Envy'

cream and white

11 Galtonia candicans
In late summer or early autumn a spike carrying 12 or more green-tinged white flowers rises from a clump of strap-like grey-green leaves. The flowers are pendent and lightly fragrant. Hardy.
General care: Plant in early spring with the top of the bulb 15cm (6in) deep. Cover ground with a mulch in winter.
Height: 1.2m (4ft) **Spread:** 15cm (6in)
Site: Sun. Fertile, moist but well-drained soil
Use: Sunny border
Good companions: *Campanula lactiflora, Geranium x magnificum, Macleaya cordata* 'Flamingo'

12 Gladiolus callianthus 'Murielae'
Narrow blade-like leaves grow from a corm. In late summer or early autumn a stem carries up to ten sweetly scented flowers, about 5cm (2in) across, on thin elegantly arching tubes. The flowers are white with a purplish red mark in the throat. Half hardy.
General care: Pot up corms in early to mid-spring and keep in a greenhouse. Plant out in late spring. Lift in autumn before the first hard frosts and store in frost-free conditions.
Height: 1m (3ft)
Spread: 8cm (3in)
Site: Sun. Well-drained soil
Use: Sunny border
Good companions: *Caryopteris x clandonensis* 'Heavenly Blue', *Gaura lindheimeri, Perovskia* 'Blue Spire'

lilies

Almost all lilies can be grown in pots – in soil-based (John Innes No. 2) or ericaceous (lime-free) compost – as well as in the garden. Plant bulbs between mid-autumn and early spring about 15cm (6in) deep; stem-rooting lilies (which produce roots above the bulb) need to be planted about 20cm (8in) deep.

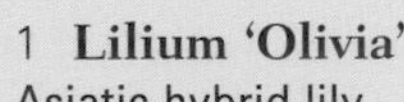

1 Lilium 'Olivia'
Asiatic hybrid lily

Large, outward-facing white flowers with orange-red anthers. The textured petals have warty protuberances. Scented. Hardy.

Height: 1m (3ft) **Spread:** 15cm (6in)

Good companions: *Choisya ternata*, *Daphne bholua* 'Jacqueline Postill', *Osmanthus delavayi*

2 Lilium 'Fire King'
Asiatic hybrid lily

An erect stem supports a head of outward-facing trumpet-shaped flowers that are orange-red with purple spots. Well suited to containers but unscented. Hardy.

Height: 1m (3ft) **Spread:** 15cm (6in)

Good companions: *Aconitum* 'Spark's Variety', *Crocosmia* 'Lucifer', *Philadelphus coronarius* 'Aureus'

3 Lilium henryi
Species lily

Easily grown stem-rooting lily with an arching stem that carries about ten deep orange flowers with dark spots. There are warty protuberances on the petals. Does best on a limy soil and usually needs staking. Hardy.

Height: 2.5m (8ft) **Spread:** 20cm (8in)

Good companions: *Paeonia delavayi* var. *ludlowii*, *Philadelphus coronarius* 'Aureus', *Thalictum flavum* subsp. *glaucum*

4 Lilium speciosum var. rubrum
Species lily

In late summer or early autumn this stem-rooting lily bears five to ten or more white or pale pink flowers with pink or crimson warty spots. Strongly fragrant. Requires lime-free soil or ericaceous compost. Hardy.

Height: 1.2m (4ft) **Spread:** 15cm (6in)

Good companions: *Abelia* x *grandiflora*, *Deutzia* x *hybrida* 'Mont Rose', *Hydrangea* 'Preziosa'

5 Lilium 'Journey's End'
Oriental hybrid lily

Vigorous strong-stemmed hybrid with a branched head of scented crimson flowers. The petals are spotted maroon and pale to white at the margins. Hardy.

Height: 1.2m (4ft) **Spread:** 20cm (8in)

Good companions: *Ceratostigma willmottianum*, *Geranium psilostemon*, *Rosa glauca*

6 Lilium 'Star Gazer'
Oriental hybrid lily

The fragrant upward-facing flowers, five to eight per stem, are deep pink with white margins and dark crimson spots. Hardy.

Height: 1m (3ft) **Spread:** 15cm (6in)

Good companions: *Nicotiana langsdorfii*, *Thalictrum delavayi* 'Hewitt's Double', *Veronica gentianoides*

7 Lilium 'Casa Blanca'
Oriental hybrid lily

This stem-rooting lily has a head of fragrant, dazzling white bowl-shaped flowers with conspicuous orange-red anthers. The petals have warty projections at the base. Hardy.

Height: 1.2m (4ft) **Spread:** 20cm (8in)

Good companions: *Fothergilla major* Monticola Group, *Fuchsia magellanica* 'Versicolor', *Hydrangea* 'Preziosa'

8 Lilium African Queen Group
Trumpet hybrid lily

Erect stems each carry a conical head of nodding, outward-facing trumpet-shaped flowers, which are apricot-yellow on the inside and shaded brown-purple on the outside. Fragrant. Not fully hardy.

Height: 1.5m (5ft) **Spread:** 20cm (8in)

Good companions: *Campanula lactiflora*, *Rosa* 'Golden Wings', *Thalictrum aquilegiifolium* 'Thundercloud'

climbers

Climbers twine, cling with aerial roots or clasp with tendrils. Trained on architectural supports or on other plants, they assert the vertical dimension of the garden. Plant in the dormant season.

purple, blue and violet

1 Clematis 'Warszawska Nike'

Large-flowered clematis

From late summer to early autumn this deciduous twiner bears deep purple velvet-textured flowers, about 15cm (6in) across. The petal-like sepals radiate from a cluster of yellow anthers. Hardy.

General care: Plant with the base in shade. Prune hard in late winter, cutting all growths back to a pair of buds 15–30cm (6–12in) above ground.

Height: 3m (10ft) **Spread:** 2m (6ft)

Site: Sun, partial shade. Fertile, humus-rich and well-drained soil. Does well on lime

Use: Screen, shrub climber, tripod, wall

Good companions: *Buddleja crispa, Clematis* 'Abundance', *Rosa* 'Parade'

pink and mauve

2 Clematis 'Comtesse de Bouchaud'

Large-flowered clematis

In summer and early autumn this deciduous twiner bears a profusion of mauve-pink flowers, about 10cm (4in) across, with cream anthers. The petal-like sepals are strongly ridged. Hardy.

General care: Plant with the base in shade. Prune hard in late winter, cutting all growths back to a pair of buds 15–30cm (6–12in) above ground.

Height: 3m (10ft) **Spread:** 2m (6ft)

Site: Sun, partial shade. Fertile, humus-rich and well-drained soil. Does well on lime

Use: Screen, shrub climber, tripod, wall

Good companions: *Clematis* 'Etoile Rose', *Clematis* 'Perle d'Azur', *Rosa* 'Madame Alfred Carrière'

3 Rosa 'Pink Perpétué'

Climbing rose

Deciduous climber with dark leathery leaves and clusters of lightly scented, bright pink double flowers. Begins flowering in early summer and repeats until the autumn. Hardy.

General care: Prune between late winter and early spring, cutting back sideshoots to three or four buds.

Height: 5m (15ft) **Spread:** 2.5m (8ft)

Site: Sun. Humus-rich, moist but well-drained soil

Use: Arbour, arch, pergola, pillar, wall

Good companions: *Clematis* 'Royal Velours', *Lonicera periclymenum* 'Serotina', *Rosa* 'Parade'

red and russet

4 Clematis 'Kermesina'

Small-flowered viticella clematis

In late summer and early autumn this slender deciduous twiner bears red single flowers with red-brown anthers. Hardy.

General care: Plant with the base in shade. Prune hard in late winter, cutting all growths back to a pair of buds 15–30cm (6–12in) above ground.

Height: 3m (10ft) **Spread:** 2m (6ft)

Site: Sun, partial shade. Fertile, humus-rich and well-drained soil. Does well on lime

Use: Screen, shrub climber, tripod, wall

Good companions: *Choisya ternata, Clematis* 'Gillian Blades', *Solanum laxum* 'Album'

5 Clematis 'Rouge Cardinal'

Large-flowered clematis

This easy and rewarding deciduous twiner flowers in late summer and early autumn. Beige anthers contrast with the deep crimson of the blunt-tipped petal-like sepals. Hardy.

General care: Plant with the base in shade. Prune hard in late winter, cutting all growths back to a pair of buds 15–30cm (6–12in) above ground.

Height: 2.5m (8ft) **Spread:** 1.5m (5ft)

Site: Sun, partial shade. Fertile, humus-rich and well-drained soil. Does well on lime

Use: Screen, shrub climber, tripod, wall

Good companions: *Buddleja crispa, Clematis* 'Abundance', *Rosa* 'Parade'

4

2

5

1

3

red and russet (continued)

1 Clematis 'Royal Velours'

Small-flowered viticella clematis

Moderately vigorous deciduous twiner with divided leaves. Bears purple-red velvet-textured flowers in late summer and early autumn. Hardy.

General care: Plant with the base in shade. Prune hard in late winter, cutting all growths back to a pair of buds 15–30cm (6–12in) above ground.

Height: 3m (10ft) **Spread:** 2m (6ft)

Site: Sun, partial shade. Fertile, humus-rich and well-drained soil. Does well on lime

Use: Screen, shrub climber, tripod, wall

Good companions: *Clematis* 'Huldine', *Cornus alba* 'Elegantissima', *Rosa* 'Aimée Vibert'

yellow and orange

2 Campsis x tagliabuana 'Madame Galen'

Trumpet creeper, Trumpet vine

This vigorous deciduous climber clings by aerial roots and has rich green leaves composed of toothed leaflets. In late summer and early autumn orange-red trumpet-shaped flowers are borne on the current season's shoots. Not fully hardy.

General care: Train in growths of young plants until aerial roots take hold. Prune established plants in late winter, cutting back sideshoots to within three or four buds of the main stems.

Height: 10m (33ft) **Spread:** 6m (20ft)

Site: Sun. Humus-rich, moist but well-drained soil

Use: Warm wall

Good companions: *Ceanothus* 'Puget Blue', *Lonicera japonica* 'Halliana', *Wisteria sinensis*

3 Rosa Golden Showers

Climbing rose

Deciduous climber with dark glossy leaves and scented, yellow semi-double flowers in summer and early autumn. The loose-shaped blooms are weather-resistant. Hardy.

General care: Prune between late winter and early spring, cutting back sideshoots to three or four buds.

Height: 3m (10ft) **Spread:** 2m (6ft)

Site: Sun. Humus-rich and moist but well-drained soil

Use: Arbour, arch, pillar, wall

Good companions: *Clematis* 'Bill MacKenzie', *Clematis* 'Perle d'Azur', *Solanum crispum* 'Glasnevin'

cream and white

4 Clematis 'Alba Luxurians'

Small-flowered viticella clematis

In late summer and early autumn this deciduous twiner bears green-tipped, white bell-shaped flowers. Short anthers make a dark eye. Hardy.

General care: Plant with the base in shade. Prune hard in late winter, cutting all growths back to a pair of buds 15–30cm (6–12in) above ground.

Height: 4m (12ft) **Spread:** 2m (6ft)

Site: Sun, partial shade. Fertile, humus-rich and well-drained soil. Does well on lime

Use: Screen, shrub climber, tripod, wall

Good companions: *Ceanothus* x *delileanus* 'Topaze', *Clematis* 'Perle d'Azur', *Solanum crispum* 'Glasnevin'

5 Rosa 'Aimée Vibert'

Rambler rose

Long-stemmed deciduous rose with glossy leaves and, from midsummer to autumn, large clusters of small, white cupped flowers that are tipped deep pink in bud. Slightly fragrant. Hardy.

General care: Prune between late winter and early spring, cutting back sideshoots to three or four buds.

Height: 5m (15ft) **Spread:** 2.5m (8ft)

Site: Sun. Humus-rich, moist but well-drained soil

Use: Arbour, arch, pillar, wall

Good companions: *Clematis* 'Huldine', *Rosa* 'Reine des Violettes', *Rosa* 'Veilchenblau'

6 Solanum laxum 'Album'

Potato vine

Evergreen or semi-evergreen, slender-stemmed climber with twining leaf stalks. From midsummer to autumn it bears sprays of small, white flowers with yellow anthers. Half hardy.

General care: In late winter prune to fit the available space and cut sideshoots to within three or four buds of the main stems.

Height: 6m (20ft) **Spread:** 2.5m (8ft)

Site: Sun. Well-drained soil

Use: Warm wall

Good companions: *Actinidia kolomikta*, *Clematis* 'Perle d'Azur', *Lonicera periclymenum* 'Serotina'

7 Trachelospermum jasminoides

Confederate jasmine, Star jasmine

This evergreen twining climber bears small, scented, white propeller-shaped flowers. The glossy dark green leaves turn bronze-red in winter. Not fully hardy.

General care: Prune in late winter; cut back side-shoots to within three or four buds of main stems.

Height: 6m (20ft) **Spread:** 2.5m (8ft)

Site: Sun. Well-drained soil

Use: Sunny wall

Good companions: *Ceanothus* 'Puget Blue', *Lonicera japonica* 'Aureoreticulata', *Solanum laxum* 'Album'

honeysuckles

These twining, mostly deciduous climbers are excellent for screens, walls and tripods. They need to have their base in shade, in humus-rich and moist but well-drained soil, but tolerate partial shade and sun. Prune from autumn to early spring as required. Honeysuckles that are not fully hardy can be grown in sheltered positions outdoors or under glass.

1 **Lonicera x brownii 'Dropmore Scarlet'**
Deciduous or semi-evergreen honeysuckle with blue-green leaves and, throughout summer, clusters of bright scarlet tubular flowers. This is a colourful climber, but it has no scent. Hardy.
Height: 5m (15ft) **Spread:** 2.5m (8ft)
Good companions: *Campsis x tagliabuana* 'Madame Galen', *Chaenomeles x superba* 'Knaphill Scarlet', *Clematis* 'Bill MacKenzie'

2 **Lonicera sempervirens**
Coral honeysuckle, Trumpet honeysuckle
In this deciduous or evergreen species one or two pairs of leaves at the shoot tips are joined to form a cup immediately below each cluster of unscented tubular flowers. These are orange-red on the outside and yellow on the inside and are borne in summer and autumn. Red berries follow. Hardy.
Height: 4m (12ft) **Spread:** 2m (6ft)
Good companions: *Humulus lupulus* 'Aureus', *Rosa* 'Maigold', *Solanum crispum* 'Glasnevin'

3 **Lonicera etrusca 'Superba'**
Etruscan honeysuckle
Deciduous or semi-evergreen honeysuckle with woody lower stems. From midsummer to mid-autumn it produces clusters of tubular flowers, which are cream at first then turn orange. Red berries follow. Not fully hardy and needs a sheltered sunny position.
Height: 4m (12ft) **Spread:** 2m (6ft)
Good companions: *Ceanothus* 'Puget Blue', *Clematis armandii, Myrtus communis* subsp. *tarentina*

4 **Lonicera x americana**
Deciduous woody climber with dark leaves. The topmost on each stem are joined to form a cup just below a large cluster of sweetly scented flowers. These are yellow flushed with red-purple and produced thoughout summer. Red berries follow. Hardy.
Height: 6m (20ft) **Spread:** 4m (12ft)
Good companions: *Clematis montana* var. *rubens* 'Elizabeth', *Rosa* 'Veilchenblau', *Vitis* 'Brant'

5 **Lonicera periclymenum 'Serotina'**
Late Dutch honeysuckle
This late-flowering form of the deciduous woodbine, or common honeysuckle, bears clusters of powerfully scented flowers that are creamy white or pale pink on the inside and red-purple on the outside. Red berries follow. Hardy.
Height: 5m (15ft) **Spread:** 2.5m (8ft)
Good companions: *Clematis tibetana* subsp. *vernayi* 'Orange Peel', *Lonicera periclymenum* 'Belgica', *Rosa* 'Gloire de Dijon'

6 **Lonicera japonica 'Halliana'**
Japanese honeysuckle
Vigorous evergreen or semi-evergreen honeysuckle with bright green leaves. From spring to late summer strongly scented pure white flowers, which age to yellow, are borne in pairs. Hardy.
Height: 10m (33ft) **Spread:** 4m (12ft)
Good companions: *Rosa banksiae* 'Lutea', *Solanum laxum* 'Album', *Vitis coignetiae*

1

2

3

4

5

6

shrubs & trees

Late-flowering trees and shrubs provide end-of-season colour, but equally important is the foliage clothing the framework of branches. Plant in the dormant season, preferably in autumn or early spring.

purple, blue and violet

1 Abies koreana
Korean fir

Slow-growing evergreen conifer of neatly symmetrical cone shape. The needles are dark green above and white on the underside. From an early age it produces erect, violet-blue cylindrical cones. The cultivar 'Silberlocke' has twisted needles, which make the contrast between the dark green and white very conspicuous. Hardy.

Height: 10m (33ft) **Spread:** 6m (20ft)
Site: Sun, partial shade. Moist but well-drained soil, preferably lime-free
Use: Specimen tree
Good companions: *Carpinus betulus, Fagus sylvatica, Taxus baccata,* all as hedges

2 Buddleja davidii 'Black Knight'
Butterfly bush

Wide-spreading deciduous shrub with lance-shaped grey-green leaves on arching stems and, in late summer and autumn, cone-shaped clusters of fragrant dark purple flowers, which are very attractive to butterflies. The colour range in other cultivars includes purple-red, pink, mauve, mauve-blue and white. Hardy.

General care: Cut back annually to a low framework of branches in early spring.
Height and spread: 3m (10ft)
Site: Sun. Well-drained soil
Use: Gravel garden, sunny border
Good companions: *Buddleja* 'Lochinch', *Cistus ladanifer, Philadelphus* 'Belle Etoile'

3 Caryopteris x clandonensis 'Heavenly Blue'

Deciduous shrub with aromatic grey-green leaves and erect stems. In late summer and autumn these bear terminal clusters of small, rich blue flowers. Hardy.

General care: In early spring cut back to a low framework of branches.
Height: 1m (3ft) **Spread:** 1.2m (4ft)
Site: Sun. Well-drained soil
Use: Gravel garden, sunny border
Good companions: *Buddleja* 'Lochinch', *Echinops ritro* 'Veitch's Blue', *Eryngium x tripartitum*

4 Ceanothus x delileanus 'Topaze'
California lilac

Dark-leaved, bushy deciduous shrub that bears large sprays of small indigo-blue flowers in summer and autumn. Hardy.

General care: In early spring cut back to a low framework of branches.
Height and spread: 1.5m (5ft)
Site: Sun. Fertile well-drained soil
Use: Sunny border
Good companions: *Lilium henryi, Rosa* Graham Thomas, *Sisyrinchium striatum* 'Aunt May'

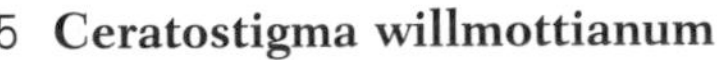

5 Ceratostigma willmottianum

Deciduous shrub with a framework of slender stems carrying sharply pointed leaves, some of which take on red tints in autumn. From midsummer to autumn it bears numerous blue saucer-shaped flowers, which open from red-purple tubes and are cut into five distinct lobes. Hardy.

General care: Trim back the previous season's growth in early to mid-spring.
Height: 1m (3ft) **Spread:** 1.5m (5ft)
Site: Sun. Moist but well-drained soil
Use: Sunny border
Good companions: *Anemone hupehensis* 'Hadspen Abundance', *Aster ericoides* 'Pink Cloud', *Spiraea japonica* 'Anthony Waterer'

6 Hibiscus syriacus 'Oiseau Bleu'

Stiffly erect deciduous shrub with dark green, deeply lobed leaves. In late summer and early autumn it bears trumpet-shaped flowers that are 5cm (2in) or more across. In this cultivar, also known as 'Blue Bird', the flowers are blue with maroon veining and cream stamens. Hardy.

Height: 3m (10ft) **Spread:** 2m (6ft)
Site: Sun. Humus-rich, moist but well-drained soil
Use: Sunny border
Good companions: *Aconitum* 'Spark's Variety', *Aster x frikartii* 'Mönch', *Geranium* 'Ann Folkard'

7 Lavandula angustifolia 'Hidcote'
Lavender

Aromatic evergreen shrub that forms a neat bush. It has grey linear leaves and produces spikes of dark purple fragrant flowers that are attractive to bees. Hardy.

General care: In spring trim back growth made in the previous year.
Height and spread: 45cm (18in)
Site: Sun. Well-drained soil. Does well on lime
Use: Gravel garden, hedge, rock garden, sunny border
Good companions: *Berberis thunbergii* 'Atropurpurea Nana', *Cistus* 'Silver Pink', *Hypericum olympicum*

8 Lavandula x intermedia Dutch Group
Lavender

Aromatic evergreen shrub that makes a rounded bush of grey-green narrowly linear or spoon-shaped leaves. In summer these are topped by spikes of small, closely packed soft blue flowers that are scented and very attractive to bees. Hardy.

5

6

7

10

11

12

8

9

General care: In spring trim back growth made in the previous year.
Height and spread: 75cm (2ft 6in)
Site: Sun. Well-drained soil. Good on lime
Use: Gravel garden, hedge, sunny border
Good companions: *Gypsophila paniculata* 'Bristol Fairy', *Knautia macedonica*, *Verbascum* Cotswold Group 'Gainsborough'

9 Perovskia 'Blue Spire'

Graceful deciduous plant with a woody base and erect, rather soft stems that carry aromatic leaves, which are grey-green on the surface and pale grey on the underside. From late summer to early autumn spires of small flowers create a violet-blue haze. Hardy.
General care: In spring cut stems back to a low woody framework.
Height: 1.2m (4ft) **Spread:** 1m (3ft)
Site: Sun. Well-drained soil
Use: Gravel garden, sunny border
Good companions: *Buddleja davidii* 'Black Knight', *Verbena bonariensis*, *Yucca gloriosa*

10 Solanum crispum 'Glasnevin'

Chilean potato tree

Bushy semi-evergreen shrub that is best grown with its branches tied in to supports on a sunny wall. Throughout summer it produces numerous clusters of purple-blue star-shaped flowers with a central cone of bright yellow anthers. Inedible yellowish white fruits follow.
General care: Tie in growths regularly and trim in mid to late spring.
Height: 6m (20ft) **Spread:** 5m (15ft)
Site: Sun. Well-drained soil
Use: Sunny wall
Good companions: *Clematis* 'Bill MacKenzie', *Clematis* 'Perle d'Azur', *Rosa* Golden Showers

pink and mauve

11 Buddleja crispa

Deciduous shrub with arching stems and toothed leaves covered in white felt. The small fragrant flowers clustered at the ends of shoots are mauve with an orange throat. Not fully hardy so best trained against a warm wall.
General care: In early spring cut back shoots to within a few buds of a permanent framework.
Height and spread: 3m (10ft)
Site: Sun. Well-drained soil
Use: Sunny wall
Good companions: *Clematis* 'Royal Velours', *Solanum laxum* 'Album', *Trachelospermum jasminoides*

12 Buddleja 'Lochinch'

Butterfly bush

Deciduous shrub with arching stems that are covered in a grey felt when young, as are the leaves. The upper surface of the stems later becomes green and smooth. In late summer and autumn there are numerous cone-shaped heads of small mauve flowers with an orange eye. Strongly fragrant and attractive to butterflies. Hardy.
General care: In early spring cut back to a low framework of branches.
Height: 2.5m (8ft) **Spread:** 3m (10ft)
Site: Sun. Well-drained soil
Use: Sunny border
Good companions: *Buddleja davidii* 'Black Knight', *Ceanothus thyrsiflorus* var. *repens*, *Potentilla fruticosa* 'Tangerine'

pink and mauve (continued)

1 Calluna vulgaris 'Darkness'
Heather, Ling

Heather is a low-growing evergreen shrub that is widely distributed through the Northern Hemisphere, where it turns large areas of acid moorland and heath a vivid purplish pink during late summer and autumn. There are hundreds of cultivars to choose from. This example has short sprays of crimson flowers and bright green foliage. Hardy.

General care: Clip over in early spring.
Height: 25cm (10in) **Spread:** 40cm (16in)
Site: Sun. Humus-rich and well-drained acid soil
Compost: Lime-free (ericaceous) soil-based
Use: Container, ground cover, heather garden
Good companions: *Betula pendula* 'Youngii', *Erica vagans* 'Mrs D.F. Maxwell', *Erica vulgaris* 'Vivelli'

2 Erica vagans 'Mrs D.F. Maxwell'
Cornish heath, Wandering heath

Vigorous evergreen shrub that bears long sprays of rich pink cylindrical to bell-shaped flowers from midsummer to late autumn, when these turn an attractive brown colour. Tolerates slightly alkaline conditions. Hardy.

Height: 75cm (2ft 6in) **Spread:** 1m (3ft)
Site: Sun. Well-drained soil
Use: Ground cover, heather garden
Good companions: *Berberis thunbergii* 'Atropurpurea Nana', *Buddleja davidii* 'Black Knight', *Cistus* 'Silver Pink'

3 Escallonia 'Apple Blossom'

Compact but bushy evergreen shrub with glossy dark leaves. From early summer onwards numerous small pink-and-white flowers are borne. These have five petals formed in a cup shape. Not fully hardy.

General care: Prune immediately after flowering.
Height and spread: 2.5m (8ft)
Site: Sun. Well-drained soil
Use: Hedge, sunny border, windbreak
Good companions: *Cistus ladanifer*, *Laurus nobilis*, *Rosa* 'Fru Dagmar Hastrup'

4 Rosa Gentle Touch
Miniature/Patio rose

Deciduous dwarf shrub with dark green leaves and sprays of pale salmon-pink semi-double flowers over a long period in summer and autumn. Hardy.

General care: Prune in late winter or early spring, cutting back all growth by up to half.
Height: 50cm (20in) **Spread:** 40cm (16in)
Site: Sun. Reasonably fertile and moist but well-drained soil
Compost: Soil-based (John Innes No. 3)
Use: Container, sunny bed or border
Good companions: *Diascia barberae* 'Ruby Field', *Lobelia erinus* 'Crystal Palace', *Viola* x *wittrockiana* 'Baby Lucia'

5 Rosa 'Louise Odier'
Bourbon rose

The Bourbon roses are a group of hybrids developed in the nineteenth century that produce double flowers in several flushes during summer and autumn. In this elegant example, arching stems carry fragrant, mauve-tinted bright pink flowers, which consist of fine-textured, neatly layered petals. Good for cutting. Hardy.

General care: Prune between late winter and early spring, cutting back main stems by up to a third and sideshoots by up to two-thirds.
Height: 2m (6ft) **Spread:** 1.2m (4ft)
Site: Sun. Reasonably fertile and moist but well-drained soil
Use: Sunny bed or border
Good companions: *Dianthus* 'Gran's Favourite', *Geranium* 'Johnson's Blue', *Lilium regale*

6 Rosa Magic Carpet
Shrub/Ground-cover rose

This is an example of a deciduous shrub rose that makes low dense growth and is wider than it is tall. It bears numerous mauve-pink semi-double flowers over a long summer and autumn season. Hardy.

General care: Prune in late winter or early spring, cutting back as required.
Height: 45cm (18in) **Spread:** 2m (6ft)
Site: Sun. Reasonably fertile and moist but well-drained soil
Compost: Soil-based (John Innes No. 3)
Use: Container, ground cover, front of sunny border
Good companions: *Alchemilla mollis*, *Nepeta* 'Six Hills Giant', *Stachys byzantina* 'Silver Carpet'

7 Spiraea japonica 'Anthony Waterer'

Deciduous twiggy shrub with lance-shaped leaves that are sometimes variegated cream and pink. Small crimson-pink flowers are packed in flat-topped heads. Hardy.
General care: Trim plants immediately after flowering.
Height and spread: 1.5m (5ft)
Site: Sun. Moist but well-drained soil
Use: Sunny border
Good companions: *Exochorda* x *macrantha* 'The Bride', *Spiraea* 'Arguta', *Viburnum opulus* 'Roseum'

8

red and russet

8 Rosa Royal William
Hybrid tea rose

A classic hybrid tea rose, this vigorous deciduous shrub is well furnished with dark green leaves. Conical buds open to shapely scented flowers, which are velvety deep red, double and about 12cm (4½in) across. Hardy.
General care: Prune between late winter and early spring, cutting main stems back to a height of about 25cm (10in) and shortening sideshoots to two or three buds.
Height: 1m (3ft)
Spread: 75cm (2ft 6in)
Site: Sun. Reasonably fertile and moist but well-drained soil
Use: Sunny bed or border
Good companions: *Lavandula* x *intermedia* Dutch Group, *Nepeta* 'Six Hills Giant', *Ruta graveolens* 'Jackman's Blue'

yellow and orange

9 Genista aetnensis
Mount Etna broom

Deciduous tree or large shrub with bright green shoots and short-lived linear leaves. Fragrant yellow pea flowers are borne abundantly in mid and late summer. Not fully hardy.
Height and spread: 8m (25ft)
Site: Sun. Light, well-drained soil
Use: Sheltered areas, gravel garden, canopy in mixed planting, specimen tree
Good companions: *Anemone blanda, Crocus speciosus, Helleborus argutifolius*

9

10 Hypericum 'Hidcote'
St John's wort

Evergreen or semi-evergreen shrub that produces bunches of large, yellow saucer-shaped flowers from midsummer to mid-autumn. Hardy.
General care: Trim lightly after flowering.
Height: 1.2m (4ft) **Spread:** 1.5m (5ft)
Site: Sun, partial shade. Moist but well-drained soil
Use: Sunny or lightly shaded border
Good companions: *Ceanothus* x *delileanus* 'Topaze', *Hydrangea macrophylla* 'Blue Wave', *Mahonia japonica*

10

11 Koelreuteria paniculata
Golden-rain tree, Pride of India

Spreading deciduous tree with attractive divided foliage that is green in summer but reddish pink when unfurling in spring and yellow in autumn. The small, yellow star-like flowers are carried in large sprays and are sometimes followed by inedible bladder-like fruit that are green at first and then tinged red. Hardy.
General care: Minimal pruning required.
Height and spread: 8m (25ft)
Site: Sun. Well-drained soil
Use: Canopy in mixed planting, specimen tree
Good companions: *Choisya ternata, Philadelphus* 'Belle Etoile', *Weigela* 'Victoria'

11

12 Rosa Graham Thomas
Shrub rose

This English rose has shiny deciduous foliage and combines in its cupped flowers old-rose qualities with rich yellow, a colour development of the twentieth century. The scented blooms are produced from summer to autumn. Hardy.
General care: Prune in late winter or early spring, cutting back by about a third.
Height and spread: 1.2m (4ft)
Site: Sun. Reasonably fertile and moist but well-drained soil
Use: Sunny bed or border
Good companions: *Campanula persicifolia, Veronica gentianoides, Viola* x *wittrockiana* 'Baby Lucia'

12

1 Aralia elata 'Variegata'
Japanese angelica tree

Large, suckering deciduous shrub with spiny stems that is best trained to form a small tree. The large leaves, which mainly grow from the ends of stems, are doubly divided and the leaflets are blotched and margined with creamy white. There are large sprays of small white flowers in early autumn. 'Aureovariegata' has yellow-variegated foliage in spring that fades to creamy white in summer. Hardy.

General care: Remove suckers to control spread and to prevent the plant from reverting to the green-leaved form.

Height and spread: 5m (15ft)

Site: Sun, partial shade. Humus-rich and moist but well-drained soil

Use: Sunny or lightly shaded border, woodland garden

Good companions: *Fuchsia* 'Riccartonii', *Hydrangea paniculata* 'Unique', *Mahonia japonica*

2 Cornus alternifolia 'Argentea'
Green osier, Pagoda dogwood

This large deciduous shrub can be trained as a small single-stemmed tree. It is grown for the tiered arrangement of the branches and the silvery effect of the white-edged leaves. There are small white flowers in early summer followed by inedible blue-black fruits. Hardy.

General care: Minimal pruning required.

Height: 3m (10ft) **Spread:** 2.5m (8ft)

Site: Sun, partial shade. Humus-rich and moist but well-drained soil

Use: Canopy in mixed border, specimen tree, woodland garden

Good companions: *Acer rubrum* 'October Glory', *Amelanchier lamarckii, Hydrangea aspera* Villosa Group

3 Eucryphia x nymansensis 'Nymansay'

Small evergreen columnar tree. In late summer and autumn the dark green, toothed leaves show off white, single cup-shaped flowers that have conspicuous stamens. Not fully hardy.

General care: Minimal pruning required.

Height: 10m (33ft) **Spread:** 3m (10ft)

Site: Partial shade, sun if roots in shade. Humus-rich and moist but well-drained soil, preferably lime-free

Use: Canopy in sheltered border, woodland garden

Good companions: *Cornus kousa* var. *chinensis* 'Satomi', *Enkianthus campanulatus, Kalmia latifolia* 'Ostbo Red'

4 Lavatera 'Barnsley'

Fast-growing and relatively short-lived semi-evergreen plant with a woody base and soft erect stems clothed with grey-green leaves. Throughout summer the stems carry numerous funnel-shaped flowers with notched petals. They are white with a red eye and age to pink. Hardy.

General care: In spring cut back to a low framework of branches.

Height and spread: 2m (6ft)

Site: Sun. Well-drained soil

Use: Gravel garden, sunny border

Good companions: *Gaura lindheimeri, Lavandula* x *intermedia* Dutch Group, *Origanum laevigatum* 'Herrenhausen'

2

1

3

5 Magnolia grandiflora
Bull bay

Evergreen tree with large dark green leaves that are glossy on the top but downy and often rust-coloured on the underside. Large fragrant flowers, up to 25cm (10in) across, are produced in late summer and autumn. The cultivars 'Exmouth' and 'Goliath' start flowering at an early age. Not fully hardy.

General care: Except where the climate is mild, train as a wall shrub.

Height: 10m (33ft) **Spread:** 6m (20ft)

Site: Sun. Humus-rich, well-drained soil

Use: Warm wall

Good companions: *Solanum laxum* 'Album', *Vitis* 'Brant', *Wisteria sinensis*

6 Myrtus communis subsp. tarentina
Tarentum myrtle

This bushy evergreen shrub is a compact, narrow-leaved cultivar of the common myrtle. In late summer and early autumn it bears masses of pink-tinged white flowers that have

4

5

6

7

8

9

10

11

12

conspicuous tufts of white stamens. The berries that follow are white. Not fully hardy.
General care: Trim lightly in the second half of spring.
Height and spread: 1.5m (5ft)
Site: Sun. Moist but well-drained soil
Compost: Soil-based (John Innes No. 3)
Use: Base of warm wall, container, sunny border
Good companions: *Passiflora caerulea, Rosmarinus officinalis, Solanum crispum* 'Glasnevin'

7 Rosa 'Blanche Double de Coubert'
Rugosa rose
Tough, dense-growing deciduous shrub with prickly stems and bright green leathery leaves. Throughout summer and into autumn it bears scented, pure white semi-double flowers, which are sometimes followed by large orange-red hips. Hardy.
General care: Prune between late winter and early spring, cutting back main stems by up to a third, other growths by as much as two-thirds.
Height: 1.5m (5ft) **Spread:** 1.2m (4ft)
Site: Sun. Well-drained soil
Use: Hedge, sunny border
Good companions: *Rosa* 'Fru Dagmar Hastrup', *Rosa glauca, Stachys byzantina* 'Silver Carpet'

8 Yucca gloriosa
Spanish dagger
Evergreen shrub with a stout, sometimes sparsely branched stem that supports jagged tufts of blade-like stiffly pointed leaves. In late summer and autumn it produces flower spikes with creamy white pendent bells that are often tinged purplish red on the outside. Not fully hardy.
General care: When flowers are spent remove the spike.
Height and spread: 2m (6ft)
Site: Sun. Well-drained soil
Compost: Soil-based (John Innes No. 2)
Use: Container, gravel garden, sunny border
Good companions: *Melianthus major, Stipa gigantea, Trachycarpus fortunei*

silver and grey

9 Pyrus salicifolia 'Pendula'
Weeping pear
This small deciduous tree has weeping branches and narrow silvery leaves that become grey-green as they age. Small, inedible green pears follow the creamy white flowers that are borne in spring. Hardy.
General care: Train and support the main stem until the tree is well established.
Height: 8m (25ft) **Spread:** 6m (20ft)
Site: Sun. Well-drained soil
Use: Specimen tree
Good companions: *Colchicum speciosum* 'Album', *Crocus tommasinianus, Muscari armeniacum*

10 Rosa glauca
Shrub rose
This deciduous shrub of arching growth is grown mainly for the grey-purple tint of its foliage. Single pink flowers are borne in early summer and followed by rounded red-brown hips. Hardy.
General care: Prune lightly in autumn.
Height: 2m (6ft) **Spread:** 1.5m (5ft)
Site: Sun. Humus-rich and moist but well-drained soil
Use: Sunny border
Good companions: *Aquilegia* 'Hensol Harebell', *Campanula lactiflora, Lilium regale*

green

11 Carpinus betulus
Common hornbeam
Deciduous tree with a grey fluted trunk and strongly veined mid-green leaves. In spring it bears fruiting catkins with conspicuous leaf-like bracts. As a specimen tree it is only suitable for large gardens, but is excellent for hedges 1.5m (5ft) or more high. Trimmed hedges retain the tawny dead leaves through winter. Hardy.
General care: Trim hedges in late summer.
Height: 25m (80ft) **Spread:** 18m (60ft)
Site: Sun, partial shade. Well-drained soil
Use: Hedge, specimen tree
Good companions: *Buxus sempervirens, Ilex aquifolium, Taxus baccata* 'Fastigiata'

12 Fargesia nitida
Fountain bamboo
Clump-forming evergreen bamboo with purple-green canes and purplish leaf sheaths. Mature canes arch over with the weight of numerous tapered narrow leaves. Hardy.
Height: 5m (15ft) **Spread:** 2m (6ft)
Site: Sun, partial shade. Moist but well-drained soil
Compost: Soil-based (John Innes No. 3) with added leaf-mould
Use: Container, hedge, screen, specimen clump, waterside, woodland garden
Good companions: *Acer rubrum* 'October Glory', *Cornus controversa* 'Variegata', *Fatsia japonica*

fuchsias

The dangling flowers of fuchsias are borne freely throughout summer and into autumn. Grow them in sunny or lightly shaded borders, in moist but well-drained soil, or in containers filled with soil-based (John Innes No. 3) or soil-less compost. Those described as not fully hardy will usually survive outdoors if planted deeply and given a winter mulch. Overwinter half hardy fuchsias under glass, above 2°C (36°F). In early spring cut back to a framework of stems or, in the case of outdoor plants, to the base. Except in very mild conditions fuchsias are deciduous shrubs.

1
2

1 **Fuchsia 'Leonora'**
Upright shrub producing numerous single pink flowers with green-tipped sepals that are swept back from the skirt of petals. Half hardy.
Height: 75cm (2ft 6in) **Spread:** 50cm (20in)
Good companions: *Fuchsia magellanica* 'Versicolor', *Hebe* 'Autumn Glory', *Hydrangea* 'Preziosa'

3

2 **Fuchsia 'La Campanella'**
Ideal for hanging baskets as the pendulous stems of this shrub trail numerous double flowers. The skirt of petals is purple and the tube and spreading sepals are white tinged with pink. Half hardy.
Height: 25cm (10in) **Spread:** 45cm (18in)
Good companions: *Fuchsia* 'Leonora', *Lobelia erinus* 'Cascade', *Pelargonium* 'L'Elégante'

3 **Fuchsia 'Red Spider'**
Spreading shrub with lax stems from which dangle numerous small single flowers in shades of crimson and red. Half hardy.
Height: 25cm (10in) **Spread:** 45cm (18in)
Good companions: *Fuchsia* 'Margaret', *Heliotropium arborescens* 'Marine', *Viola* x *wittrockiana* 'Baby Lucia'

4 **Fuchsia 'Mrs Popple'**
This upright vigorous bush freely produces medium-sized single flowers. The tube and sepals are scarlet, the skirt, or corolla, is dark violet. Not fully hardy.
Height and spread: 1m (3ft)
Good companions: *Hosta* 'Snowden', *Hydrangea macrophylla* 'Ayesha', *Spiraea japonica* 'Anthony Waterer'

5 **Fuchsia magellanica 'Versicolor'**
Shrub of gracefully arching growth with small, pointed variegated leaves that are predominantly grey-green but often tinged with pink. It bears numerous slender, dangling crimson flowers with a purple skirt. Not fully hardy.
Height: 1.5m (5ft)
Spread: 1.2m (4ft)
Good companions: *Hebe* 'Autumn Glory', *Hydrangea macrophylla* 'Madame Emile Mouillère', *Viola cornuta* Alba Group

6 **Fuchsia 'Annabel'**
Very free-flowering upright bush that produces white double flowers. These are veined and flushed pink while the anthers provide a pink accent. Half hardy.
Height: 60cm (2ft) **Spread:** 45cm (18in)
Good companions: *Geranium wallichianum* 'Buxton's Variety', *Hebe* 'Midsummer Beauty', *Lilium regale*

4

5

6

hydrangeas

Many shrubby hydrangeas flower over a long period in late summer and autumn. The heads are composed of small, fertile central flowers surrounded by larger sterile flowers, or ray-florets, which sometimes fill the whole head, as in hortensias, or mophead hydrangeas. Grow hydrangeas in partial shade or sun in humus-rich, moist but well-drained soil. In pots use soil-based (John Innes No. 3) compost with added leaf-mould, or ericaceous compost. The soil's alkalinity affects the colours of *Hydrangea macrophylla* cultivars.

3

1 **Hydrangea macrophylla 'Altona'**
Hortensia, Mophead hydrangea
Rounded deciduous shrub with large flowerheads composed of overlapping sterile flowers. These are rich pink on neutral to alkaline soils but blue on acid soils, and age to purple. Best in partial shade. Suitable for containers. Hardy.
Height: 1m (3ft) **Spread:** 1.5m (5ft)
Good companions: *Fuchsia* 'Riccartonii', *Hydrangea macrophylla* 'Ayesha', *Lilium* 'Journey's End'

2 **Hydrangea arborescens 'Annabelle'**
Somewhat open deciduous shrub with bright green leaves and 20cm (8in) heads packed with creamy white sterile flowers. These are tinted green at first and age to pale brown. Hardy.
Height and spread: 2.5m (8ft)
Good companions: *Cornus alternifolia* 'Argentea', *Hydrangea* 'Blue Wave', *Magnolia stellata*

3 **Hydrangea serrata 'Bluebird'**
Compact deciduous shrub with somewhat pointed leaves that turn red in autumn. The flowerheads are composed of rich blue fertile flowers surrounded by pale mauve-blue sterile ones. Remains attractive over a long season. Not fully hardy.
Height and spread: 1.2m (4ft)
Good companions: *Acer palmatum* 'Bloodgood', *Amelanchier lamarckii*, *Osmanthus delavayi*

4 **Hydrangea macrophylla 'Blue Wave'**
Lacecap hydrangea
This rounded deciduous shrub has flattened lacecap flowerheads that consist of closely packed fertile flowers surrounded by a ring of paler-coloured sterile flowers – rich blue on acid soils, mauve to pink on alkaline ones. Hardy.
Height: 2m (6ft) **Spread:** 2.5m (8ft)
Good companions: *Cercidiphyllum japonicum*, *Hamamelis* x *intermedia* 'Pallida', *Hydrangea macrophylla* 'Madame Emile Mouillère'

5 **Hydrangea macrophylla 'Ayesha'**
Hortensia, Mophead hydrangea
Rounded deciduous shrub with glossy, coarsely toothed egg-shaped leaves. The rather open flowerheads are composed of cupped florets that are grey-mauve or pink on alkaline soils but blue on acid ones. Suitable for containers. Hardy.
Height: 2m (6ft) **Spread:** 2.5m (8ft)
Good companions: *Deutzia* x *hybrida* 'Mont Rose', *Hydrangea paniculata* 'Unique', *Spiraea japonica* 'Anthony Waterer'

6 **Hydrangea paniculata 'Unique'**
Upright deciduous shrub with pointed egg-shaped leaves. The large conical flowerheads are packed with small fertile flowers and larger, more conspicuous sterile flowers that at first are creamy white but age to purplish pink. Suitable for growing in containers. Hardy.
Height and spread: 5m (15ft)
Good companions: *Acer griseum*, *Cornus alba* 'Variegata', *Hydrangea* 'Preziosa'

7 **Hydrangea aspera Villosa Group**
Deciduous shrub or small tree with velvety dark green leaves and flowerheads, 15cm (6in) across, composed of small, purplish blue central flowers and larger flowers that are pale mauve with a darker eye. Best in partial shade. Hardy.
Height: 2.5m (8ft) **Spread:** 3m (10ft)
Good companions: *Cornus alternifolia* 'Argentea', *Fargesia murieliae*, *Hydrangea serrata* 'Bluebird'

4

5

6

7

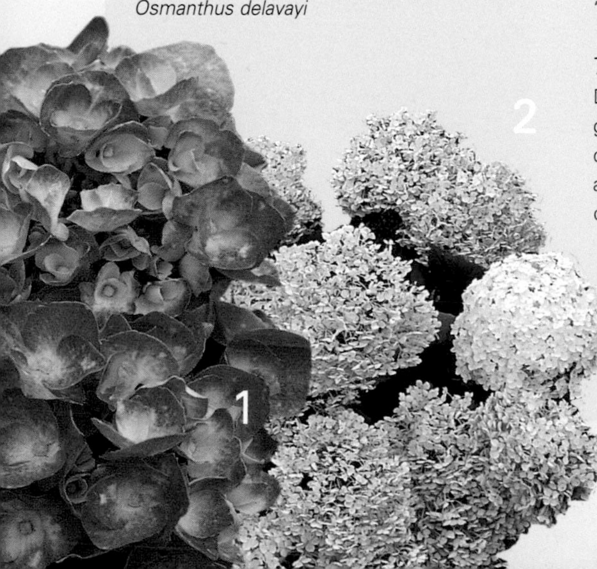

1 2

alpines

Most small perennials and shrubs that thrive in well-drained conditions do not need a rock garden. Many are suitable for raised beds, containers and paving. Plant in mild weather between autumn and early spring.

purple, blue and violet

1 Acaena saccaticupula 'Blue Haze'
Bidi-bidi, New zealand burr

The toothed leaves of this vigorous creeping evergreen perennial are pewter-blue with blue and bronze tints. In midsummer red burrs follow small round flowerheads. Hardy.

Height: 15cm (6in) **Spread:** 1m (3ft)
Site: Sun, partial shade. Well-drained soil
Use: Ground cover, paving, raised bed, rock garden
Good companions: *Cytisus* x *beanii, Hebe ochracea* 'James Stirling', *Juniperus communis* 'Green Carpet'

2 Campanula carpatica
Bellflower

Compact clump-forming perennial with toothed, usually heart-shaped leaves. In the second half of summer these are almost hidden by upturned blue bell-shaped flowers. Hardy.

Height: 25cm (10in) **Spread:** 40cm (16in)
Site: Sun, partial shade. Moist, well-drained soil
Use: Dry-stone wall, front of border, paving, raised bed, rock garden
Good companions: *Alchemilla conjuncta, Diascia* 'Salmon Supreme', *Geranium cinereum* 'Ballerina'

3 Convolvulus sabatius
Bindweed

Woody-based perennial with trailing stems and mid-green leaves. Throughout summer and into autumn the stems carry satiny blue or purple-blue flowers of shallow funnel shape. Not fully hardy.

Height: 10cm (4in) **Spread:** 60cm (2ft)
Site: Sun. Well-drained soil
Compost: Soil-based (John Innes No. 2) with added grit
Use: Container, paving, raised bed, rock garden
Good companions: *Achillea* x *lewisii* 'King Edward', *Lavandula angustifolia* 'Hidcote', *Oenothera macrocarpa*

4 Gentiana septemfida
Gentian

This easy-to-grow gentian makes a mound of leafy stems, at the end of which are clustered bell-shaped flowers, bright blue in the best forms.

Height: 20cm (8in) **Spread:** 30cm (12in)
Site: Sun, partial shade. Humus-rich and moist but well-drained soil
Compost: Soil-based (John Innes No. 2) with added leaf-mould
Use: Raised bed, rock garden, trough
Good companions: *Alchemilla conjuncta, Astilbe chinensis* var. *pumila, Saxifraga* 'Peter Pan'

pink and mauve

1

5 Diascia barberae 'Ruby Field'

This perennial makes low mats of heart-shaped leaves, over which float salmon-pink spurred flowers in summer and autumn. Not fully hardy.

General care: To encourage fresh flushes trim off old flower stems during the growing season.
Height: 25cm (10in)
Spread: 60cm (2ft)
Site: Sun. Moist but well-drained soil
Use: Front of sunny border, raised bed, rock garden
Good companions: *Campanula carpatica, Geranium cinereum* 'Ballerina', *Hebe cupressoides* 'Boughton Dome'

2

3

4

6 Geranium cinereum subsp. subcaulescens
Cranesbill

This compact evergreen perennial forms a mound of lobed grey-green leaves. Throughout summer it produces black-eyed magenta flowers.

Height: 15cm (6in) **Spread:** 30cm (12in)
Site: Sun, partial shade. Well-drained soil
Use: Paving, raised bed, rock garden
Good companions: *Crocus ancyrensis* 'Golden Bunch', *Pulsatilla vulgaris, Rhodanthemum hosmariense*

7 Silene schafta
Campion, Catchfly

This easily grown perennial makes a broad tuft of semi-evergreen narrow leaves. The sprays of magenta-pink flowers last into autumn. Hardy.

Height: 15cm (6in) **Spread:** 30cm (12in)
Site: Sun. Well-drained soil. Good on lime
Use: Front of sunny border, paving, raised bed, rock garden
Good companions: *Artemisia stelleriana* 'Boughton Silver', *Gypsophila repens* 'Rosa Schönheit', *Sedum* 'Bertram Anderson'

red and russet

8 Berberis thunbergii 'Atropurpurea Nana'
Barberry

Deciduous dwarf shrub with spiny twigs and rich purple-red leaves, which are at their best in late summer and turn red in autumn. Red berries may follow the small yellow spring flowers. Excellent as a low hedge or specimen. Hardy.

General care: Trim hedges in summer.
Height: 60cm (2ft) **Spread:** 75cm (2ft 6in)
Site: Sun, partial shade. Well-drained soil
Use: Front of border, hedge, raised bed, rock garden
Good companions: *Chamaecyparis lawsoniana* 'Green Globe', *Hypericum olympicum, Lavandula angustifolia* 'Nana Alba'

9 **Sedum spathulifolium 'Purpureum'**
Stonecrop
The fleshy spoon-shaped leaves of this ground-hugging evergreen succulent are arranged in a crowded rosette, usually with a silver-grey centre and contrasting purple-red outer leaves. There are yellow starry flowers in spring. Hardy.
Height: 10cm (4in) **Spread:** 60cm (2ft)
Site: Sun. Well-drained soil
Use: Paving, raised bed, rock garden
Good companions: *Artemisia stelleriana* 'Boughton Silver', *Festuca glauca* 'Seeigel', *Sempervivum tectorum*

10 **Sempervivum tectorum**
Common houseleek
Evergreen succulent with rosettes usually marked with red or chocolate. Stiff stems bear purplish red starry flowers in midsummer. Hardy.
Height: 15cm (6in) **Spread:** 50cm (20in)
Site: Sun. Sharply drained soil
Compost: Soil-based (John Innes No. 2) with equal quantity of grit
Use: Container, dry-stone wall, paving, raised bed, rock garden
Good companions: *Aubrieta* 'Doctor Mules', *Helianthemum* 'Wisley Primrose', *Sedum* 'Bertram Anderson'

yellow and orange

11 **Hypericum olympicum**
St John's wort
Low-growing deciduous shrub with erect stems covered in small, grey-green pointed leaves. In summer it bears numerous rich yellow flowers.
Height: 25cm (10in) **Spread:** 30cm (12in)
Site: Sun. Well-drained soil
Use: Front of sunny border, paving, raised bed, rock garden
Good companions: *Berberis thunbergii* 'Atropurpurea Nana', *Helianthemum* 'Wisley Primrose', *Lavandula angustifolia* 'Hidcote'

12 **Oenothera macrocarpa**
Evening primrose, Ozark sundrops
Perennial with red-tinted lax stems and narrow leaves with a white midrib. Throughout summer it bears yellow cup-shaped flowers. Hardy.
Height: 15cm (6in) **Spread:** 50cm (20in)
Site: Sun. Well-drained soil
Use: Front of sunny border, raised bed, rock garden
Good companions: *Aubrieta* 'Greencourt Purple', *Campanula poscharskyana* 'Stella', *Helianthemum* 'Wisley Primrose'

silver and grey

13 **Artemisia stelleriana 'Boughton Silver'**
Mugwort, Sagebrush, Wormwood
Sprawling evergreen perennial grown for its grey felted foliage, which becomes silvery white in hot summers. The yellow flowerheads in late summer are of little ornamental value. Hardy.
Height: 15cm (6in) **Spread:** 40cm (16in)
Site: Sun. Well-drained soil
Compost: Soil-based (John Innes No. 2)
Use: Container, front of sunny border, raised bed, rock garden
Good companions: *Campanula carpatica, Geranium cinereum* subsp. *subcaulescens, Lavandula angustifolia* 'Nana Alba'

waterside & water plants

All the perennials described here either require reliably moist soil or like to float on the surface of a pool with their roots anchored in the mud below. Plant in the dormant season, in spring or autumn.

purple, blue and violet

1 Pontederia cordata
Pickerel weed

This perennial is for the water's edge. It has glossy, rather arrow-like leaves that are heart-shaped at the base. In late summer and early autumn spikes of bright blue tubular flowers rise above the foliage. Hardy.

Height: 1m (3ft) **Spread:** 75cm (2ft 6in)
Site: Sun. Still water about 10–15cm (4–6in) deep
Compost: Soil-based aquatic compost
Use: Margin of pool
Good companions: *Iris laevigata* 'Variegata', *Myosotis scorpioides* 'Mermaid', *Nymphaea* 'Gonnère'

1

2

pink and mauve

2 Filipendula rubra 'Venusta'
Queen of the prairies

Large stately perennial with vine-like leaves. In midsummer red stems carry large heads, up to 30cm (12in) across, crowded with small pink flowers. Spreads to form large clumps. Hardy.

Height: 2.5m (8ft) **Spread:** 1.2m (4ft)
Site: Sun, partial shade. Fertile, reliably moist or wet soil
Use: Bog garden, moist border, waterside
Good companions: *Eupatorium purpureum*, *Gunnera manicata*, *Osmunda regalis*

3 Lythrum salicaria 'Feuerkerze'
Purple loosestrife

The stiff stems of this erect perennial are set with narrow pointed leaves. From late summer to early autumn clumps are topped by spikes of small, vivid deep pink starry flowers. Hardy.

3

4

5

Height: 1m (3ft) **Spread:** 45cm (18in)
Site: Sun, partial shade. Reliably moist soil
Use: Bog garden, moist border, waterside
Good companions: *Eupatorium purpureum*, *Filipendula rubra* 'Venusta', *Rodgersia aesculifolia*

4 Nymphaea 'Frobelii'
Water lily

The rounded floating leaves are bronze at first, then purplish green. Flowers are red-pink with orange-yellow stamens and produced throughout summer. They open from cup shapes into stars. Suitable for a medium-sized pool. Hardy.

Spread: 1.2m (4ft)
Site: Sun. Still water 45–75cm (18–30in) deep
Compost: Soil-based aquatic
Use: Pond or pool
Good companions: *Nymphaea* 'James Brydon', *Pontederia cordata*, *Zantedeschia aethiopica*

5 Rodgersia pinnata 'Superba'

This clump-forming perennial makes an impressive foliage plant. The large leaves are burnished, heavily veined and usually divided into five or more leaflets. A plume of tiny pink flowers appears in midsummer and is followed by a bold seed head. Hardy.

Height: 1.2m (4ft) **Spread:** 75cm (2ft 6in)
Site: Sun, partial shade. Humus-rich and reliably moist soil
Use: Bog garden, moist border, waterside, woodland garden
Good companions: *Hosta sieboldiana* var. *elegans*, *Matteuccia struthiopteris*, *Rheum palmatum* 'Atrosanguineum'

red and russet

6 Lobelia 'Queen Victoria'

Short-lived perennial, but a striking plant for moist soils. The stems and lance-shaped leaves are

6

7

9

8

10

11

12

beetroot-red and from late summer to mid-autumn they flaunt bright scarlet flowers. Hardy.
General care: Cut down after flowering and cover base with a mulch.
Height: 1m (3ft) **Spread:** 30cm (12in)
Site: Sun, partial shade. Fertile and reliably moist soil
Use: Moist border, waterside
Good companions: *Iris sibirica* 'Ego', *Primula pulverulenta, Rodgersia pinnata* 'Superba'

yellow and orange

7 Ligularia 'Gregynog Gold'

This large perennial forms an impressive mound of heart-shaped leaves and reaches its full stature in late summer with conical spikes of orange-yellow daisy-like flowers. Hardy.
Height: 2m (6ft) **Spread:** 1m (3ft)
Site: Sun. Fertile and reliably moist soil
Use: Moist border, waterside
Good companions: *Ligularia dentata* 'Desdemona', *Miscanthus sacchariflorus, Osmunda regalis*

8 Ligularia 'The Rocket'

This perennial makes a mound of dark green, boldly cut leaves, from which soar nearly black stems brightened by small yellow flowers. Hardy.
Height: 2m (6ft) **Spread:** 1m (3ft)
Site: Sun. Fertile and reliably moist soil
Use: Moist border, waterside
Good companions: *Ligularia* 'Gregynog Gold', *Rodgersia aesculifolia, Trollius europaeus*

cream and white

9 Nymphaea 'Gonnère'

Water lily

The floating leaves of this water lily, bronze at first and then pea green, show off the white fully double flowers with yellow stamens that are produced throughout summer. Fragrant. Suitable for a medium-sized pool. Hardy.
Spread: 1.2m (4ft)
Site: Sun. Still water 60–75cm (24–30in) deep
Compost: Soil-based aquatic
Use: Pool or pond
Good companions: *Acorus calamus* 'Argenteostriatus', *Caltha palustris* 'Flore Pleno', *Iris ensata*

10 Rodgersia aesculifolia

The giant fingered leaves of this clump-forming perennial are deeply veined and crinkled and have a bronzed metallic lustre. The small star-shaped flowers are cream, sometimes tinted pink, and make tall plumes above the foliage. Hardy.
Height: 2m (6ft) **Spread:** 1m (3ft)
Site: Sun, partial shade. Humus-rich, reliably moist soil
Use: Bog garden, moist border, waterside, woodland garden
Good companions: *Hosta* 'Honeybells', *Matteuccia struthiopteris, Rodgersia podophylla*

green

11 Carex pendula

Drooping sedge, Pendulous sedge, Weeping sedge

The grass-like clump of this evergreen perennial consists of shiny green, rather broad leaves with blue-green undersides. Arching stems bear brown flower spikes, which are erect from late spring to early summer but then hang vertically. Hardy.
Height: 1m (3ft) **Spread:** 1.2m (4ft)
Site: Sun, partial shade. Fertile, reliably moist or wet soil
Use: Bog garden, waterside
Good companions: *Iris pseudacorus* 'Variegata', *Matteuccia struthiopteris, Sagittaria sagittifolia*

12 Sagittaria sagittifolia

Common arrowhead

Perennial for pool margins that has distinctive arrow-shaped leaves with extended pointed lobes at the base. Spikes with tiers of small white flowers appear in summer. Hardy.
Height: 1m (3ft) **Spread:** Indefinite
Site: Sun. Still water about 25cm (10in) deep
Compost: Soil-based aquatic compost
Use: Wildlife pond
Good companions: *Carex pendula, Eupatorium purpureum, Iris pseudacorus* 'Variegata'

herbs, vegetables & fruit

In late summer many useful plants make the garden look attractive as they reach maturity, but in most cases, for produce to be of high quality, crops need to be harvested promptly.

herbs

1 Angelica
Angelica archangelica

This tall biennial makes a large leafy clump in its first year and bears flowerheads the following summer. The young scented leaves are used in salads and for flavouring cooked rhubarb. Candied stems are used for cake decoration. Hardy.
General care: Sow fresh seeds *in situ* or allow plants to self-seed and thin to 1m (3ft) apart.
Height: 1.2–1.5m (4–5ft) **Spread:** 1m (3ft)
Site: Shade. Humus-rich and moist soil
Compost: Soil-based (John Innes No. 3) or soil-less
Use: Back of border, large container

2 Basil
Ocimum basilicum

Bushy annual with aromatic green or purple leaves used as an accompaniment to tomatoes, in many Italian dishes and as an ingredient of pesto. Some ornamental varieties are cinnamon, aniseed or lemon flavoured. Often best in pots on a patio or windowsill. Tender.
General care: Shelter from wind and avoid over-watering. Remove flower buds and pick leaves frequently.
Height: 30–45cm (12–18in)
Spread: 23–30cm (9–12in)
Site: Sun. Fertile, well-drained soil
Compost: Soil-based (John Innes No. 3) or soil-less with added grit
Use: Border edging, greenhouse, container

3 Coriander
Coriandrum sativum

This Mediterranean annual has two distinctly different crops: the finely cut pungent leaves and the round, orange-scented seeds, which are an essential ingredient of many Oriental dishes. Grows best in hot dry conditions. Tender.
General care: Do not transplant or over-water. Pick leaves frequently and support seed-bearing plants. Harvest seeds in autumn.
Height: 60cm (2ft) **Spread:** 45cm (18in)
Site: Sun. Light, well-drained soil.
Compost: Soil-less with added grit and extra bottom drainage
Use: Border, container

4 Marjoram
Origanum species

The three main kinds of culinary marjoram, all perennial plants that thrive in containers, are sweet marjoram (*O. majorana*), the warmer pot marjoram (*O. onites*) and pungent oregano (*O. vulgare*). The leaves aid digestion and are an ingredient of bouquet garni. Generally hardy, although sweet marjoram is slightly tender.
General care: Avoid over-watering. Trim after flowering and cut back to 5cm (2in) high in late autumn. Divide or take cuttings every two years.
Height: 15–45cm (6–18in)
Spread: Up to 45cm (18in)
Site: Sun. Dry, well-drained soil
Compost: Soil-based (John Innes No. 3) or soil-less with added grit
Use: Border, edging, container

5 Parsley
Petroselinum crispum

Dark green biennial commonly grown in two forms: the tightly curled version used for garnishing, and the more strongly flavoured French or flat-leaved variety used for both garnishing and cooking. For a year-round supply sow in spring and again in midsummer for growing under cover. Hardy.
General care: Harvest regularly and remove flower stems, leaving one or two plants to self-seed if required.
Height: 40–60cm (16–24in)
Spread: 30–45cm (12–18in)
Site: Light shade in summer, but sun for winter crops. Deep, fertile soil with added compost or rotted manure
Compost: Soil-based (John Innes No. 3) with added bark, or soil-less
Use: Border, container, edging

6 Savory, summer
Satureja hortensis

Annual often referred to as the bean herb as it aids digestion when cooked with beans. Its strong peppery flavour can be added sparingly to rich meat dishes, vegetables and pulses. Tender.
General care: Sow indoors and plant out in a sheltered position when there is no longer a risk of frost. Pick regularly to prevent flowering, and protect in autumn to extend use. Do not feed.
Height: 30cm (12in)
Spread: 20–23cm (8–9in)
Site: Sun. Poor, well-drained soil
Compost: Soil-based (John Innes No. 3) or soil-less with plenty of added grit
Use: Border, container

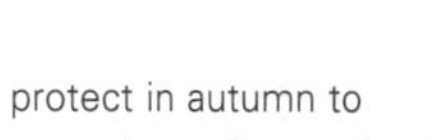

vegetables

7 Aubergine
Solanum melongena

This has large felty leaves and purple to black or white, generally pear-shaped, fruits. Can be grown under glass or outdoors in a sheltered position. Striking as a container plant for a sunny patio. Tender.
Site: Sun. Rich, well-drained soil
Compost: Soil-based (John Innes No. 3)
How to grow: Sow and grow on as for tomatoes (see 3, Tomato, page 114). Plant out 45cm (18in) apart when there is no longer a risk of frost. Pinch out growing tips when plants are 30cm (12in) high. Allow five or six fruits to set, then pinch out the branch tips. Stake large plants and feed once or twice with high-potash fertiliser when fruits are swelling. Harvest while young.

8 Broccoli, Calabrese
Brassica oleracea Italica Group

This quick-growing plant produces a large central head of tight buds, usually blue-green but sometimes purple or golden yellow. There are many varieties, all highly nutritious and well flavoured: 'Trixie' is particularly fast growing and tolerates club root disease. Not fully hardy.

Site: Sun. Rich firm soil

How to grow: Sow small batches from six to eight weeks before the last frosts until early summer. Make the earliest sowings in small pots under glass and plant out 23–30cm (9–12in) apart each way when there is no longer a risk of frost; make later sowings *in situ* and thin seedlings to the above planting distances. Water regularly and mulch to encourage fast, even growth. Cut the central head before the flower buds open and apply a high-nitrogen feed. Cut the later sideshoots when about 10cm (4in) long.

9 French bean, climbing
Phaseolus vulgaris

This tender annual is related to the dwarf french bean but is more productive and so useful where space is limited. Early sowings in a greenhouse can be harvested until outdoor beans are available, and, if cut back and fed, will crop again after open-air plants are finished. Varieties with gold, purple or speckled pods, such as 'Borlotto', 'Viola Cornetti' and 'Rob Roy', make decorative features on tall cane wigwams in flower borders.

Site: Sun. Fertile and well-drained soil

How to grow: Sow indoors in small pots in mid-spring or outdoors from late spring until midsummer. Sow greenhouse crops in early spring. Space plants 15cm (6in) apart in rows 20cm (8in) apart or in a 1m (3ft) circle. Provide each plant with a sturdy 2.5m (8ft) cane crossed and tied in rows or as a wigwam. Keep moist, especially once flowering starts. Start picking while beans are young (eight to ten weeks after sowing) and repeat every two to three days.

10 Pepper
Capsicum annuum

Both large-fruited sweet peppers and slimmer hot peppers, or chillies, grow on sun and heat-loving bushy plants. Where summers are cool, peppers are best grown under glass or on a warm patio sheltered from cool winds. Tender.

Site: Sun. Rich well-drained soil

Compost: Soil-based (John Innes No. 3)

How to grow: Sow in late winter as for tomatoes (see 3, Tomato, page 114) or buy young plants in late spring. Pot up seedlings into 8cm (3in) pots, moving them into larger ones as they grow. Harden off outdoor plants and plant out 45cm (18in) apart when there is no longer a risk of frost. Pinch out growing tips when 38cm (15in) high. Water regularly during flowering and fruiting, and feed every 10–14 days. Harvest sweet peppers green or fully coloured; let chillies ripen and then dry on strings for two weeks before storing.

11 Potato, second early
Solanum tuberosum

Ready two to three weeks after 'first earlies', varieties like 'Catriona', 'Marfona' and the salad type 'Belle de Fontenay' give slightly heavier yields of 'new' potatoes or can be left until larger and dug up for storing. Not fully hardy.

Site: Sun. Deeply dug fertile and well-drained soil

How to grow: Sprout tubers in late winter, as for first earlies, and plant in mid-spring 10–15cm (4–6in) deep and 38cm (15in) apart each way. Water and mound soil halfway up the stems every two to three weeks. Start lifting tubers with a fork when flowers are fully open.

1 Runner bean
Phaseolus coccineus

A popular tender perennial, usually grown as a half-hardy annual, with lush foliage and decorative scarlet, white, pink or bicoloured flowers. Most varieties are climbers, but a few, such as 'Gulliver' and 'Pickwick', are naturally dwarf, and all can be grown as 45cm (18in) high plants by pinching out growing tips regularly. Train on sunflowers to make a feature. Tender.

Site: Sun, light shade, sheltered from strong winds. Deep, moist and fertile soil

How to grow: Sow as for climbing beans (see 9, French bean, page 113), and plant out after the last frosts, 15cm (6in) apart in rows or circles. Water freely in dry weather, especially during flowering, and mulch. Start harvesting before the seeds are visible through the pods, and pick every few days until the autumn frosts.

2 Sweetcorn
Zea mays

This is a superb crop for home-growing because the flavour and sweetness of the cobs start to deteriorate minutes after picking. The tall plants are decorative and sturdy enough to support climbing beans (see 9, French bean, page 113) planted at their base. In cool gardens, choose early-ripening varieties. Tender.

Site: Sun. Rich, firm well-drained soil

How to grow: Sow seeds individually in small pots in a warm place indoors, about six weeks before the last frosts occur. Harden off outdoors and plant out 35cm (14in) apart each way in blocks. Water well when flowers appear and again when cobs are swelling. Harvest cobs when their tassels turn brown and the kernel contents are milky. Use immediately.

3 Tomato
Lycopersicon esculentum

For the best flavour, tomatoes should be grown outdoors, sheltered from cool winds, but where summers are cool they are an ideal crop for greenhouse borders, containers or growing bags. The most productive kinds are tall varieties, grown on canes or strings as single stems; naturally bushy varieties crop earlier and make decorative pot or hanging basket plants. There is a huge choice available, including red, yellow, green or striped fruits in a range of sizes from small 'cherries' to enormous 'beefsteak' kinds for slicing. Tender.

Site: Sun. Fertile, well-drained soil with plenty of humus

How to grow: Sow indoor crops between midwinter and early spring according to the amount of heat you can provide; sow outdoor varieties 8 weeks before the last frosts. Germinate seed at 15°C (59°F) and prick out seedlings into small pots. Plant out when the first flower truss is visible, after hardening off outdoor plants. Train tall varieties on supports, removing sideshoots; leave bush types unpruned. Water regularly and feed every 10–14 days after flowering starts. Harvest fruits when fully coloured.

fruit

4 Apple
Malus domestica

Apples can be grown in even the smallest garden if the right rootstock is chosen and plants are trained as cordons or espaliers against a fence or wall; if grafted on a very dwarfing rootstock, they will even thrive in large containers. Depending on the variety, apples ripen from late summer until late autumn; later varieties often store until the following year. Early frosts can damage the blossom. Hardy.

Site: Sun. Deep, humus-rich and well-drained soil

How to grow: Plant trees while dormant (spacing will depend on the chosen rootstock). Feed and mulch every spring. Prune trained trees in mid or late summer.

5 Blackcurrant
Ribes nigrum

Blackcurrants are easy to grow and one of the richest sources of vitamin C. They need plenty of space and lavish annual feeding or manuring. 'Ben Sarek' forms a compact bush, but 'Laxton's Giant' has the largest currants. Hardy.

Site: Sun, light shade. Deeply dug, rich soil
How to grow: Plant while dormant, 1.5m (5ft) apart and 10cm (4in) deeper than the previous soil level on the plant; cut down to 8cm (3in) high. Feed and mulch in spring, and water in dry weather. Prune after fruiting, cutting out a third of the old, darker stems. Harvest complete bunches of fruit when fully coloured.

6 Fig
Ficus carica

A handsome Mediterranean tree, this makes an attractive fan when trained on a warm garden or conservatory wall. Figs fruit best when the roots are confined in a large container or a pit lined with buried slabs. Not fully hardy.

Site: Sun. Well-dug soil with a restricted root run
Compost: Soil based (John Innes No. 3)
How to grow: Plant in spring. Mulch heavily each spring with rotted manure or garden compost. Prune damaged and surplus branches in late spring, and shorten sideshoots in summer. Pick fruits when fully coloured and starting to split. Protect in a hard winter with layers of fleece or by wrapping branches in straw.

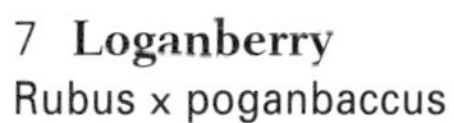

7 Loganberry
Rubus x poganbaccus

The long canes of this vigorous raspberry-blackberry hybrid make an excellent screen when trained on a fence of wires. Alternatively, grow it on a wall or training wires. Choose a thornless variety such as 'LY 654' for comfortable harvesting of the richly flavoured berries. Hardy.
Site: Sun. Fertile, well-drained soil
How to grow: Plant while dormant, 3–4m (10–12ft) apart. Mulch with rotted manure or compost each spring, and water in dry weather. Tie in new canes as they develop, and prune out all the old canes after harvesting. Pick fruits when fully ripe and almost purple in colour.

8 Peach
Prunus persica

These attractive trees have a froth of soft pink blossom in late spring followed by richly flavoured fruits. Best grown on a warm sheltered wall where the blossom can be protected from frost. Dwarf plants grow 1.5m (5ft) high and are excellent for large containers. Hardy.
Site: Sun. Fertile, well-drained soil
How to grow: Plant in autumn, spacing full-size trees 4m (12ft) apart. Mulch in spring with well-rotted manure and water in dry weather. Protect against frost and peach leaf curl in late winter and early spring with a sheet of polythene. Prune out surplus growth in spring, leaving a new shoot at the base of each flowering shoot. Pollinate flowers on indoor plants using a soft brush, and thin fruit clusters until fruitlets are about 10cm (4in) apart. Harvest when soft around the stalk.

9 Pear
Pyrus communis

Pears need warm summers for perfection and crop best if fan-trained on warm walls and sheltered from spring frost. Most need a compatible partner for cross-fertilisation. Hardy.
Site: Sun. Fertile, very well-drained soil
How to grow: Plant, grow and prune pears as for apples (see 4, Apple, page 114). Start picking from late summer, while fruits are still hard: test every week and harvest any that come away easily. Store in a cool place until fruits ripen.

10 Plum
Prunus domestica

Plums, gages and damsons are all vigorous trees, even when grafted on a semi-dwarfing rootstock, and are best trained on a wall as fans or left to make large specimen trees, sheltered from cold spring winds. A few varieties like 'Victoria' are self-fertile but most need a pollen partner. Dessert, cooking and dual-purpose varieties are available. Hardy.
Site: Sun. Rich, deep moist soil
How to grow: Plant in late autumn, spacing bushes 2.5m (8ft) apart and other kinds 4.5m (15ft) apart. Mulch generously each spring with rotted manure. Thin fruits in early summer and support heavily laden branches. Only prune trees in leaf, removing misplaced shoots and some that have carried fruit. Harvest ripe fruits, checking every two to three days, and use immediately.

11 Strawberry, alpine
Fragaria vesca

This compact perennial bears flushes of small, intensely fragrant red, yellow or white berries from midsummer until the autumn frosts. The berries are usually overlooked by birds, so rarely need netting. Excellent for edging and containers and as ground cover under fruit trees. Hardy.
Site: Sun, light shade. Well-dug, fertile soil
How to grow: Buy young plants or sow seeds in warmth or outdoors from early spring onwards. Plant out in late spring, about 30cm (12in) apart. Feed each spring and mulch with compost or grass clippings. Water fruiting plants regularly. Harvest fruit when fully coloured and soft. Divide and replant every three to four years.

the greenhouse

Many of the tender plants that flourish in a protected environment can be moved outdoors to a warm sheltered position during summer. Dimensions given here indicate average sizes for container-grown plants.

purple, blue and violet

1 Tibouchina urvilleana
Brazilian spider flower, Glory bush

Hairy evergreen shrub with veined, velvety leaves and in summer and autumn satiny, violet-purple saucer-shaped flowers, 10cm (4in) across. Move pot-grown plants outdoors in summer. Tender.

General care: Protect from hot sun. Trim lightly in late winter.

Height and spread: 5m (15ft)

Under glass: Full light. Soil-based compost (John Innes No. 3)

Use: Conservatory or greenhouse minimum 5°C (41°F), sunny patio

pink and mauve

2 Anisodontea capensis

Evergreen, bushy shrub with hairy leaves and, in summer and autumn, veined pink flowers. Move pot-grown plants outdoors in summer. Half hardy.

General care: Trim lightly in late winter to encourage bushy growth.

Height: 1m (3ft) **Spread:** 75cm (2ft 6in)

Under glass: Full light. Soil-based compost (John Innes No. 2)

Use: Conservatory or greenhouse minimum 2°C (36°F), sunny patio

3 Nerium oleander
Oleander

Evergreen leathery-leaved shrub with pink, red or white tubular flowers, often with twisted lobes. Move pot-grown plants outdoors in summer. In a mild climate can be grown outdoors in a sheltered site. Poisonous if ingested. Tender.

General care: Keep well ventilated. Trim in late winter or early spring. Tolerant of hard pruning.

Height: 5m (15ft) **Spread:** 3m (10ft)

Under glass: Full light. Soil-based compost (John Innes No. 3)

Outdoor site: Sun. Well-drained soil

Use: Conservatory or greenhouse minimum 2°C (36°F), sunny border, sunny patio

bronze and maroon

4 Aeonium 'Zwartkop'

Rosette-forming succulent with fleshy, purplish black leaves. Individual rosettes die after flowering in spring. Move pot-grown plants outdoors in summer. Tender.

General care: Shade from hot sun. Keep dry during the dormant season.

Height: 1m (3ft) **Spread:** 1.2m (4ft)

Under glass: Full light. Soil-based compost (John Innes No. 2) with added grit

Use: Conservatory or greenhouse minimum 10°C (50°F), sunny patio

5 Cobaea scandens
Cathedral bell, Cup-and-saucer plant

This softly woody, perennial climber has dark green leaves and clings to supports by tendrils. Can be grown outdoors as an annual or as a longer-lived plant under glass. The flower 'cup', or 'bell', opens yellow-green then turns purple. The 'saucer' is a green and wavy calyx. Flowers outdoors from late summer until the frosts, or under glass from spring to early winter. Tender.

General care: Sow seed under glass in early to mid-spring. Prune plants under glass in autumn or early spring.

Height: 5m (15ft) **Spread:** 3m (10ft)

Under glass: Full light. Soil-based compost (John Innes No. 3) with added leaf-mould and grit

Outdoor site: Sun. Well-drained soil

Use: Conservatory or greenhouse minimum 5°C (41°F), warm wall outdoors

6 Ricinus communis 'Impala'
Castor oil plant

Fast-growing evergreen shrub valued for its maroon-purple fingered foliage and often grown as an annual for summer bedding. Red-brown spiny seed capsules follow male and female flowers. Poisonous if ingested and contact with leaves may cause skin reactions. Half hardy.

General care: Prune in late winter or early spring.

Height: 1.2m (4ft) **Spread:** 1m (3ft)

Under glass: Full light. Soil-based compost (John Innes No. 2)

Outdoor site: Sun. Fertile and humus-rich but well-drained soil

Use: Conservatory or greenhouse minimum 2°C (36°F), formal or tropical bedding

red and russet

7 Abutilon megapotamicum
Trailing abutilon

Slender evergreen or semi-evergreen shrub that can be grown outdoors in a mild climate. The protective base of the dangling flowers is an inflated red calyx, from which protrude twisted yellow petals and purple stamens. Not fully hardy.

General care: Train stems into supports. Prune in late winter or early spring, cutting back sideshoots to about four buds.

Height and spread: 2m (6ft)

Under glass: Full light. Soil-based compost (John Innes No. 2)

Outdoor site: Sun. Well-drained soil

Use: Conservatory or greenhouse minimum 2°C (36°F), warm wall

8 Bougainvillea 'San Diego Red'

The hybrid bougainvilleas are usually evergreen. In temperatures below 10°C (50°F) they lose their leaves but survive in frost-free conditions. They make new growth in spring, then flower in very frequent flushes while in leaf. Three long-lasting petal-like bracts surround each small tubular flower, which opens white at the tip. Those of this cultivar are magenta-red ageing to pink. Tender to half hardy.

1

2

3

4

General care: Prune lightly after each flush. Hard prune in early spring to check growth or to train standards and restricted shapes.
Height: 10m (30ft) **Spread:** 6m (20ft)
Under glass: Full light. Soil-based compost (John Innes No. 3)
Use: Conservatory or greenhouse minimum 2°C (36°F)

9 Fuchsia 'Gartenmeister Bonstedt'
Triphylla Group fuchsia

Fuchsias in the Triphylla Group are evergreen shrubs that bear dangling clusters of long-tubed flowers. 'Gartenmeister Bonstedt' has deep bronze-red foliage, purple on the underside, and small, bright red flowers. Plants can be moved outdoors in summer. Tender.
General care: To keep plants in flower all year maintain a temperature of 15°C (59°F).
Height: 75cm (2ft 6in) **Spread:** 50cm (20in)
Under glass: Full light. Soil-based compost (John Innes No. 3) or soil-less
Outdoor site: Sun, partial shade. Fertile and moist but well-drained soil
Use: Conservatory or greenhouse minimum 5°C (41°F), sunny or lightly shaded patio

10 Solenostemon 'Crimson Ruffles'
Coleus, Flame nettle, Painted nettle

Flame nettles are woody-based perennials grown for their colourful leaves, which are attractively toothed, scalloped or lobed and often strongly patterned. They can be treated as annuals and grown under glass or outdoors. 'Crimson Ruffles' has deep red-and-purple waved leaves.
General care: Shade from hot sun. Pinch out the flower spikes before they develop.
Height: 50cm (20in)
Spread: 35cm (14in)
Under glass: Full light. Soil-based compost (John Innes No. 3) or soil-less
Outdoor site: Sun, partial shade. Humus-rich and moist but well-drained soil
Use: Container, conservatory or greenhouse minimum 10°C (50°F), formal bedding, patio

yellow and orange

11 Brugmansia x candida 'Grand Marnier'
Angels' trumpets, Datura

Evergreen shrub with large, usually toothed leaves and night-scented trumpet-shaped flowers. These are creamy apricot and hang almost vertically. Can be moved outdoors in summer. All parts are poisonous if ingested. Tender.
General care: Prune hard after flowering or in late winter.
Height: 4m (12ft) **Spread:** 2.5m (8ft)
Under glass: Full light. Soil-based compost (John Innes No. 3)
Use: Conservatory or greenhouse minimum 7°C (45°F), sunny patio

green

12 Cycas revoluta
Japanese sago palm

Slow-growing plant with a stout trunk crowned by glossy green leaves up to 1.5m (5ft) long and composed of numerous narrow leaflets and a sturdy midrib. Move outdoors in summer. Tender.
General care: Water sparingly in winter.
Height and spread: 2m (6ft)
Under glass: Bright indirect light. Soil-based compost (John Innes No. 1) with added grit
Use: Conservatory or greenhouse minimum 7°C (45°F), houseplant, sunny patio

5

7

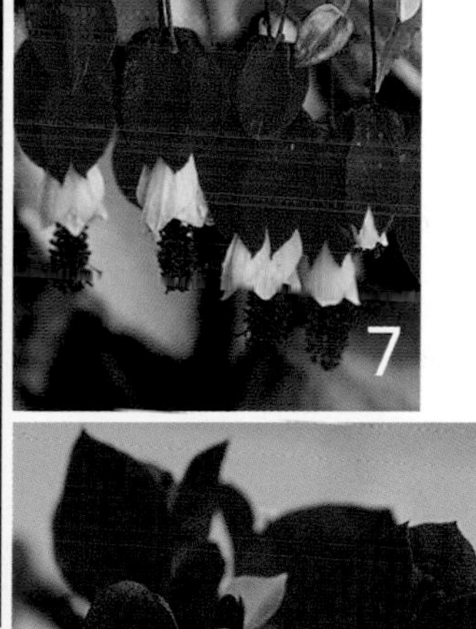
8

6

9

10

11

12

choosing the best plants

The following plant lists draw on all the plants described in the preceding pages of the Plant Selector, but they are grouped together here to help you choose plants for particular conditions, situations and uses.

plants for clay soil

Although the following plants generally succeed on close-textured clay soils, they do better when the ground has been improved by the addition of grit and organic matter such as well-rotted garden compost.

- *Abies koreana*
- *Acanthus mollis* Latifolius Group
- *Anemone hupehensis* 'Hadspen Abundance'
- *Anemone* x *hybrida* 'Whirlwind'
- *Aralia elata* (all cultivars)
- *Asplenium scolopendrium*
- *Berberis thunbergii* 'Atropurpurea Nana'
- *Campsis* x *tagliabuana* 'Madame Galen'
- *Carex comans* 'Frosted Curls'
- *Carpinus betulus*
- *Cornus alternifolia* 'Argentea'
- *Deschampsia cespitosa* 'Goldschleier'
- *Escallonia* 'Apple Blossom'
- *Fargesia nitida*
- *Hemerocallis* (all)
- *Hibiscus syriacus* 'Oiseau Bleu'
- *Hosta* (all)
- *Hypericum* (all)
- *Kniphofia* (all)
- *Lonicera* (most)
- *Magnolia grandiflora*
- *Rodgersia pinnata* 'Superba'
- *Rosa* (all)

Kniphofia 'Percy's Pride'

plants for dry chalky soil

A large number of plants are automatically excluded from this list because they will not tolerate alkaline (limy) soil. The improvement of shallow chalky soil by the addition of moisture-retaining organic matter allows lime-tolerant but moisture-loving plants, notably clematis, to be grown successfully.

- *Acanthus mollis* Latifolius Group
- *Artemisia stelleriana* 'Boughton Silver'
- *Buddleja* (all)
- *Berberis thunbergii* 'Atropurpurea Nana'
- *Caryopteris* x *clandonensis*
- *Ceanothus* x *delileanus* 'Topaze'
- *Convolvulus sabatius*
- *Coreopsis verticillata* 'Grandiflora'
- *Dianthus chinensis* Baby Doll Series
- *Echinops ritro* 'Veitch's Blue'
- *Eryngium* (all)
- *Gypsophila* (all)
- *Hypericum* (all)
- *Lavandula* (all)
- *Lavatera trimestris* 'Mont Blanc'
- *Origanum* (all)
- *Osteospermum* 'Jucundum'
- *Salvia viridis* 'Oxford Blue'
- *Scabiosa caucasica* 'Moerheim Blue'
- *Sedum* (all)
- *Sempervivum tectorum*
- *Silene schafta*
- *Verbena bonariensis*
- *Yucca gloriosa*

Echinops ritro 'Veitch's Blue'

plants for sandy or gravelly soil

The following plants require free drainage and are generally drought tolerant. The range of plants that can be grown in dry sunny gardens can be enlarged if the soil is improved by the addition of well-rotted organic matter.

- *Agapanthus* (all)
- *Artemisia stelleriana* 'Boughton Silver'
- *Berberis thunbergii* 'Atropurpurea Nana'
- *Brachyscome iberidifolia* Splendour Series
- *Buddleja* (all)
- *Calendula officinalis* 'Fiesta Gitana'
- *Calluna vulgaris* 'Darkness'
- *Caryopteris* x *clandonensis* 'Heavenly Blue'
- *Centaurea hypoleuca* 'John Coutts'
- *Convolvulus sabatius*
- *Coreopsis verticillata* 'Grandiflora'
- *Echinops ritro* 'Veitch's Blue'
- *Erica vagans* 'Mrs D.F. Maxwell'
- *Eryngium* (all)
- *Gaura lindheimeri*
- *Genista aetnensis*
- *Gypsophila* (all)
- *Knautia macedonica*
- *Lavandula* (all)
- *Lavatera* 'Barnsley'
- *Lavatera trimestris* 'Mont Blanc'
- *Oenothera macrocarpa*
- *Origanum* (all)
- *Perovskia* 'Blue Spire'
- *Ruta graveolens* 'Jackman's Blue'
- *Salvia viridis* 'Oxford Blue'
- *Sedum* (all)
- *Sempervivum tectorum*
- *Stipa gigantea*
- *Tagetes* (all)
- *Verbena bonariensis*
- *Yucca gloriosa*

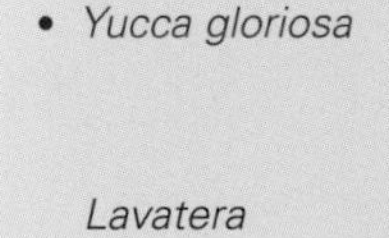

Lavatera 'Barnsley'

plants for moist shade

The following plants tolerate or more commonly thrive in moist shade, although many will also grow in full sun provided the soil is reliably moist.

- *Alstroemeria* ligtu hybrids
- *Astilbe* (all)
- *Carex pendula*
- *Fargesia nitida*
- *Filipendula rubra* 'Venusta'
- *Fuchsia* (all)
- *Gentiana asclepiadea*
- *Gentiana septemfida*
- *Hosta* (all)
- *Hydrangea* (all)
- *Kirengeshoma palmata*
- *Impatiens walleriana* Tempo Series
- *Lobelia* 'Queen Victoria'
- *Lonicera* (most)
- *Lythrum salicaria* 'Feuerkerze'
- *Rodgersia* (all)
- *Thalictrum delavayi* 'Hewitt's Double'
- *Viola* x *wittrockiana* Crystal Bowl Series

Astilbe 'Professor Van de Wielen'

plants for coastal sites

Where windbreaks and hedges give protection from salt-laden winds, a wide range of plants can be grown in coastal gardens, including many that benefit from the sea's moderating influence on temperatures.

- *Achillea* 'Coronation Gold'
- *Agapanthus* (all)
- *Alstroemeria* ligtu hybrids
- *Antirrhinum* Tahiti Series
- *Argyranthemum* (all)
- *Artemisia stelleriana* 'Boughton Silver'
- *Aster* x *frikartii* 'Mönch'
- *Aster novi-belgii* 'Heinz Richard'
- *Buddleja* (all)
- *Calendula officinalis* 'Fiesta Gitana'
- *Calluna vulgaris* 'Darkness'
- *Caryopteris* x *clandonensis* 'Heavenly Blue'
- *Convolvulus sabatius*
- *Crocosmia* (all)
- *Dianthus chinensis* Baby Doll Series
- *Echinops ritro* 'Veitch's Blue'
- *Erica vagans* 'Mrs D.F. Maxwell'
- *Eryngium* (all)
- *Escallonia* 'Apple Blossom'
- *Fuchsia* (all)
- *Geranium* (all)
- *Gypsophila paniculata* 'Bristol Fairy'
- *Heuchera micrantha* var. *diversifolia* 'Palace Purple'
- *Hydrangea macrophylla* (all)
- *Hypericum* (all)
- *Kniphofia* (all)
- *Lavandula* (all)
- *Lavatera* 'Barnsley'
- *Lavatera trimestris* 'Mont Blanc'
- *Oenothera macrocarpa*
- *Origanum laevigatum* 'Herrenhausen'
- *Osteospermum* 'Jucundum'
- *Penstemon* (all)
- *Rosa* 'Blanche Double de Coubert'
- *Rosa* Magic Carpet
- *Scabiosa* (all)
- *Scaevola aemula* 'Blue Wonder'
- *Sedum* (all)
- *Sempervivum tectorum*
- x *Solidaster luteus* 'Lemore'
- *Spiraea japonica* 'Anthony Waterer'
- *Yucca gloriosa*

plants for acid soils

Plants in the following list that are marked with an asterisk* will only grow satisfactorily on soils that are free of lime. Other plants in the list thrive on acid soils, although they may also grow satisfactorily on soils that are neutral or to some degree alkaline.

- *Abies koreana*
- *Calluna vulgaris* 'Darkness'*
- *Erica vagans* 'Mrs D.F. Maxwell'
- *Eucryphia* x *nymansensis* 'Nymansay'
- *Kirengeshoma palmata**

plants for ground cover

Close planting of shrubs and perennials will help to create an attractive weed-excluding cover. However, effective cover can only be achieved by planting into soil from which perennial weeds have been eliminated. The following plants are particularly useful because of their dense foliage.

- *Calluna vulgaris* 'Darkness'
- *Geranium* x *riversleaianum* 'Russell Prichard'
- *Heuchera micrantha* var. *diversifolia* 'Palace Purple'
- *Hosta* (all)
- *Erica vagans* 'Mrs D.F. Maxwell'
- *Rosa* Magic Carpet

Rosa Magic Carpet

choosing the best plants/2

trees for small gardens

None of the following is suitable for very small gardens, where climbers on structures such as arches are a better way of creating height and shade.

- *Abies koreana* 'Silberlocke'
- *Aralia elata* 'Variegata'
- *Cornus alternifolia* 'Argentea'
- *Eucryphia* x *nymansensis* 'Nymansay'
- *Genista aetnensis*
- *Koelreuteria paniculata*
- *Pyrus salicifolia* 'Pendula'

flowering plants for containers

As well as the plants listed here, many alpine, or rock garden, plants are suitable for troughs, and all the greenhouse plants listed can be grown in containers.

- *Agapanthus* (all)
- *Amaranthus caudatus*
- *Antirrhinum* Tahiti Series
- *Argyranthemum* (all)
- *Begonia* 'Orange Cascade'
- *Brachyscome iberidifolia* Splendour Series
- *Calendula officinalis* 'Fiesta Gitana'
- *Calluna vulgaris* 'Darkness'
- *Cleome hasslereana* 'Rose Queen'
- *Dianthus chinensis* Baby Doll Series
- *Fuchsia* (most)
- *Hemerocallis* 'Stella de Oro'
- *Hydrangea macrophylla* 'Blue Wave'
- *Hydrangea paniculata* 'Unique'
- *Impatiens walleriana* Tempo Series
- *Lilium* (all)
- *Lobelia erinus* 'Crystal Palace'
- *Myrtus communis* subsp. *tarentina*
- *Nemesia* 'Carnival'
- *Nicotiana* Domino Series
- *Osteospermum* 'Jucundum'
- *Pelargonium* (all)
- *Petunia* Surfinia Series
- *Rosa* Gentle Touch
- *Rosa* Magic Carpet
- *Scaevola aemula* 'Blue Wonder'
- *Tagetes* (all)
- *Tropaeolum* Alaska Series
- *Verbena* (most)
- *Viola* x *wittrockiana* Crystal Bowl Series
- *Zinnia* 'Envy'

flowers for cutting

In addition to the following, many other plants provide material for small, sometimes short-lived, displays.
The flowers of plants marked with an asterisk* are suitable for drying.

- *Acanthus mollis* Latifolius Group
- *Achillea* 'Coronation Gold'*
- *Aconitum* 'Spark's Variety'
- *Agapanthus* (all)
- *Alstroemeria* ligtu hybrids
- *Amaranthus caudatus**
- *Anaphalis triplinervis* 'Sommerschnee'
- *Aster novi-belgii* 'Heinz Richard'
- *Calendula officinalis* 'Fiesta Gitana'
- *Chrysanthemum* 'Clara Curtis'
- *Cleome hassleriana* 'Rose Queen'
- *Coreopsis verticillata* 'Grandiflora'
- *Cortaderia selloana* 'Sunningdale Silver'*
- *Cosmos bipinnatus* Sensation Series
- *Cynara cardunculus**
- *Dahlia* (all)
- *Delphinium* Belladonna Group
- *Deschampsia cespitosa* 'Goldschleier'*
- *Eryngium* (all)
- *Gladiolus* (all)
- *Helenium* 'Moerheim Beauty'
- *Hydrangea macrophylla* (all)
- *Lathyrus odoratus* 'Noel Sutton'
- *Lilium* (all)
- *Lonicera* (most)
- *Molucella laevis*
- *Monarda* 'Prärienacht'
- *Phlox paniculata* (all)
- *Rosa* (most)
- *Scabiosa caucasica* 'Moerheim Blue'
- *Stipa gigantea**
- *Zinnia* 'Envy'

Gladiolus 'Woodpecker'

plants with variegated foliage

The leaves of the following plants are edged, spotted or otherwise marked in white, cream or yellow.

- *Aralia elata* 'Aureovariegata'
- *Aralia elata* 'Variegata'
- *Cornus alternifolia* 'Argentea'
- *Fuchsia magellanica* 'Versicolor'
- *Hosta fortunei* var. *aureomarginata*
- *Tropaeolum* Alaska Series

plants with aromatic foliage

In the case of many aromatic plants the scent of the leaves is only detectable when they are bruised.

- Angelica (*Angelica archangelica*)
- Basil (*Ocimum basilicum*)
- *Caryopteris* x *clandonensis* 'Heavenly Blue'
- Coriander (*Coriandrum sativum*)
- *Lavandula* (all)
- Marjoram (*Origanum* spp.)
- *Monarda* 'Prärienacht'
- *Myrtus communis* subsp. *tarentina*
- Parsley (*Petroselinum crispum*)
- *Pelargonium* 'Apple Blossom Rosebud'
- *Pelargonium* 'Rouletta'
- *Perovskia* 'Blue Spire'
- *Ruta graveolens* 'Jackman's Blue'
- Summer savory (*Satureja hortensis*)
- *Tagetes* (all pungent)

Lavandula x *intermedia*

plants with fragrant flowers

Age of flower, time of day, temperature and other factors affect the strength of floral scents and their appreciation is highly personal. Some of the following are worth siting to give the best chance of their perfumes being enjoyed, but the fragrance of others can only be fully appreciated close to.

- *Brachyscome iberidifolia* Splendour Series
- *Brugmansia* x *candida* 'Grand Marnier'
- *Buddleja crispa*
- *Buddleja davidii* 'Black Knight'
- *Buddleja* 'Lochinch'
- *Cosmos atrosanguineus*
- *Cyclamen purpurascens*
- *Genista aetnensis*
- *Gladiolus callianthus* 'Murielae'
- *Hosta* 'Honeybells'
- *Lathyrus odoratus* 'Noel Sutton'
- *Lavandula angustifolia* 'Hidcote'
- *Lavandula* x *intermedia* Dutch Group
- *Lilium* 'Casa Blanca'
- *Lilium* 'Star Gazer'
- *Lonicera* x *americana*
- *Lonicera etrusca* 'Superba'
- *Lonicera* x *heckrottii*
- *Lonicera japonica* 'Halliana'
- *Lonicera periclymenum* 'Serotina'
- *Magnolia grandiflora*
- *Nymphaea* 'Gonnère'
- *Rosa* 'Blanche Double de Coubert'
- *Rosa* Golden Showers
- *Rosa* Graham Thomas
- *Rosa* 'Louise Odier'
- *Rosa* 'Pink Perpétué'
- *Rosa* Royal William
- *Trachelospermum jasminoides*
- *Tropaeolum* Alaska Series
- *Verbena bonariensis*
- *Verbena* 'Silver Anne'

Rosa Royal William

evergreen shrubs and trees

The following are useful for creating a year-round structure for the garden.

- *Abies koreana*
- *Calluna vulgaris* 'Darkness'
- *Erica vagans* 'Mrs D.F. Maxwell'
- *Escallonia* 'Apple Blossom'
- *Eucryphia* x *nymansensis* 'Nymansay'
- *Fargesia nitida*
- *Hypericum* 'Hidcote'
- *Lavandula* x *intermedia* Dutch Group
- *Magnolia grandiflora*
- *Myrtus communis* subsp. *tarentina*
- *Ruta graveolens* 'Jackman's Blue'
- *Yucca gloriosa*

plants with large or boldly shaped leaves

The leaves of the following plants are of architectural value in the garden and in most cases are useful as cut foliage too.

- *Acanthus mollis* Latifolius Group
- *Aralia elata* 'Variegata'
- *Brugmansia* x *candida* 'Grand Marnier'
- *Campsis* x *tagliabuana* 'Madame Galen'
- *Cycas revoluta*
- *Cynara cardunculus*
- *Heuchera micrantha* var. *diversifolia*
- *Koelreuteria paniculata*
- *Ligularia* 'Gregynog Gold'
- *Ligularia* 'The Rocket'
- *Magnolia grandiflora*
- *Phormium* 'Sundowner'
- *Pontederia cordata*
- *Ricinus communis* 'Impala'
- *Rodgersia pinnata* 'Superba'
- *Yucca gloriosa*

Ricinus communis 'Impala'

plants with fruit, berries and seed heads

The plants in the following list are of value because they have more than one feature of ornamental value.

- *Abies koreana*
- *Acanthus mollis* Latifolius Group
- *Carpinus betulus*
- *Cortaderia selloana* 'Sunningdale Silver'
- *Cynara cardunculus*
- *Heuchera micrantha* var. *diversifolia* 'Palace Purple'
- *Koelreuteria paniculata*
- *Lonicera* x *americana*
- *Lonicera etrusca* 'Superba'
- *Lonicera periclymenum* 'Serotina'
- *Lonicera sempervirens*
- *Pyrus salicifolia* 'Pendula'
- *Rodgersia pinnata* 'Superba'
- *Rosa* 'Blanche Double de Coubert'
- *Rosa glauca*
- *Stipa gigantea*

plants with colourful foliage

The red, purple, copper, yellow, blue or cream foliage colour of plants in the following list is generally strongest in spring and early summer. Plants marked with an asterisk* have grey or white-backed leaves. For other colourful foliage see Plants with Variegated Foliage.

- *Abies koreana* 'Silberlocke'*
- *Aeonium* 'Zwartkop'
- *Artemisia stelleriana* 'Boughton Silver'*
- *Astilbe* 'Bronce Elegans'
- *Berberis thunbergii* 'Atropurpurea Nana'
- *Carex comans* 'Frosted Curls'*
- *Cynara cardunculus**
- *Geranium* 'Ann Folkard'
- *Heuchera micrantha* var. *diversifolia* 'Palace Purple'
- *Lobelia* 'Queen Victoria'
- *Nymphaea* 'Frobelii'
- *Phormium* 'Sundowner'
- *Pyrus salicifolia* 'Pendula'*
- *Ricinus communis* 'Impala'
- *Sedum* 'Ruby Glow'
- *Sedum spathulifolium* 'Purpureum'
- *Solenostemon* 'Crimson Ruffles'

garden projects

Late summer is a good time to design a new planting area or embark on a construction project. How about laying out a new herb garden, or planting up a perennial border that will come into its own next year. Much of the growing season still remains, giving the new plants time to establish before winter sets in. You may be tempted to install a modest water feature, such as a rill or a simple fountain. And how about your front garden – is it time for an overhaul? Edgings to pathways and beds can make a huge difference to your garden's appearance.

designing with plants

Plants are beautiful in so many different ways that they are extremely versatile in their use in the garden. The key to successful planting lies in establishing a good basic framework and building up a balanced collection of permanent and seasonal-interest plants.

choosing key plants

To give your garden a firm structure, which will keep it looking attractive all year with minimal maintenance, select a few key plants (see below) to form the 'backbone' of your garden planting. These structural ingredients will be medium and large evergreen plants – mostly shrubs, trees, conifers and bamboos. Due to the space they take up, structural plants need to have long-term appeal, so try to see beyond the immediate appeal of their flowers. Look for attributes such as handsome evergreen foliage, attractively shaped or coloured leaves, interesting bark or more than one season of interest – like spring flowers and autumn fruit.

a garden for all seasons

Ensuring that your garden looks good throughout the year is a balancing act between choosing large, 'backbone' plants and leaving enough room for infill plants that will provide a succession of colour. Decide first what to grow for winter and early spring interest, when there is a scarcity of plants looking their best. After selecting and placing them, choose plants for autumn, late spring and summer – in that order.

first things first

If your garden is big enough for trees, choose these first and take their shape into consideration – their many forms include columnar, upright, wide-spreading and weeping. Then decide on evergreen shrubs and conifers. These plants, which are wonderful for providing year-round structure and of great value in winter, should make up around one-third of all your medium-sized to large plants. Try not to increase that proportion, or the garden will start to appear static and boring. Include a few bold and architectural evergreens, with large or spiky leaves or a striking shape. Finally, incorporate deciduous shrubs with attractive foliage that looks its best from spring to autumn. These make a fantastic backdrop to a variety of different flowers.

When choosing and positioning your larger plants, take into account their eventual height and spread, and allow them room to fill out. Correctly spaced plants look very 'gappy' at first but will grow surprisingly quickly.

infill planting

Once you have positioned the key plants, move on to perennials, roses, small shrubs and ornamental grasses. A few should have long-lasting, attractive foliage, but many can give shorter, showier bursts of colour at different times of the year.

It generally works best to place the large plants towards the back of a border and grade down to the smaller ones at the front, but it pays to have an occasional tall plant at the front, if it has a light, airy habit, like giant oat grass (*Stipa gigantea*) or *Verbena bonariensis*.

Leave a few spaces for seasonal performers, those annuals and bedding plants that will bloom for months on end, at least until the end of summer.

key plants

• bamboos such as *Fargesia murielae* and *Phyllostachys* • *Berberis* • conifers: many of medium size such as *Juniperus scopulorum* 'Skyrocket', *Taxus baccata* 'Standishii' and *Thuja occidentalis* 'Rheingold' • *Cordyline* • *Cornus alba* varieties • hollies: *Ilex* x *altaclerensis* and *I. aquifolium* varieties • *Ligustrum ovalifolium* 'Aureum' • *Mahonia* • *Phormium* • *Rhamnus* • *Sambucus*: varieties with coloured leaves • viburnums such as *V.* x *burkwoodii*, *V. davidii* and *V. tinus*

Tall plants do not always have to go at the back. Here, *Salvia* x *superba*, *Leucanthemum* x *superbum* and red *Helenium autumnale* are seen through a foreground veil of *Verbena bonariensis*.

Plants are graded by height in this yellow border. In front of a shrub rose are *Phlomis longifolia, Potentilla recta, Helichrysum angustifolia* and *Linaria dalmatica.*

Sow hardy annuals, which are tolerant of frost, directly into the ground, and plant out tender perennials and half-hardy annuals once all danger of frost is past.

planting in layers

In a small garden or where you want to pack in more plants, maximise colour in the available space by 'layering' the different-sized plants in tiers. You might start with a tree like a birch or sorbus that casts only a light, dappled shade so that you can plant underneath it. There put in medium-sized shrubs that thrive in dappled shade, such as dogwoods (*Cornus alba* varieties), philadelphus and viburnums. Beneath these, plant a carpet of shade-tolerant perennials or plants at their best in winter or spring, before the large shrubs start to produce leaves. Suitable plants include vincas, epimediums, winter heathers (*Erica carnea*), hellebores and pulmonarias. Plant colourful spring bulbs in between.

using climbers

After several years, when the large plants are well established, it is possible to squeeze in more flowers by planting climbers to grow through these living supports. Choose them with care, as some vigorous climbers will overwhelm their hosts. Well-behaved climbers include large-flowered hybrid clematis, *C. viticella* varieties, the perennial pea (*Lathyrus latifolius*) and golden hop (*Humulus lupulus* 'Aureus'). In a very small garden with no room for trees, climbers are invaluable for bringing interest to walls and fences.

Shapely maples and hydrangeas endow this garden with form and structure, while the mophead flowers add colour in late summer.

using shape & texture

Given that flowers are a relatively short-lived occurrence in the yearly life of a plant, it pays to concentrate on getting the best combinations of plant shapes and foliage for your garden.

Shape and texture play a vital role in successful planting schemes, helping to guarantee the long-term interest of your borders. Not only does each plant have an overall shape, which can be distinctive, but individual leaves also differ greatly in size, shape and texture.

Putting together plants of contrasting shape will contribute enormously to the year-round good looks of your garden. Although a rounded habit is most common among plants, there are upright, weeping, wide-spreading and other different outlines. Strong outlines and bold foliage make 'architectural' plants that can provide a striking backdrop for flowers in any season, or, when carefully sited, establish a dramatic focal point.

architectural plants

Since architectural plants naturally draw attention to themselves, you will need to exercise care when placing them. It is preferable to position them near to the house or just a little way down the garden, where they will catch the eye before anything else. If you use such strong shapes in the distance, they will immediately draw the attention and make the intervening space appear smaller than it really is. Be wary of having too many bold plants in the garden as it could easily end up looking distracting and over-dramatic.

varied outlines

Since most plants have a rounded habit, it is all too easy to end up with an uninteresting border of bun-shaped bushes. If this has happened, simply take out a few of the dullest plants and replace them with plants of a spiky, vertical or low-growing habit.

changing shape

There are plants, not naturally architectural in habit, that can have form thrust upon them by being trimmed to a certain shape. This usually involves training, in particular the art of topiary, by which small-leaved plants such as box (*Buxus sempervirens*) are clipped into crisply defined shapes like spirals. Or it may simply involve pruning to give an amenable plant a little more shape and character than it would have if left to its own devices. For example, you can clip tall plants such as holly (*Ilex*), golden privet (*Ligustrum ovalifolium* 'Aureum') and Italian buckthorn (*Rhamnus alaternus* 'Argenteovariegata') into broad cones or pyramids, medium ones like *Lonicera nitida* 'Baggesen's Gold' into upright domes, and small shrubs like lavender and santolina into neat mounds.

focus on foliage

Take a close look at a random selection of leaves to see what variety there is in their size and shape alone, from the fine filigree leaves of artemisias and the slender ornamental grasses to the palmate, glossy, plate-sized leaves of *Fatsia japonica*. Moisture-loving plants for the edges of ponds and boggy soil have some of the largest leaves of all, such as the huge, dramatic *Gunnera manicata* and *Rheum palmatum*. Smaller but still of distinctive shape are hostas and ligularias.

Texture adds yet another facet to a planting. Soft-textured foliage is irresistible to the touch, as in the

dramatic plant shapes

VERTICAL • bamboos (many varieties including *Fargesia murieliae* and *Phyllostachys*) • *Crocosmia* • irises • ornamental grasses • plume poppy (*Macleaya cordata*)
NARROW AND UPRIGHT (FASTIGIATE) • *Berberis thunbergii* 'Helmond Pillar' • *Juniperus scopulorum* 'Skyrocket' • *Malus* 'Van Eseltine' • *Sorbus aucuparia* 'Fastigiata'
SPIKY • cordylines • new zealand flax (*Phormium tenax*) • yuccas
WEEPING OR ARCHING • japanese maples (*Acer palmatum* Dissectum varieties) • weeping crab apple (*Malus* 'Royal Beauty') • weeping purple beech (*Fagus sylvatica* 'Purpurea Pendula') • weeping purple willow (*Salix purpurea* 'Pendula')

New zealand flax (*Phormium tenax*)

In a bed in a large garden (right), the emphasis is on foliage. The blue-green lobes of the tall plume poppy contrast with the strap-shaped leaves of *Iris sibirica* and the bright green strands of the fern *Matteuccia struthiopteris*.

The globe-flowers of agapanthus add form and intense colour to the feathery plumes of *Stipa tenuissima* and the sword-like iris (below right).

The tall silver-leaved thistle (*Onopordum acanthium)* draws the eye among softer clumps of deep pink astilbes and airy, white-flowered gypsophila (below).

woolly leaves of lamb's ears (*Stachys byzantina*) or the shaggy mop shape of the little conifer *Chamaecyparis pisifera* 'Filifera Aurea'. If you place these close to paths and patios they are readily accessible for stroking as you pass.

special effects

Create lively effects by partnering delicate-looking leaves or flowers with large or coarsely textured foliage. For example, a hazy cloud of *Gypsophila paniculata* or thalictrum makes a dynamic contrast with the corrugated leaves of *Viburnum rhytidophyllum* or *V. davidii*. Conversely, place plants with big blooms like peonies and echinacea next to feathery-leaved purple fennel (*Foeniculum vulgare* 'Purpureum') and conifers with needle-like leaves. Growing large-flowered hybrid clematis, with their plate-sized blooms, through different shrubs makes an eye-catching contrast of shape as well as colour.

using colour

One of the joys of gardening is that it adds colour to our lives, and by planning the use of colour you can produce a garden to match your personal style, or create areas with entirely different atmospheres.

choosing a colour scheme

Creating distinct colour schemes will bring harmony to the garden and give a sense of cohesion to different areas. As the colours you choose are immensely personal, this can often be the most emphatic way of stamping your taste on the garden. Colour influences our moods and, depending on the colours we select and the way in which we put them together, a garden can vary from being restful and soothing to being upbeat and lively.

Colours fall into two main groups: strong and warm, and soft and cool. Strong colours, such as red, orange, bright yellow and purple, are dynamic, stepping up the tempo to create a sense of drama, excitement and exhilaration. By comparison, soft blues, mauves, pale yellows and pinks are calm and peaceful, blending gently into the surrounding landscape.

putting colours together

While the choice of colours is a personal matter, you need to exploit the way colours work together in order to achieve the best effects in your garden. One way to do this is with a design device known as the 'colour wheel', an aid to using different colours usually depicted in books on this subject.

Harmonious colours are those adjacent or close to each other in the spectrum, such as blue with green and violet. Contrasting colours – blue and orange, for example, or red and green – lie opposite each other on the wheel. When planning a colour scheme, decide whether you want the boldness of contrast or the softness of harmony and select planting partners accordingly.

the importance of foliage

Green, the most restful and essential of nature's colours, should be used in quantity as a 'buffer' between brighter-hued plants. There is also plenty of attractive and colourful foliage that can be chosen to tone in with the main colour scheme. You might put blue-grey and silver foliage with blue flowers, or lime-green leaves with yellow flowers.

effective colour schemes

The most successful schemes are often those based on simple yet striking colour combinations. Although single-colour borders such as white may sound attractive and sophisticated, such plantings are difficult to achieve and you may tire of them quickly. The following are examples of well-tried or dramatic combinations.

- red with green and creamy white
- red with yellow and lime-green
- yellow and blue
- yellow with orange and lime-green
- orange with blue
- blue with pink and silver
- blue with red and white
- purple with blue and silver
- white with yellow and pale blue
- white with purple and dark red

In a harmonious pink-themed planting, *Dahlia* 'Fascination', with its dark foliage, takes centre stage in front of *Achillea millefolium* 'Cerise Queen' and the spires of *Lythrum salicaria* 'Feuerkerze'.

In a soft colour scheme, the flat flowerheads of creamy achillea and the erect spires of foxtail lilies (*Eremurus* 'Cleopatra') are cloaked by a haze of the grass *Calamagrostis hortorum.*

light-reflecting plants for shady places

• *Arum italicum* subsp. *italicum* 'Marmoratum' • *Aucuba japonica* 'Crotonifolia' • *bergenia* • busy lizzie (*Impatiens*): varieties with pale flowers • Christmas box (*Sarcococca*) • clematis: varieties with pale flowers such as 'Nelly Moser'• *Daphne laureola* • *Euonymus fortunei* 'Emerald Gaiety', *E.* 'Emerald 'n' Gold' and *E.* 'Silver Queen' • *Fatsia japonica* • foxglove, white (*Digitalis purpurea* f. *albiflora*) • hellebores: *H. foetidus* and Lenten rose (*H. hybridus*) • *Iris foetidissima* var. *citrina* • ivies: with variegated leaves (*Hedera colchica* and *H. helix* varieties) • pulmonarias • spring bulbs including winter aconite (*Eranthis hyemalis*), snowdrops (*Galanthus*) and *Narcissus* • vincas: variegated varieties

creating illusions

You can use colour to fool the eye and create illusions of scale and distance. Bright colours appear to 'leap' forward, while cool ones recede and look farther away. To create a sense of distance in a small space, gather the bright, attention-seeking colours near the house and place pale ones farther away. Most effective of all is to plant the end of the garden with foliage in muted shades, such as blue-green or green tinged with purple, together with plants that have small flowers in soft shades. This will create the impression of a misty, subtle vista that disappears into the distance.

colour in bright light

Gardens that are in the sun for all or most of the day look best planted with flowers and foliage in vivid, bold hues, such as red, orange, purple or bright blue. When the sun is high in the sky and the light is bright and hard, light-coloured flowers and airy foliage would simply pale into insignificance.

lightening dark spaces

Gardens that receive little or no sun can be transformed by using plenty of pale flowers and variegated foliage to dispel the gloom. Evergreens with glossy, light-reflecting leaves are invaluable for cheering up a shady spot (see above). Pale flowers also look lovely in a garden used primarily in the evening, as they remain visible at dusk, long after all the other colours have disappeared from view.

The silvery foliage of the shapely weeping pear (*Pyrus salicifolia* 'Pendula') is echoed at its foot by other silver-leaved low shrubs.

designing a herb garden

Herbs are adaptable plants that will blend in almost anywhere, from a clump of fennel in a flower bed to a border edging of parsley or a pot of sweet cicely by the back door. But herbs are compelling plants, too, and you may soon find that you amass an expanding collection that deserves a garden setting of its own.

choosing a site

In assessing your garden to find the most suitable place for growing herbs, bear in mind the following points:

- **most herbs prefer heat and sun,** as they come from the Mediterranean. Heat concentrates their aromatic oils. Avoid planting in areas of deep shade.
- **shelter from cold** drying winds is vital, especially for evergreens. A hedge, fence or nearby shrubs will protect them.
- **good drainage** is important, so improve heavy ground with compost or leaf-mould, or make a raised bed to increase the depth of well-drained soil.
- **some herbs** are drought-tolerant but others prefer moist soil.
- **avoid frost pockets,** as damp, cold conditions can be lethal in winter, and overhanging deciduous trees can shed leaves and drip water onto plants.
- **for convenience,** position culinary herbs as near to the kitchen as possible.

themed herb gardens

There are so many herbs to choose from you might want to theme your collection. Here are some suggestions.

FRAGRANT GARDEN: include traditional strewing herbs such as rosemary, thyme and rue, aromatherapy plants like lavender, clary sage (*Salvia sclarea*) and roses, and bergamot or wild strawberries for pot pourri

MEDICINAL BORDER: include sage, valerian, feverfew and calendula

DYE GARDEN: include madder (red), agrimony (yellow), meadowsweet (black), rudbeckia (orange), woad (blue) and lily of the valley (green)

BEE GARDEN: include good flowering herbs such as bergamot, borage and lavender

choosing a style

Think about the herbs you would like to grow and how much space you can allocate to them. You can grow a few basic culinary varieties, such as parsley, sage, thyme, marjoram, savory and bay, in a small rectangular or circular bed up to 1.2m (4ft) wide; arrange the plants according to their heights (see opposite) as well as their soil requirements. A larger collection of herbs will require more planning.

formal herb gardens

These traditional gardens are based on symmetrical geometric shapes, such as squares, triangles or segments of a circle. Herb plants are organised in structured groups within the beds, separated by a pattern of paths in the classic potager, or divided by neatly clipped hedges in a knot garden. This kind of garden needs regular trimming to maintain its disciplined formality.

informal herb gardens

The plants in an informal herb garden are laid out in a relaxed, cottage-garden style, growing and spreading freely as they would in the wild. Although charming in appearance, this style of planting also needs careful planning and maintenance, to avoid a free-for-all of competitive, sometimes invasive plants.

In a scented herb garden based on a circular design, shrubby herbs such as rosemary, thyme and marjoram surround the stems of standard holly centrepieces. In the foreground, meadow plants such as annual poppies and biennial clary (*Salvia sclarea*) bring additional colour.

making a plan

Armed with a clear idea of the proposed layout, draw up a plan on graph paper. Mark in existing features, such as paths, walls or the full spread of a tree – these may need to be incorporated into the design and could affect the final layout. Scale is important, too: it is easy to assume that you have more space than actually exists, so measure the site carefully and use the same scale when adding details like paths to your plan.

To permit easy harvesting and maintenance, make sure that the beds are no more than 1–1.2m (3–4ft) wide, unless you can include stepping stones to give you access without treading on the soil. Try to arrange for frequently used herbs to be no more than 60–75cm (2ft–2ft 6in) from a path or a stepping stone. If you are edging beds with hedges of germander, box or a similar dwarf evergreen, mark in the space that these will occupy to show how much ground is left for planting.

A large pot of nicotiana (right) creates a focus in an informal cottage garden, where herbs including rosemary, rue, golden and purple sage, and thyme spill softly over the paving.

the role of paths

Paths divide beds into manageable units, establish the outline of a formal plan and encourage air circulation around plants, which helps to prevent disease. They need to be a realistic width, ranging from 30cm (12in) for occasional access to 1m (3ft) for main pathways where you might wish to use a wheelbarrow. This is not wasted space because the paths can be edged with rows of chives or sweet violets, or interplanted like an alpine pavement with spreading herbs, such as pennyroyal and creeping thymes.

plants for a herb bed

A herb bed is usually designed so that plants of similar height are gathered together in ranks, with the tallest at the back and the shortest at the front, as in a group photograph. In island beds, the tallest plants go in the centre.

TALL HERBS, 1m (3ft) or more
• angelica • bergamot • fennel • foxgloves • liquorice • lovage • meadowsweet • mullein • rosemary • sea holly • sweet cicely

HERBS FOR THE MIDDLE RANKS, 45cm–1m (18in–3ft) • agrimony • borage • bugloss • caraway • comfrey • curry plant • dill • lavender • lemon balm • rue • sage • santolina • tansy • tarragon • valerian

FRONT RANK AND EDGING HERBS, up to 45cm (18in) • anise • basil • calendula • chamomile • chervil • chives • clary • coriander • cumin • hyssop • marjoram • parsley • savory • sorrel • thyme

In a formally planned herb garden (below), the plants have been allowed to form clumps and to flower, following their natural inclination, to soften the hard edges.

building a herb garden

As soon as you are confident about the shape and style of your new herb garden, you can start constructing it. The best time to do this is in late summer or early autumn, when the weather is still warm enough for you to cultivate in comfort.

preparing the ground

Thorough ground preparation is especially important when constructing a herb garden: you may need to adjust the texture or acidity of the soil, and eliminate any weeds before planting to avoid difficulties later on.

If the ground has already been cultivated, start by marking out the overall shape with pegs and string. Fork over the soil to turn in annual weeds and remove perennials, such as docks, dandelions, bindweed and creeping buttercups. Loosen any deep-rooted weeds first, so that you can lift them out intact, and pick out any small root fragments that might regenerate.

Uncultivated and weed-infested ground will need more extensive preparation. Fork out any perennial weeds, then double-dig the whole bed (see Autumn); add well-rotted manure or garden compost below the topsoil as you go. If you do this in late summer or autumn, you can leave the soil to settle over winter and then plant in spring.

path materials

It is best to construct new paths before planting, using any excavated soil to raise the level of the beds. There are several suitable materials you can use.

- **paving stones** are expensive but quick to lay and hard-wearing, although they need a solid, level foundation. They suit formal, squared layouts and allow for prostrate herbs to be grown between them.
- **bricks** are perhaps the most attractive paving material, suitable for both formal and informal gardens.
- **coarse bark** may be laid in an 8cm (3in) layer over landscape fabric.
- **gravel** provides a hard-wearing surface that you can define with edging or allow to merge softly with edging plants (see Late Spring). Although a seedbed for weeds, gravel is ideal for planting informally with a range of small herbs.
- **grass** is inexpensive to lay and easy to maintain, but it is not an all-weather surface. It also requires edging, either with a hard material, such as bricks or timber boards, or with regular trimming.

Chamomile (above) forms the centre of a little-used brick path flanked by lavenders.

Part of a potager (left), a geometric bed with a bay tree in the middle, is filled with a mix of herbs, salad crops and flowers. Chives fill one bed, lemon balm is surrounded by marigolds and rue has an edging of lavender.

a herb wheel

A circular island bed of kitchen herbs is attractive and easy to make.

- Mark out a circle 2–2.5m (6–8ft) in diameter. Arrange an edging of frost-resistant tiles or bricks laid flat or wedged at an angle (see page 151).
- Divide the circle into four or eight with straight paths of stone slabs or bricks, leaving space in the centre to plant a rosemary or bay tree.
- Plant up the beds with basil, parsley, marjoram, sage, thyme, chives, chervil, rosemary and savory for a good selection.

herb lawns and seats

Certain creeping herbs can be used as a good-looking and fragrant alternative to grass for a small lawn or for transforming a raised bed into a perfumed seat. Traditional plants for this are pennyroyal, Corsican mint (*Mentha requienii*), creeping *Thymus serpyllum* varieties, such as 'Goldstream', 'Minimus' or 'Rainbow Falls', and the non-flowering chamomile 'Treneague'. Bear in mind that these herbs cannot withstand heavy traffic and need completely weed-free soil. Space chamomile 10cm (4in) apart, the other herbs 20cm (8in) apart.

planting a box-edged herb bed

YOU WILL NEED
• digging or border fork and spade
• well-rotted garden compost • rake
• trowel • dwarf box plants for edging • specimen centrepiece
• assorted herbs for filling in

1 Dig over the soil and fork plenty of well-rotted garden compost into the top layer. Rake level and firm by tamping the soil with the rake head.

2 Plant dwarf box plants 8–10cm (3–4in) in from the permanent boards edging the bed. Space them about 15cm (6in) apart, round all four sides.

3 Find the centre of the bed by marking where diagonal lines from the corners cross, and plant the centrepiece at the same level that it was growing previously.

4 Plot the positions of the remaining herbs by standing them out in their pots at least 10cm (4in) apart. Dig holes and plant each herb firmly. If planting in dry weather, water the whole bed afterwards.

before planting

• **carry out a soil test** with a simple pH kit. If the reading is 6.5 or below, which indicates acid soil, fork a dressing of garden lime into the top 10cm (4in) of the soil. Repeat every two to three years.

• **improve the drainage of clay** soils by incorporating plenty of garden compost, and add lime to the surface in autumn. The compost will aerate and open up the structure, and the lime will help to reduce stickiness. Prepare individual planting areas with plenty of sharp sand or grit. Check the drainage: if the ground stays very wet after rain, consider making a raised bed.

• **sandy soils** can be hungry and will dry out fast in summer, so work in liberal amounts of well-rotted garden compost where you will grow leaf and salad herbs. After planting apply a bark or gravel mulch to conserve moisture.

The square and rectangular beds are laid in a cruciform pattern, separated by 60cm (2ft) wide paths covered with coarse bark. Treated 10cm (4in) timber boards keep the soil in place.

herbs in containers

Many herbs are drought-tolerant and so are ideal for growing in containers: this is the perfect solution if you have difficult soil or insufficient growing space. Grouped together, decorative pots make an eye-catching feature.

A really large container (above) will support a collection of herbs to give aromatic pickings for the kitchen. This pot holds thymes, curry plant and a small bay tree.

Individually pot-grown herbs – rosemary, parsley, thyme and mint – look pretty lining the sides of a flight of steps (left).

care guide

SPRING: trim off old and frosted growth • pot on or divide large plants • top-dress large containers by replacing the top 5cm (2in) with fresh compost • increase watering • top up mulches

SUMMER: water if necessary and feed occasionally • move plants into sun or shade, according to needs • harvest regularly

AUTUMN: reduce watering and stop feeding • trim perennial herbs • move tender varieties indoors, together with those still being harvested

WINTER: gather containers into large groups in a sheltered place, and insulate against frost • water only enough to keep the compost barely moist

advantages of pot culture

- **mobility** You can position kitchen herbs near the house for easy access during the picking season, and move them around the garden as the seasons change, to follow the sun or protect them from cold winds and frost.
- **restraint** You can control the root growth of mint, tarragon and similar spreading herbs, which are potentially invasive in the open ground.
- **individuality** It is easy to treat plants that need special conditions (for example, more or less water, frequent feeding or lime-free compost) separately from other herbs.
- **creativity** You are free to assemble and change groupings at will, moving individual plants out of sight when they are past their ornamental best.

practical considerations

The choice of container is a personal one, but you should always set practical criteria above appearances to ensure healthy growth.

- **make sure that drainage** is adequate, with at least one large hole at the base of the container covered with a layer of stones, gravel or crocks (broken flowerpots).
- **containers must be big enough** to accommodate plants comfortably.
- **stability is important** outdoors. Use wide containers and soil-based compost for taller herbs to prevent them from toppling over in the wind. Select deep pots for tap-rooted plants, such as fennel and lovage.
- **try to match the container** to the type of plant. Decorative herbaceous herbs look good in terracotta, while tubs or wooden Versailles boxes suit formal

shrubs like rosemary or a topiary bay tree. Confine invasive herbs like mint to utilitarian containers such as bottomless buckets or large paint cans.

- **if you are grouping** different herbs in one container, try to match their feeding and watering requirements, and their growth rates, to avoid problems caused by strongly rooting herbs like lemon balm infiltrating less vigorous, mat-forming herbs such as thyme.

regional cooking with herbs

Some herbs are typical of certain cuisines, and make all the difference in achieving an authentic flavour. Plant your pots to supply your favourite herbs for use in cooking.

FRENCH: bay, chervil, fennel, parsley, tarragon, thyme

GREEK: cumin, dill, marjoram, mint, oregano, parsley

ITALIAN: basil, bay, oregano, flat-leaved parsley, sage

MIDDLE EASTERN: basil, coriander, cumin, dill, fennel, marjoram, mint, parsley, rosemary, sage, thyme

NORTH AFRICAN: anise, caraway, coriander, chives, cumin, fenugreek, lavender, mint

NORTH EUROPEAN: bay, dill, fennel, horseradish, parsley, sorrel, tarragon, thyme

choosing containers

You can grow a complete collection of herbs in large containers such as half-barrels, stone sinks and wooden troughs or window boxes. If you have less space, gather together compact or creeping herbs in a strawberry barrel or herb pot equipped with several planting pockets.

window boxes

These are ideal for smaller herbs. Make sure that the box is well secured, supported on strong brackets, and that there is enough depth for a good root-run; about 20–25cm (8–10in) is suitable for most plants.

For a continuous harvest, grow herbs individually in 10cm (4in) plastic pots, plunging these to their rims in the window box compost. When they are exhausted, you can replace them with other pots of the same herb grown on elsewhere. Include larger herbs such as rosemary and bay, rooted as cuttings in small pots, until they outgrow the box.

sinks and troughs

These are large enough to contain a basic range of herbs or a collection of dwarf species. For efficient drainage, raise the container off the ground on tiles, pieces of slate or decorative wedges, and spread a 5cm (2in) layer of gravel or pebbles in the bottom before filling to the rim with soil-based compost. Plunge in a trowel repeatedly to settle the contents. Mulch after planting with a decorative finish such as stone chippings, to allow free drainage and to conserve moisture.

hanging baskets

Many herbs will grow happily in hanging baskets (see below). To allow enough space for healthy root growth, you need a minimum size basket of 35cm (14in) diameter. Fit it with a liner and fill with soil-less compost to which you have added water-retaining granules, to prevent rapid drying out. Check for watering needs at least once a day during hot weather, and feed the hanging basket with a general liquid fertiliser every 10–14 days.

planting a herb window box

1 **Make sure there are drainage holes** in the base of the box and cover these with broken crocks. Fill to within 5cm (2in) of the top with soil-based compost, then plant the herbs.

2 **Leave enough space** around each plant for it to grow and thicken up. Small-leaved plants like marjoram can be clipped into a dome.

herbs and edible flowers for hanging baskets

- alpine strawberries • basil
- chamomile • chives • compact and golden marjoram • creeping thymes
- pennyroyal • pineapple mint
- low-growing rosemary such as Prostratus Group • prostrate savory (*Satureja spicigera*) • scented-leaved pelargoniums • sweet violets
- trailing nasturtiums

moving water features

Running water brings its own special magic to a garden. It provides interest, sound and light and promotes an air of tranquillity, as well as attracting birds and a variety of animals.

designing a water feature

Features that rely on moving water can be used to create different effects. They include streams, rills, canals and chutes as well as fountains, waterfalls and cascades. There are also smaller features like bubble or millstone fountains, brimming urns and Japanese deer scarers. Whether they form the central theme of a garden design or are simply an embellishment, they must always be in proportion and in keeping with the rest of the garden.

A long, slim water feature, such as a narrow waterfall or a rill (see pages 138–9), may be used to draw attention to the source of the flow, whereas a broad expanse of water can itself be the central part of the design and create a mirror effect. A fountain with a high narrow jet will direct the eye skywards, while a lower, multi-headed fountain will draw the eye down to the patterns formed on the water below. When active, these features bring sound to the garden and attract attention.

fountains

A fountain is a jet of water pumped under pressure through a head or nozzle to give a spray; and spray patterns can be varied by fitting nozzles of different designs. The height of the jet depends on the capacity of the pump. To avoid water loss caused by spray splashing over the sides, the jet of water should ideally not reach higher than the distance equal to half the width of the pond or reservoir. The higher the operating pressure and the finer the water droplet size, the greater is the chance of water drifting in the wind.

waterfalls and watercourses

Most of these features rely on gravity to achieve their effect, with water flowing down a planned route through a formal or informal setting. The source of water will normally originate from some form of reservoir and it is recycled via a pump to run through the watercourse. The speed at which the water runs is determined by the flow rate of the pump and the arrangement of pools and waterfalls along the sloping watercourse.

A stream built to soften the formality of a garden room is bordered by hedges. Lining the banks are moisture-loving plants, including rodgersias and astilbes.

keeping the water moving

Most moving water features rely on a pump. This is to circulate the water, which has to be moved from the reservoir where it is collected and held – usually at the lowest point – up to the highest point. From there the water either flows back down as a stream or rill, or is pushed out as a fountain.

The pump, operated by an electric motor, draws the water through a filter and forces it through an outlet fitted with an adjuster to regulate flow rate and pressure. Pumps fall into two broad categories:

- **submersible pumps** are positioned underwater, usually within the water feature itself, hidden from view. They push the water to the point where it will be discharged. They are simple to install and quiet in operation.
- **surface pumps** are protected by well-ventilated housings and their only contact with water is through the pipework. They are usually larger, more powerful and often much more noisy than submersible pumps. They are also more expensive to run.

 tip

Young children are naturally drawn to water features, so safety has to be a major consideration. A mesh fence up to 60cm (2ft) in height will keep young children away from a watercourse, while ponds can be made safe by fixing strong, plastic-covered metal mesh or a metal grill just below the water surface. If in any doubt, do not install a watercourse or a pond where children under five will be either using or visiting the garden.

A tiered fountain plays over pebbles (left). Ornamental grasses include *Pennisetum, Festuca glauca* and *Carex* 'Frosted Curls'.

Water sheets through a slit into a raised pool (below), constantly circulated by a submersible pump.

selecting a pump

The choice of pump for a water feature will depend on a number of factors. Its output capacity – that is, the amount of water it can move per hour over a certain height – must be sufficient for the job; your supplier will advise you. The following factors all need to be taken into consideration:

- **the dimensions** of the water feature.
- **the type of outlet feature** planned: fountain, watercourse or waterfall.
- **for a fountain,** the height of the jet.
- **for a watercourse,** the distance the water will have to be pumped and the diameter of pipe used.
- **whether the pump** will run continuously or intermittently.

pump maintenance

Although most modern submersible pumps need little regular maintenance, they should be lifted out of the pond at least once a year in order to clean the filter and check the casing and cables for cracks and splits. If the water is less than 30cm (12in) deep, the pump must be removed before winter, dried out and stored in a dry place until spring. Otherwise the pump housing might split if the water freezes.

Few aquatic plants like fast-moving water, so position them where the water is calmest and always well away from playing fountains.

rates of flow

For moving water, a pump should have sufficient output capacity to give the right flow rate for the feature in question. A small feature like a pebble fountain requires a flow rate of 450 litres an hour; large features, such as a display fountain, need 650 litres an hour; and waterfalls require at least 950 litres an hour.

watercourses

A watercourse can vary from a simple straight rill or meandering stream to a more sophisticated course involving different levels and falling water. Whatever kind of watercourse you choose, the attraction always has to be the water and its movement, whether it is rushing along or moving slowly.

natural-looking streams

A natural stream running through a garden is a rare asset, but it is possible to create a self-contained watercourse and keep the water moving with the help of a pump. The channel should look as natural as possible: avoid making it too winding or too intricate, as this would appear contrived and spoil the effect. The water storage area can be placed at either the top or the bottom of a watercourse, but it must be of sufficient capacity to prevent a discernible drop in water level when the pump is started and avoid the need for constant topping up in hot weather.

The contours of your garden will determine the line and flow of a stream. On a steeply sloping site the water will flow more rapidly, so a larger pump will be required to maintain a continuous supply. Or you could incorporate a number of areas where the water flow will be restricted. These may take the form of pools or changes in direction, which act as collection points and check the water flow for a short while. Varying the depth and size of the pools will help to create a more natural appearance.

reproducing a stream

A stream can be constructed in much the same way as a pond by using a flexible liner (see Late Spring), but this will need to be cut into strips. Always start at the bottom of the stream and work up to the top. The strips can be stuck together with a mastic-type glue, but since every join is a potential leakage point, try to minimise the number of joins by cutting the liner into lengths that fit the spaces between the pools. When joining strips of flexible liner, make sure that the upper strip always overlaps the lower one by at least 75mm (3in).

After digging out the channel for a stream (as for the rill, see opposite), line it with damp sand, liner underlay or loft insulation to prevent the liner from being punctured by stones. Then lay the liner before carefully placing any large rocks or stones around the edge of the pool.

rills and canals

A rill is a shallow channel of slowly running water, narrow enough to step over and constructed to provide a reflective element within the garden. The feature originates in eastern cultures and has a symbolic place in Islamic gardens where it is intended to create a sense of peace and tranquillity. Usually geometric in shape, it is often designed to fit into a formal setting and may mirror nearby planting. In its simplest form, it suits small urban gardens and city courtyards. A rill can be made more interesting if the water runs along a series of level planes, the falls in level being emphasised by incorporating steps over which the water flows down from one level to the next. This is more complicated to construct, however.

The linear nature of a rill in itself suggests movement, which means that large volumes of water are not needed. A shallow rill, for instance, can consist of a slick of water not much more than 2–3cm (1in) deep, constantly moving over the liner, but a depth of 8–10cm (3–4in) is more usual. A deeper rill, or a canal, holds continually flowing water that is 15–30cm (6–12in) deep. When constructing a rill, remember that the top surface of the edging needs to end up at the same level as the existing surface – of soil, gravel or paving – in the rest of the garden. Take this into account when excavating and checking the levels.

The sound of a watercourse, which is one of its attractions, is dependent on the distance the water has to fall from one level to the next. Water falling onto another body of water makes the loudest noise.

In this stepped rill with a fountain at one end, a lip at the edge of each section allows the water level to build up slightly before it spills over and down onto the next level.

constructing a rill

YOU WILL NEED • string and pegs for marking out • spade • spirit level • soft sand • tamping tool or rammer • flexible liner • submersible pump • black flexible pipe, the length of the rill plus 45cm (18in) • reservoir tank (a 30 litre (6½ gallon) plastic header tank measuring 45 x 37 x 35cm/18 x 16 x 14in is ideal for most situations) • paving slabs or bricks • gravel, stones or slate chips • mesh grating, cut to the size of the reservoir • cobbles or pebbles to disguise grating

1 **If necessary, remove** the existing surface – turf, gravel or paving – to expose the soil. Mark out the width and course of the rill and its edging using string lines and wooden pegs or canes. Dig to the correct depth for the edging, then make a trench 10–15cm (4–6in) deeper for the rill. Rake the soil at the base roughly to level it, then compact the base with a rammer. Using a spirit level, add or remove soil to equalise the level along the length of the trench.

2 **Cover the base of the trench** with a 2–3cm (1in) layer of soft sand and compact it down to about 2cm (¾in), using a rammer, until it is firm and level.

3 **At the bottom end of the rill,** dig a hole large enough to accommodate the reservoir tank. Make the hole approximately 5cm (2in) longer and deeper than the header tank and about 45cm (18in) deep. Sink the tank into the hole until its rim is level with the base of the trench. Fill in any gaps around the tank with loose soil and pack it firmly into place.

4 **Place the waterproof liner** in the trench, leaving about 45cm (18in) protruding from each narrow end. Press down well to ensure that the liner is in close contact with the base and sides. Bring the surplus up either side of the trench, and at top narrow end, and lay it on the soil surface. Cut the surplus to leave about 10cm (4in), which will later be hidden under a paved edge. Lay the other end of the liner over the edge of the tank and fold the edge under, to direct water into the reservoir.

5 **Lay paving slabs** or bricks as an edging along both sides and the top narrow end of the trench, trapping the liner between soil and paving. Use a mix of one part cement to four parts sand to form a layer of mortar 2–3cm (1in) thick, and bed the slabs onto this; use this mixture to fill the joints.

With cobbles in place (right), the water appears to gurgle down into a 'hole' in the ground.

6 **Lay out the flexible pipe,** positioning it along one side of the trench, then place the submersible pump into the reservoir tank. Trim the flexible pipe to the correct length with a sharp knife before fitting one end onto the pump's outlet. Run the supply cable from the pump to its transformer, which should be housed in a dry and sheltered position.

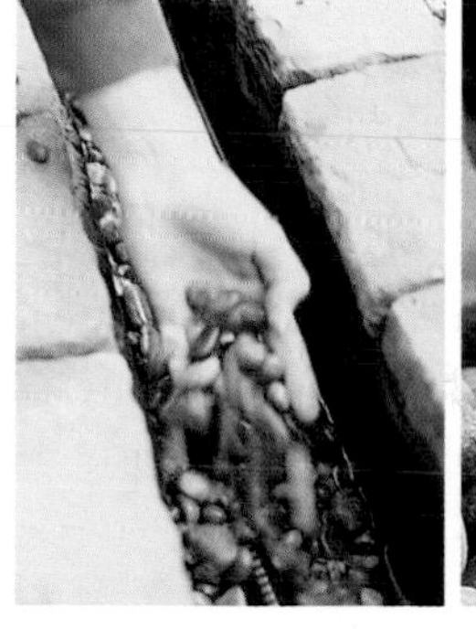

7 **Cover the base of the rill** with a layer of gravel, stones or slate chips. Lay the mesh grating over the reservoir and cover it with cobbles to hide the tank.

waterfalls & cascades

Water can be directed to spill over almost any surface to provide both visual and audible attractions in a garden. The style of waterfall should be chosen to fit the situation and can consist of a single fall or several linked together to form a cascade. A high, narrow fall draws the eye upwards, while a broad, low fall will create a feeling of width.

installing a waterfall over a retaining wall

YOU WILL NEED: club hammer and bolster chisel • flexible liner for top pool • flexible liner or small plastic header tank of 22 litres/5 gallons capacity for bottom pool • liner underlay • spillstone • submersible pump • flexible pipe • spade • spirit level • sharp knife or scissors • waterproof mastic • bricks for edging • sand and cement • gravel for surround • slate chips or small stones to disguise liner

1 **Dig a hole** about 5cm (2in) bigger than the tank you are using just behind the retaining wall, to accommodate the header pool. Check the edges are level.

2 **Using a club hammer** and bolster chisel, remove a brick or two from the top of the wall to form an opening for the water to flow through from the header pool.

3 **Line the hole** with a piece of underlay (to prevent the flexible liner from being punctured by stones), then cover with flexible pond liner. There should be an overlap of at least 10cm (4in) around the edge of the hole.

4 **Lay out the flexible pipe,** running it behind the wall. At the front of the wall, it is laid under the paving slabs and at the back of the wall it is buried, apart from the section that runs into the header pool.

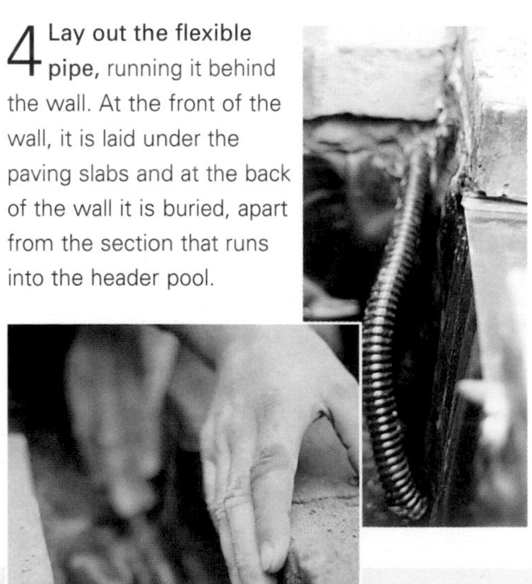

5 **Apply waterproof mastic** to the top of the wall where the brick was removed in step 2. Fold one edge of the liner over this opening and press it onto the mastic, then apply more mastic onto the liner before positioning the spillstone – in this case, a rigid sheet of stainless steel – across the opening. Check the level.

6 **Fold the edges** of the liner onto the soil before part-filling the pool with water to settle the liner. Then lay a course of bricks around the rim of the header pool to hide the liner and hold it in place. Using a mixture of one part cement to four parts sand, spread a mortar layer 2–5cm (1–2in) thick onto which to bed the bricks. Use this mixture to fill the joints between the bricks. A layer of gravel finishes the area round the pool.

7 **At the base** of the wall, dig out another hole about 45cm (18in) long and wide and at least 45cm (18in) deep or big enough to accommodate the footer tank. You may need to remove paving stones to do this.

8 **Line the hole** with flexible liner, or a rigid tank, to form the base pool or reservoir. If a rigid tank is used, make sure that the rim is level. With flexible liner, fold the edges over at the top, as in step 6; they will be covered by paving.

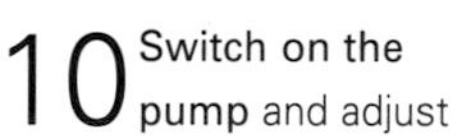

9 **Install the pump** in the base pool and attach the flexible pipe to its outlet. Fill the base pool with water and top up the header pool.

10 **Switch on the pump** and adjust the pump's flow rate (see right) until it reaches the desired level, after positioning the spillstone as described in step 5. Finish with paving stones around the lower pool and slate chips or small stones to disguise the liner at the back of the wall.

An even flow of water depends on the stainless steel 'spillstone' being completely level.

how a waterfall works

A simple waterfall has four components:

- two pools or reservoirs, one at the head of the fall and the other at the foot
- a spillstone – the large, flat surface or 'lip' over which the water falls
- a submersible pump with a flexible pipe to return water to the top of the waterfall.

The water in the header pool is initially held back by the spillstone until the level in the header pool rises and spills over it to create the fall – the wider the spillstone, the wider the curtain of water. At the bottom of the fall the water is collected in the second pool or reservoir, where it is pumped back up to the header pool. You can increase the splashing sound of a waterfall by placing the spillstone so that it juts out over the water below. It is easiest to create a waterfall where there is already a vertical drop from one level to another. This may be an existing feature of the garden, like a retaining wall, which would be enhanced by the introduction of moving water.

flow rates for waterfalls

Choose a pump with the correct output capacity (see page 137). The wider the fall, the greater the flow needed to feed it. A 2–3cm (1in) wide waterfall takes about 270 litres (60 gallons) of water per hour. For every extra 2–3cm (1in) width, an increased flow rate of about 270 litres (60 gallons) per hour is required.

cascades

On sloping ground several waterfalls can be linked to create a cascade, with water falling from one level to the next as a series of short falls rather than one continuous sheet. These may be designed as a series of steps, linked by a stream or other watercourse. As well as providing a visual focus, cascades create a splashing sound, useful to counter background noise such as the hum of traffic.

The easiest way to make a cascade is to use the construction technique for building a stream using flexible liner (see page 138). Start from the bottom of the watercourse and work up to the top.

designing front gardens

First impressions really do count, yet the front garden is all too often the poor relation of the back, where we spend much more of our time. However, an attractive and well-planned front garden is a real asset, giving a warm and welcoming face to your home.

finding the right style

Whatever the size of garden, try to match its style to that of the house. A smart town house calls for a neat, formal garden with a symmetrical layout, containing low clipped hedges and strongly architectural plants. On an estate of modern houses, the planting can be more informal, but still within a structured design. By contrast, a country cottage demands an informal and colourful style, with lots of flowers and low-growing plants spilling out onto curving paths.

If you are not sure where to start, walk round the houses in your area and see how your neighbours have tackled their plots. Then browse through some well-illustrated gardening books to see how you might develop ideas you like.

Paving slabs (left above) make 'stepping stones' through an attractive bed of cobbles, leading from the gate to the front door.

In a tiny city front garden topiary box and gravel keep the formal design uncluttered.

a path to the door

The path is usually the main element of a front garden. Be sure to make it wide enough – the minimum practical width is 60cm (2ft), but it will need to be 1–1.2m (3–4ft) wide if plants spill over the edges.

The wide range of materials for paths includes tiles, paving slabs and brick paviors. If possible, choose materials that echo the colour of the house in order to create a harmonious impression, or at least make sure the colours will not clash. The surface must be reasonably smooth for easy walking, so avoid any lumpy material such as cobbles. But very smooth surfaces such as stone and concrete slabs are unsuitable, as they become dangerously slippery in the wet.

Design the path to take a reasonably direct route to the front door, although it need not be an absolutely straight line. Make it diagonal or slightly angled in a formal garden, or curving in an informal design. Avoid making the angles or curves too severe, as visitors will then ignore the path and simply take the shortest route to the front door.

the practicalities

All paths must have a firm foundation of hardcore that has been packed down with a plate vibrator to a thickness of 80mm (3in). Add a 5cm (2in) layer of sand if using paviors, or a 2.5cm (1in) layer of mortar for slabs or tiles. When laying the path, check for levels: take care to avoid leaving any dips where water could lie and form dangerous icy patches in winter.

front garden storage

The front garden often has to fulfil a practical role by providing convenient storage for rubbish bins and bicycles. Tuck unsightly bins behind a screen made of trellis clothed with plants or ready-made ones of willow or bamboo, but make sure they are no higher than necessary, so that they do not call attention to themselves. As well as protection from the weather, bicycles also need secure storage – a low, wooden or metal shed is the best solution.

Planting pockets have been left in an expanse of paving so that low-growing shrubs such as sedums and lavenders can soften its edges.

design ideas

- **unless your front garden** is large, cut down on maintenance by doing away with a lawn. Replace it with a hard surface, such as paving slabs, brick paviors, stone setts, gravel, stone chippings or glass 'gravel'.
- **combine two or three** different hard materials for maximum interest. For example, surround gravel with edging tiles or bricks, or intersperse paving with sections of stone chippings and plants.
- **make a boundary fence** an open design so that the garden can be partially seen from the outside. This will create a welcoming impression, unlike a solid fence, which looks distinctly unfriendly. Open designs are better from a security point of view, too.
- **make the gate** the same height as the boundary fence or wall. Fix a self-closing spring so that it shuts automatically if you have small children or pets that must be kept in.
- **a pair of well-planted containers** flanking the doorway always looks attractive and welcoming. Either choose permanent plants for all-year structure or go for changing displays of seasonal flowers, from bulbs to summer bedding.
- **add interest at eye level** with hanging baskets, wall pots and climbing plants.
- **in very small gardens,** keep the colours low-key to avoid foreshortening distances and making the space look even smaller.
- **choose climbing plants** to contrast with the colour of the house wall: pale flowers and foliage against red brick, for example, and deep, rich colours on white paintwork or pale stone.

A rose tumbles over a white-painted picket fence in a classically welcoming front garden.

easy-care planting

The front garden, unlike the back, is on permanent public display, so it is crucial to have a high proportion of plants that perform well for as much of the year as possible and which involve minimal maintenance.

matching plants to site

Nowhere is more demanding of easy-care and year-round solutions than the front garden. Much can be achieved by using structural evergreens and enlivening them with small shrubs, roses, herbaceous perennials and ornamental grasses. Before choosing which plants to grow, assess the growing conditions. The influence of the building itself often results in extremes of shade or hot sun. If there is heavy traffic close by, take this into account too.

The plants listed in the boxes opposite have been divided according to their preference for shade, partial shade and full sun. Key plants give structure, colour and interest for most or all of the year. The smaller infill plants go between or in front of the larger plants. Edging plants are neat growers that will not spread vigorously underfoot and will perform well for a length of time.

All the plants in this gravel garden (above) are sun-loving species and many have interesting year-round foliage, including hebes, dwarf conifers, dwarf bamboos and yucca.

noise and pollution

If your front garden adjoins a busy road, you can use plants to help mitigate traffic noise and pollution. Where space permits, have a tall, densely planted border or hedge of tough evergreens, such as holly (*Ilex*), laurel (*Prunus laurocerasus*), western red cedar (*Thuja plicata* 'Atrovirens') or *Viburnum rhytidophyllum*, to absorb some of the sound and dirt. Trees with dense foliage, such as varieties of *Acer platanoides*, *A. pseudoplatanus* and *Sorbus aria*, will also help to block out noise. Give these plants an occasional and thorough rinse with a hose to prevent thick deposits of grime from building up on the leaves.

exposed gardens

Plants in a coastal situation, or in a city where they are likely to be showered with salt from treated roads in winter, must be exceptionally tough or be shielded from the worst of the salt spray by a low fence. The most resilient plants for exposed sites are sea buckthorn (*Hippophae rhamnoides*), wayfaring tree (*Viburnum lantana*), guelder rose (*V. opulus*) and sweet briar (*Rosa rubiginosa*).

A simple planting of dome-shaped hebes and ground-covering *Geranium macrorrhizum* 'Ingwersen's Variety' (below) is an easy, low-maintenance solution for a front garden.

easy-care plants for partial shade

When the garden receives sun for part of the day, the range of plants to choose from widens considerably. You can also add plants for shade in such a garden.

KEY PLANTS • *Acer palmatum* varieties • bamboos • box (*Buxus*) • *Cornus alba* varieties with coloured or variegated leaves • *Elaeagnus* x *ebbingei* • hollies (*Ilex* varieties) • *Osmanthus* x *burkwoodii* and *O. decorus* • *Photinia* x *fraseri* 'Red Robin' • *Phyllostachys aurea* and *P. nigra* • *Viburnum davidii* • yews (*Taxus*)

INFILL PLANTS • *Berberis candidula* and *B. verruculosa* • *Deschampsia cespitosa* • geraniums (all but dwarf species and varieties) • *Hakonechloa macra* 'Aureola' • *Philadelphus* 'Manteau d'Hermine' • *Potentilla fruticosa* varieties

EDGING PLANTS • *Carex oshimensis* 'Evergold' • heathers (*Erica carnea* varieties) • *Heuchera* varieties • *Ophiopogon planiscapus* 'Nigrescens'

CLIMBERS AND WALL SHRUBS • *Clematis:* large-flowered hybrids with flowers in all but the deepest or brightest shades • golden hop (*Humulus lupulus* 'Aureus') • *Jasminum officinale* and varieties • *Parthenocissus henryana*

Cornus alba

Fargesia murielae

easy-care plants for shade

While there are few bright flowers to be found among shade-loving plants, there is plenty of colour and interest from a wealth of attractive foliage as well as many delicately coloured blooms.

KEY PLANTS • *Aucuba japonica* 'Crotonifolia' and *A. japonica* 'Variegata' • bamboos (*Fargesia murielae*) • camellias (acid soil only) • *Fatsia japonica* • *Mahonia* • rhododendrons (acid soil only) • privet (*Ligustrum ovalifolium* 'Aureum')

INFILL PLANTS • *Acanthus mollis* • *Daphne laureola* • *Dryopteris filix-mas* • *Helleborus foetidus* • pulmonarias • *Sarcococca* • *Skimmia*

EDGING PLANTS • *Alchemilla mollis* • *Bergenia* • *Euonymus fortunei* varieties • *Pachysandra* • *Vinca minor* varieties

CLIMBERS AND WALL SHRUBS • *Chaenomeles* • *Clematis alpina* and *C. macropetala* varieties • *Hydrangea anomala* subsp. *petiolaris* • ivies with decorative or variegated leaves (*Hedera* varieties) • winter jasmine (*Jasminum nudiflorum*)

easy-care plants for full sun

A front garden that gets the sun all day needs real sun-lovers to cope with the hot conditions, which will be intensified by the storage-heater effect of brick or stone walls. Take full advantage of this by growing some plants that are on the borderline of hardiness and will relish the extra warmth and protection.

KEY PLANTS • *Choisya* • *Cordyline australis* varieties • *Elaeagnus pungens* 'Maculata' • *Laurus nobilis* • *Phormium cookianum* and *P. tenax* varieties • *Rhamnus alaternus* 'Argenteovariegata' • *Yucca filamentosa*

INFILL PLANTS • *Daphne odora* 'Aureomarginata' • hebes • junipers: low-growing types such as varieties of *Juniperus communis* and *J. horizontalis* • *Olearia* x *haastii* • *Pennisetum* species and varieties • roses: repeat-flowering compact bush and ground-cover varieties • *Stipa tenuissima*

EDGING PLANTS • *Euphorbia myrsinites* • *Festuca glauca* • *Gaura lindheimeri* varieties • *Helianthemum* varieties • lavenders • *Santolina* • *Stachys byzantina* • thymes

CLIMBERS AND WALL SHRUBS • *Ceanothus* (except low-growing varieties) • *Fremontodendron* 'California Glory' • *Magnolia grandiflora* • *Passiflora caerulea* • *Trachelospermum*

Magnolia grandiflora

changes of level

Uneven ground in a garden can often be used to introduce interesting features, while a sloping garden provides opportunities for creating dramatic effects – all you need to do is make minor adjustments to the levels.

steps in a slope

A flight of wide, shallow steps meandering up and across a gradual slope can be a pleasing sight. For a steeper slope, there are several possibilities. You might opt for a staircase effect, but another solution would be to introduce short flights of steps and separate these with a series of level 'landings'; the flights could enter and leave each landing in varying directions. Or you could create terraces across the full width of the slope, with their own beds, borders and areas of garden, linked at different points by short flights of steps.

materials for steps

Various types of material are suitable for making steps, but the surface should ideally be slightly rough or roughened to provide good grip in wet weather.

- **timber** has increased in popularity as a garden flooring material for decking, walkways and steps. In an informal garden, log steps make an attractive and practical feature (see page 148). They can be used as risers, retaining the backfill material (usually hardcore or gravel) that forms the tread of each step. Wooden posts driven into the ground in front of the logs will hold them in place. To keep the steps as even in height as possible, select logs of fairly uniform size. Log cross-sections can also be set into a slope so that the exposed grain forms the tread, while the side (with or without bark) forms the riser.
- **railway sleepers** make excellent steps, either used whole or cut into sections. Their proportions are ideal for both the tread and riser of a step.
- **paving slabs** made from concrete or stone are ideal for steps. Large slabs are best as they cover a bigger surface area, which makes them more stable and less likely to settle or tip. Stone blocks or bricks are most commonly used as risers with paving slab treads.
- **concrete** is a very resilient, if not particularly attractive, material and can be used to make steps in a wide range of shapes and sizes. Usually, some type of formwork, or shuttering, must be constructed to hold the wet concrete in place after it is poured and until it has set and cured. Make concrete more interesting and attractive by brushing its surface while still damp to expose the aggregate. Use a stiff brush.
- **bricks and paviors** can be used for treads and/or risers and offer a wide range of textures and colours. Bricks need careful thought as a material for steps. As they are about 21cm (8½in) long, 10cm (4in) wide and 6.5cm (2½in) deep, each step tread must be at least one brick's length plus one width deep to make a safe minimum tread (see page 148).
- **slate** is sometimes used for making steps as it has a very attractive surface. However, it may become slippery when wet, so use this material with caution.
- **compacted soil** can be used for steps but it is really only a short-term solution, as the soil will soon erode and cannot survive heavy traffic. Simply cut the steps into the slope – you may need to re-cut them frequently. If you bed a timber riser into the front of each step, this will reduce the amount of erosion.

SAFETY TIP Wooden surfaces can be slippery when wet. Nail chicken wire over timber steps to provide extra grip.

In a small formal garden on two levels (right), the flight of brick steps is broken by a landing halfway up, paved in a herringbone pattern for contrast.

Suiting their informal rural setting, these curved steps (far right) are constructed of gravel and old railway sleepers, with plants spilling over them.

The shallow steps (below) are made up of a row of bricks laid lengthways and one laid widthways to achieve a comfortable depth of tread. Wooden sleepers edge the steps and form the risers.

changes of level/2

constructing steps

Steps are comprised of risers (the vertical sections) and treads (the horizontal parts you step on). For safety and comfort risers should be 8–18cm (3–7in), while the depth of a tread should never be less than 30cm (12in). Make sure their dimensions are not so large that they dominate the garden.

It is important to keep the steps as uniform in size as possible. To work out exactly how many steps you require you need to measure the height and length of the slope and divide this by the dimensions of the steps (see opposite). To check your calculations, mark out the position and route of the steps and roughly dig out the soil to see how they fit.

rustic steps

In an informal setting, where brick, concrete or stone steps can look out of place, wooden steps may be a solution. These are simply made by cutting into the bank and building the flight of steps over the existing contours of the land. Logs – either single thick ones or several small ones – are used as risers and the treads can be finished off with a layer of turf or bark chips, or simply left as soil. Soil will encourage plant growth and help the steps to blend in quickly with informal surroundings, which is why cut-in steps are popular for woodland settings and wildflower gardens. To increase their useful life, use hardwood logs such as oak, or wood treated with preservative.

The risers for cut-in steps are held in place by strong upright wooden stakes, which prevent the logs from rolling down the slope. The space behind is packed with hardcore or gravel, which helps to improve drainage as well as forming the tread of each step before the final surface is in place.

making cut-in steps

YOU WILL NEED

• canes and string • spade • rammer (a flat metal plate on the end of a heavy-duty broom handle or a length of wood with a flat base of at least 10 x 10cm (4 x 4in) • wood saw • stout wooden stakes 2–3cm (1in) square x 60cm (2ft) long • wooden logs minimum size 10cm (4in) diameter x 75cm (2ft 6in) long • hardcore or rubble • spirit level

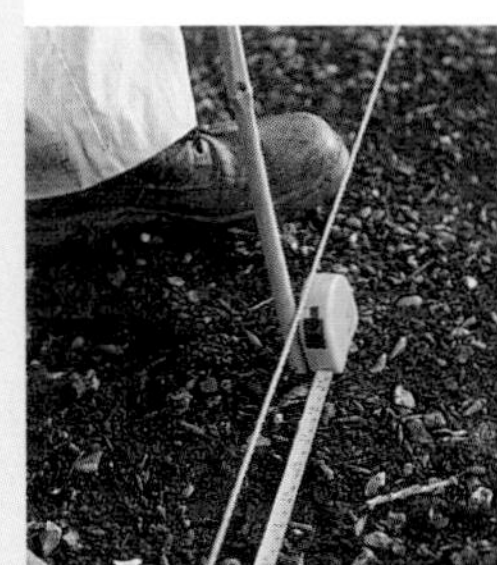

1 **Mark out the line** of the flight of steps and the position of each step, using canes and string. Then dig out the bottom step to roughly half the depth of the riser.

2 **About 10cm (4in) in front** of the edge of the bottom step, knock two stakes into the ground, about 15cm (6in) in from each end of the step, and position one or more wooden logs horizontally behind the stakes to form the riser.

3 **Back-fill the area** behind the logs with a layer of hardcore. Its thickness will depend on the depth of the riser, but hardcore usually compacts down to half its original depth. Using a rammer, compact it to within 5cm (2in) of the top of the upper horizontal log. On the bottom steps it may be necessary to provide some shuttering (flat wooden boards laid on edge) to hold in the soil and prevent it from spreading.

4 **Cut the upright support stakes** to length just below the horizontal log risers. These are often cut at an angle to prevent any sharp edges protruding.

proportions for steps

The deeper the tread, the shallower the riser needs to be. The following formula is an easy guide to working out safe, well-proportioned steps for an average-sized garden:

the depth of the tread + twice the height of the riser = 65cm (26in).

For example, if you want a 30cm (12in) tread, then twice the riser height = 65cm (26in) minus 30cm (12in) = 35cm (14in), so the risers will be 17.5cm (7in) high.

5 **Cover the compacted hardcore** with a layer of soil 5cm (2in) deep, to form the tread of each step. This can be left bare to allow native plants to establish or be covered with turf or bark chips; you should allow for this in working out the height of the risers – the new surface must be level with the top of the riser.

6 **Continue this process** up the bank until the flight of steps is complete. The soil being excavated for the upper steps can be used to cover the hardcore on the steps lower down.

calculating the number of steps

Drive a wooden peg vertically into the ground at the top of the slope, where you want the flight of steps to end, and push a long cane into the ground at the base of the slope. Tie a length of string to the bottom of the wooden peg and stretch it to a point on the cane where the string is roughly horizontal (check with a spirit level). To work out the number of steps, measure from this point down to the base of the cane, and divide this figure by the desired height of a single riser. Then measure the horizontal string from the peg to the cane and divide this by the number of steps to get the depth of the tread. You may need to adjust the proportions slightly.

terraces

An informal garden can easily accommodate a slope, but in a more formal design, a terrace – a large flat area cut into or constructed on a slope like a very wide step – may be a better solution. Terraces break up a slope into a series of banks and level areas, and provide a far greater range of planting opportunities than a sloping site could.

Below each level, the soil needs to be held back by a retaining wall (see Autumn). The depth of the terraces and the height of the walls will vary according to the angle of slope and the garden's design. The gentler the slope, the wider and shallower the terraces are likely to be. The steeper the slope, the higher and thicker the walls must be in order to hold back the weight of soil.

Before you start work on designing or constructing terraces, mark out the site and check the intended levels to make sure the proposed number of retaining walls will provide the terraces required. Plan the work so that as little movement of earth is involved as possible. The depth of foundations will be determined by the height and thickness of the retaining walls themselves. For steep sites and large schemes seek the advice of a structural engineer.

Wooden logs are an appropriate material for steps leading up to a wilder woodland area at the top of the garden (right).

edging beds

The edge of a bed or a border is like a picture frame. There are aesthetic considerations but it must be practical, help to confine the plants or create a useful divider – an interim zone that separates one part of the garden from another.

formal edgings

Straight formal edgings emphasise the geometry of a design. Their presence defines the shape of a bed or border and must be clearly visible. This is true of constructed edgings or those using plants. Plants make a very visible edging and must be kept in trim so as not to blur the outline. This is why they are often clipped to form a hedge (see page 152).

Formal lines are usually straight, but you can curve them symmetrically or make them follow a set pattern that is replicated. A garden made up of a series of symmetrical beds has a pleasing rhythm and creates delightful planting opportunities within the formal confines. It is perfectly possible to use formal edging to retain highly informal planting. A mixed border, for example, could be bounded by clipped hedges or subdivided into neat, low-walled compartments, each one holding a different array of plants.

informal edgings

In more naturalistic gardens there will still be boundaries between borders and other surfaces, and therefore edgings. The aim here is to allow for a gentle or contrasting transition between one part of the garden and another. Where an informal border runs alongside a lawn, for instance, there could be an area of difficulty unless the design is modified. Plants will naturally flop and flow over the edge of the bed onto the lawn. But how can you mow the grass without spoiling the flowers? The solution is a mowing edge.

edging a lawn

Where beds or borders edge a lawn, mowing will be made easier if you make a hard edge of paving slabs or

A brick mowing edge (left), set slightly lower than the lawn itself, makes mowing easier.

A gravel path (below) is retained and edged on the lawn side by a decorative tiled mosaic.

A low wattle panel (top right) edges a vegetable bed in which ruby chard is growing.

A raised bed with alchemilla (centre right) is edged with a line of treated timber logs.

Low 'rope' tiles decoratively finish off a box-edged bed (below right).

bricks. Although you can lay these on firmed and levelled soil, you will get more stability if you first prepare a dry mortar or hardcore base (see page 143). Set the slabs at a level so the mower skims cleanly over them without going too close to the plants. The result is a softened, beautiful line with a groomed lawn running alongside it.

- **cut the turf back** to accommodate the paving slabs. Lay the slabs so that they are level, but set them just below the level of the lawn.
- **take strips of turf** and back-fill the gap between lawn and slabs, firming down. Brush soil into any remaining gaps.
- **sweep off** surplus soil using a broom.

materials for edging

You can make edgings in a range of bought materials or grow them (see page 152) to delineate beds or borders, paths, a patio, lawn or terrace.

- **specially manufactured Victorian-style tiles,** with crenellated or 'rope' tops, or rounded topped kerbstones, are set in soil to make an obvious line.
- **treated softwood** or, if you can afford it, hardwood sawn as planks makes a functional edging for paths or may be set up as retaining boards for raised beds in the kitchen garden, for example (see page 133). If you find the unweathered wood unattractive, most of it can be hidden with a thick mulch of bark chips. Alternatively, you can stain it in the colour of your choice.

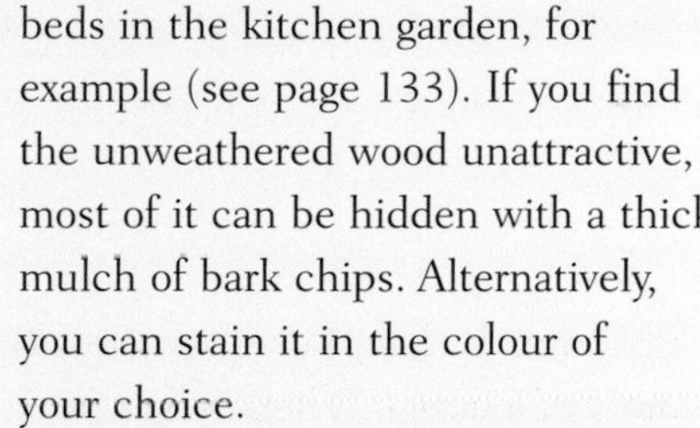

- **natural logs** combine well with bark chips and make a charming informal edging in a woodland garden, where primroses or violets can nestle into the crooks and crevices.
- **railway sleepers** are heavyweight soil retainers for raised beds. They are very durable and their dark tones will lighten with age.
- **metal** suits certain styles of modern town garden. It is usually galvanised or painted.
- **dressed natural building stone** is one of the most attractive edgings for raised beds. However, before you buy, make sure it is suitable for this role, as some oolithic limestones, for example, though they may survive as part of a building for centuries, can perish and crumble in the course of a single winter when in constant contact with damp ground.
- **engineering bricks,** set diagonally into the ground so that their tops form a 'cockscomb', were a popular edging in Victorian times. Use good-quality frost-proof bricks made to last, as cheaper house bricks will eventually crumble if used in this way.
- **concrete edgings** are cheap and functional, and it is possible to achieve a range of finishes by exposing the aggregate and adding colour.

TIP If a raised bed is next to your lawn, you will know how awkward it is to mow close to the retaining stones. You can either lay a mowing edge, or leave clear a narrow strip of earth, no more than 5–8cm (2–3in) wide, and keep it continually weed-free.

edging with plants

Plants are used to mark edges in much the same way as hard materials. They may be clipped as a low formal hedge, or a row of low plants can be allowed to grow informally to achieve a very different effect.

making a box hedge

Ever since the Romans brought their style of formal gardening to Britain, clipped box has been the favourite species for edging. It is used not only to edge the sides of borders, but to pick out pathways and for such period pieces as knot gardens, which can be all edging and no bed. Box is hardy, evergreen, aromatic and slow-growing, it keeps its shape well and is relatively easy to clip. It is also simple to propagate, if a little slow. If you buy well-grown plants for a box hedge, expect to pay a high price. If you have patience, you can buy a few plants and propagate your own.

Box hedging is useful in both formal and informal designs. Where plants in informal borders are inclined to tumble, the low hedge corrals them within its enclosure. It is important not to allow other plants to lie on top of box for too long; prune them back to prevent them from damaging the hedge.

The most widely used box species for dwarf hedging is the small-leaved *Buxus sempervirens* 'Suffruticosa', but there are others. *Buxus balearica* is upright-growing with slightly longer and narrower blue-green leaves. On a smaller scale, *Buxus microphylla* 'Green Pillow' is suitable for miniaturised edging.

Grey-leaved cotton lavender has been clipped into neat mounds (top right) to make an eye-catching edging to a bed on one side of an informal path.

Lamb's ears (*Stachys byzantina*) surround a mound of *Berberis thunbergii* (centre right).

Deep slate and cobble steps (bottom right) are softened by a low edging of dwarf *Geranium endressii.*

Low box hedges give a neat finish to the beds in this light-reflecting green and white city-basement garden (below).

taking box cuttings

- **take small shoots** any time from September to April (October is best) and remove the lower leaves.
- **select a shaded spot,** preferably north-facing, where the soil is rich, moist and well drained.
- **insert the cuttings** in rows, 2–3cm (1in) apart, and make sure they never dry out, especially through summer.
- **after about 12 months** the cuttings should have rooted and the resulting young box plants are ready, either to pot up or to plant in their growing positions. They will be very small, so need to be kept clear of competing weeds or other plants.

planting a low box hedge

Measure out the exact line of the hedge. Mark it with a string held taut between stakes. If you are making a complicated curve or pattern, for a knot garden, for example, you can trace the line of the hedge with silver sand dribbled on the soil.

- Dig a trench for the plants. If the plants are small, fill the trench and position each plant with a hand trowel along the line. Sprinkle potting compost or sieved garden compost along the trench and some bone meal at a rate of 50–75g per m (¾–1oz per ft); fork in.
- For a dense hedge, space small plants 15cm (6in) apart. As an economy, you could increase this to 25cm (10in), although the resulting hedge will take a season or two longer to fill out. When planting bare-rooted specimens, never let the roots dry out. The plants can be kept in a bucket of water for an hour or two, or be temporarily planted (heeled in) into soil nearby until you are ready to plant.
- Firm in each plant securely, making sure they are exactly in line and equally spaced. Then water thoroughly.

other plants for low hedges

Lavender, particularly *Lavandula angustifolia* 'Hidcote' and 'Twickel Purple', and cotton lavenders (*Santolina chamaecyparissus* or *S. pinnata*) make low billowy hedges and are flowering.

Rosemary clips into a beautiful and aromatic hedge. Wall germander (*Teucrium chamaedrys*) was popular in Elizabethan times and, though less disciplined than the plants above, has triangular, shiny evergreen leaves and pink deadnettle-like blooms.

hedge maintenance

All low hedges require clipping at least once a year (see page 41). Box needs clipping once, preferably in August. Lavender and santolina are more difficult to keep in a neat shape. Clip off the faded flowers in late summer, but also trim them over each spring, especially if damp weather has caused excessive growth.

In time lavenders become old and leggy. Then you need to decide whether to enjoy the gnarled, dishevelled look of maturity or if you prefer to remove and replace the plants. Replacement is best carried out in early spring or mid-autumn. You can easily layer old lavender plants in spring, or take cuttings (see page 43).

informal edging plants

Edging need not take the form of a hedge. A large number of well-disciplined, low-growing plants make charming border markers and they will not need trimming. Hardy geraniums make soft mounds, while lilyturf (*Liriope muscari*) forms a line of green grassy leaves, as does the darker foliage of *Ophiopogon planiscapus*, the 'black' grass. For summer, the spider plant, *Chlorophytum comosum* also makes a distinctive edge.

late summer index

D

E

F

acknowledgments

Photographs were supplied by the following people and organisations. Where relevant, the number of a picture as it appears on a page is given. Abbreviations are used as follows: t top, c centre, b bottom, l left, r right. DA David Askham, JB Jonathan Buckley, MB Mark Bolton, MBr Martin Brigdale, CB Chris Burrows, PB Philippe Bonduel, BC Brian Carter, HSC Harry Smith Collection, EC Eric Crichton, SC Sarah Cuttle, RE Ron Evans, RD Reader's Digest, CF Christopher Fairweather, FH Fran Harpur, JH Jerry Harpur, MH Marcus Harpur, NH Neil Holmes, SH Sunniva Harte, GPL Garden Picture Library, JG John Glover, AL Andrew Lawson, MM Marianne Majerus, S&OM S & O Mathews, CN Clive Nichols, MLS Mayer Le Scanff, MN Mike Newton, JP Jerry Pavia, HR Howard Rice, GR Gary Rogers, JS J Sira, RS Ron Sutherland, SSP Sea Spring Photos, BT Brigitte Thomas, MT Maddie Thornhill, DW Didier Willery, SW Steven Wooster, JW Justyn Willsmore, JWh Jo Whitworth, MW Mark Winwood.

Front cover Flowerphotos, photographer Carol Sharp **Back cover tl** MW, **cl** RD, **tcr** MW, **tr** SC, **br** GPL/CN, **bl** MW **1** MW **2–3** GPL/JG **4–5** GPL/SW **8–9** GPL/SW (Priory, Kemerton) **10 tl** JH (Great Dixter, E. Sussex), **tr** JB (Design: S Raven), **b** JH (Wollerton Old Hall, Shropshire) **11 tl** MH (Lakemount, Co. Cork, Ireland), **tr** MT, **bl** JH (Kettle Hill, Norfolk), **br** MM (Old Vicarage, East Ruston, Norfolk) **12 t** GPL/SW (Priory, Kemerton), **bl** MM (Old Vicarage, East Ruston, Norfolk) **br** MN **13 tl** MM (Design: W Giles) **tr** MH (Lakemount, Co. Cork, Ireland), **b** JB (Great Dixter, E. Sussex) **14 l** GPL/JG, **tr** JH, **br** GPL/BT **15 tl** SC, **tr** GPL/JP, **br** S&OM, **bl** GPL/SW **16 tl** CN (Sticky Wicket, Dorset) **tr** S&OM, **b** CN (Design: S Hammond, USA) **17 l** AL, **tr** JB (Hollington Herbs, Berks), **br** JB (Clinton Lodge, Sussex) **18 tl** JH (Design: R Hudson, RSA), **tc** MH (Design: J Baillie), **tr** S&OM (Hamilton Botanic Garden, NZ), **br** AL (RHS Chelsea 2000. Design: P Oudolf & A Maynard), **bl** CN (Design: A Armour-Wilson, RHS Chelsea 2001) **19 t** JH (Montecito, CA, USA), **br** CN (RHS Chelsea 2001 Design: G Whiten), **bl** JH (Little & Lewis, Washington, USA) **20 tl** JH (D Dalbok, USA), **tr** JH (Design: G Pickard, Essex), **br** JH (M Barzi & J Casares, Argentina), **bl** MT **21 tl** MM (Design: E & J Follas), **tr** MM (Design: P Southern), **br** JB (Design: G Wilson, Merton Hall Rd. Ldn), **bl** CN (Design: L Pleasance, Ldn) **22 l** JH (E Ossart, France), **r** JH (Pettifers, Oxon) **23 tl, bl, cr** S&OM (RHS Garden, Wisley), **tr** MH (Lakemount, Co Cork, Ireland), **br** S&OM (Rozelle Close, Hants) **24 tl** MH (RHS Chelsea 1999, Design: Sir Terence Conran), **tr** JB (Warren Farm Cottages, Hants), **bl** CN (Design: Hedens Lustgard, Sweden) **24-25** JB (Design: H Yemm. Ketley's, E. Sussex) **25 tl** JB (West Dean, Sussex), **r** AL (Barnsley House, Glos.), **c** GPL/J Sira **26-27** MW **28** MB **29 tl** MT (Cokes Barn, W. Burton, W. Sussex), **tr** SC, **b** MW **30** MW **31 tl & tr** MW, **tc** MN, **b** SC **32 l** MT, **tr & br** SC **33** MT **34** MW **35 t** GPL/D England, **b** SC **36 l** SC, **r** MB **37 all** MW **38 l** MW, **r** SC **39** MW **40** GPL/MLS **41 t all** MW, **br** MT, **bl** JW **42 l** JWh, **r** MW **43 all** MW except **tr** GPL/MB **44 all** MW **45** JH (King Henry's Hunting Lodge) **46** SC **47 all** SC except **r** FH **48** SC **49 tl** N Browne, **br** S&OM (Lower Mill, Hants), **bc & bl** MW **50** SC **51 tl** JWh (Little Brook Fuchsias, Ash Green, Hants), **br** CN (Design: L Pleasance, Ldn), **bl** SC **52 t** MW, **b** MH (Design: J Baillie) **53** MW **54 l** GPL/MLS, **r** GPL/Lamontagne **55** GPL/J Hurst **56 l** SC, **b** MT **56-57** GPL/E Craddock **57 b** MW **58 l** MT, **r** MW **59** GPL/HR **60** MW **61** JH (Barnsley House, Glos.) **62 l** MT, **r** GPL/R Butcher **63 t** MN, **b** CN (Design: Hedens Lustgard, Sweden) **64** MW **65** CN (Little Court, Hants) **66** CN (RHS Chelsea 1993, National Asthma Campaign. Design: Lucy Huntington) **67 l** GPL/RS, **r** JB (Hollington Herbs, Berks) **68** GPL/NH **69** MW **70 l** GPL/R Asser, **r** MW **71** SC **72 l** S&OM (Les Moutiers, Normandy), **r** MT **73** GPL/RS **74 t** GPL/PB, **b** MW **75** MN **76-77** RD **78-79 (1, 5, 8, 10, 11)** RD, **(2)** AL, **(3, 4, 6)** MT, **(7)** SC, **(9)** GPL/RE, **(12)** HSC **80-81 (1, 2, 5, 7, 8, 9,12)** RD, **(3)** GPL/M Watson, **(4)** GPL/JG, **(6)** GPL/MB, **(10)**GPL/DW, **(11)** GPL/SH **82-83 (1, 2, 5, 7, 10)** RD, **(3)** GPL/PB, **(4)** GPL/SH, **(6)** GPL/J Greene, **(8)** GPL/J Sorrell, **(9, 11)** MT, **(12)** GPL/CB **84-85 (1, 4, 9, 10, 11)** RD, **(2, 3, 5, 7, 8, 12)** MT, **(6)** GPL/HR **86-87 (1)** GPL/DW, **(2)** MT, **(3, 4, 5, 8, 9, 11)** RD, **(6, 12)** HSC, **(7)** GPL/BC, **(10)** GPL/DA **88-89 (1, 3, 4, 7, 8)** RD, **(2, 5, 9, 10)** MT, **(6)** GPL/MB, **(11)** AL, **(12)** GPL/JG **90-91 (1, 2, 3, 9, 10)** HSC, **(4)** MT, **(5)** GPL/N Kemp, **(6, 7)** GPL/JP, **(8)** MW, **(11)** GPL/EC,**(12)** GPL/HR **92-93 (1)** RD, **(2, 5, 6 ,11)** MW, **(3)** GPL/BC, **(4)** MT, **(7)** GPL/HR, **(8)** GPL/D Cavagnaro, **(9)** GPL/NH, **(10, 12)** HSC **94-95 (1, 2, 9, 10)** RD, **(3)** GPL/M Howes, **(4)** GPL/NH, **(5)** GPL/BC, **(6)** MW, **(7)** JW, **(8)** HSC, **(11)** GPL/PB, **(12)** GPL/JG **96 (1)** GPL/JS, **(2)** GPL/B Forsberg, **(3, 4, 7)** RD, **(5)** GPL/CB, **(6, 8)** GPL/JG **97 (1, 3)** RD, **(2, 5)** MT, **(4)** GPL/BC **98 (1)** S&OM, **(2)** MT, **(3)** GPL/Z McCalmont, **(4)** RD, **(5)** HSC **99 (1, 2, 6)** RD, **(3)** GPL/HR, **(4)** GPL/J Ferro Sims, **(5)** MT **100-101 (1, 2, 3, 4, 5, 8, 9, 10, 11)** RD, **(6, 12)** JWh, **(7)** GPL/HR **102-103 (1, 7)** GPL/NH, **(2, 10)** JWh **(3)** GPL/CF, **(4)** HSC, **(5, 6)** JWh (Seale Nursery, Surrey), **(8, 12)** JWh (Apuldram Roses, Chichester, W. Sussex), **(9)** GPL/JS, **(11)** A-Z Botanical **104-105 (1, 2, 5, 10)** JWh, **(3,7, 8, 9)** RD, **(4, 12)** GPL/JG, **(6)** HSC, **(11)** GPL/MB **106 (1, 2)** JWh (LittleBrook Fuchsias, Hants), **(3)** JWh (Seale Nursery, Surrey), **(4)** GPL/JS, **(5)** JWh, **(6)** GPL/JG **107 (1)** GPL/MB, **(2)** GPL/NH, **(3)** GPL/MLS, **(4)** GPL/JG, **(5)** JWh, **(6, 7)** RD **108-109 (1, 2, 3, 4, 8, 9, 12, 13)** RD, **(5)** A-Z Botanical,**(6)** HSC, **(7, 11)** GPL/BC, **(10)** MN **110-111 (1, 2, 3, 4, 5, 6, 7, 9, 11)** RD, **(8)** GPL/MB, **(10)** GPL/BT, **(12)** HSC **112-113 (1, 3)** GPL/JP, **(2)** GPL/D Cavagnaro, **(4, 7)** GPL/MLS, **(5, 6)** GPL/JG, **(8, 11)** SSP, **(9)** GPL/DA, **(10)** GPL/C Carter **114-115 (1)** MW, **(2, 5)** GPL/M Howes, **(3)** GPL/SH, **(4, 10)** RD, **(6)** GPL/HR, **(7)** GPL/Lamontagne, **(8)** GPL/JS, **(9)** MT, **(11)** SSP **116-117 (1, 3, 4, 6, 7, 10)** RD, **(2)** GPL/NH, **(5, 9)** GPL/JS, **(8)** HSC, **(11)** GPL/BT, **(12)** GPL/Lamontagne **118 l** GPL/JG, **c** RD, **r** GPL/JG **119 l** RD, **r** JWh (Seale Nursery,Surrey) **120** RD **121 l** JWh, **r** RD **122-123** SC **124** GPL/P Baistow **125 t** CN (Hadspen House, Somerset) **b** JH **126** GPL/HR **127 l** JH (Ton Ter Linden, NL), **tr** GPL/SW, **br** S&OM (Rozelle Close, Hants) **128-129** MM (Old Vicarage, East Ruston, Norfolk) **129 t** GPL/A Scaresbrook, **b** GPL/RE **130** AL **131t** JH (Design: M Runge), **b** AL **132 l** AL (RHS Chelsea 1992. Design: D Pearson), **r** JB (Clinton Lodge, Sussex) **133** SC **134 l** MN, **r** AL **135** MBr **136** MM (Design: B Guinness) **137 l** GPL/L Pullen, **r** JH (Design: T Hobbs, Seattle) **138** GPL/RS (RHS Chelsea 1999 Design: P McCann. Hope Springs Eternal Garden) **139** MW **140-141** MW **142 t** JH (Design: J Sharpe, London), **b** AL **142-143** JH (Design: J Fearney-Whittingstall) **143** GPL/JP **144 t** CN (Design: R Green & R Cade, London), **b** AL **145 l br** JWh, **tr** AL **146-147** CN (Design: V Shanley, Ldn), **147 t** AL (Design: P Hobhouse), **br** AL **148-149 all** MW except **br** CN (Design: J Billington, Ldn) **150 l** JH (Design: G Pickard, Essex), **br** JB(Design: J Pickett-Baker) **151 tl** GPL/SH, **c** GPL/GR, **b** GPL/BC **152** JH (Design: S Woodhams, Ldn) **153 t** AL (Design: E Clarke) **c & b** AL

Front cover: *Echinops bannaticus.*
Back cover, clockwise from top left: planting bulbs in grass; *Knautia macedonica*; twisting off an apple; *Papaver somniferum* seed heads; *Clematis* 'Bill MacKenzie'; bee on cosmos flower

Amazon Publishing would like to thank Adrian Hall Garden Centres. Thanks also to the following individuals who allowed us to use their gardens for photography: Bridget Heal, Martin Brigdale & Helen Trent.

Late Summer is part of a series of gardening books called the **All-Season Guide to Gardening**. It was created for Reader's Digest by Amazon Publishing Limited.

Series Editor Carole McGlynn
Art Director Ruth Prentice

Editors Barbara Haynes, Alison Freegard, Jackie Matthews; also Norma MacMillan
Design Jo Grey, Mary Staples
Photographic art direction Ruth Prentice
Special photography Sarah Cuttle, Mark Winwood, Martin Brigdale
Writers Steve Bradley, Andi Clevely, Nigel Colborn, Sue Fisher, David Joyce
Picture research Clare Limpus, Mel Watson, Sarah Wilson
Consultants Jonathan Edwards, Mike Lawrence
DTP Felix Gannon, Claire Graham
Editorial Assistant Elizabeth Woodland

FOR READER'S DIGEST
Project Editor Christine Noble
Project Art Editor Kate Harris
Pre-press Accounts Manager Penny Grose

READER'S DIGEST GENERAL BOOKS
Editorial Director Cortina Butler
Art Director Nick Clark

First Edition Copyright © 2002
The Reader's Digest Association Limited,
11 Westferry Circus, Canary Wharf,
London E14 4HE
www.readersdigest.co.uk
Reprinted with amendments 2003

Copyright © 2002 Reader's Digest Association Far East Limited
Philippines copyright © 2002 Reader's Digest Association Far East Limited

All rights reserved. No part of this book may be reproduced, stored in a retrieval system or transmitted in any form or by any means, electronic, electrostatic, magnetic tape, mechanical, photocopying, recording or otherwise, without permission in writing from the publishers.

® Reader's Digest, The Digest and the Pegasus logo are registered trademarks of The Reader's Digest Association, Inc, of Pleasantville, New York, USA.

We are committed to both the quality of our products and the service we provide to our customers. We value your comments, so please feel free to contact us on **08705 113366**, or via our website at **www.readersdigest.co.uk** If you have any comments about the content of our books, you can email us at **gbeditorial@readersdigest.co.uk**

Origination Colour Systems Limited, London
Printed and bound in the EEC by Arvato Iberia

ISBN 0 276 42710 6
BOOK CODE 621-003-2
CONCEPT CODE UK0087